America and China

America and China

Asia-Pacific Rim Hegemony in the Twenty-first Century

Randall Doyle

LEXINGTON BOOKS

A division of
ROWMAN & LITTLEFIELD PUBLISHERS, INC.
Lanham • Boulder • New York • Toronto • Plymouth, UK

LEXINGTON BOOKS

A division of Rowman & Littlefield Publishers, Inc.
A wholly owned subsidary of The Rowman & Littlefield Publishing Group, Inc.
4501 Forbes Boulevard, Suite 200, Lanham, MD 20706

Estover Road, Plymouth PL6 7PY, United Kingdom

British Library Cataloguing in Publication Information Available

Library of Congress Cataloging-in-Publication Data
Doyle, Randall Jordan.
  America and China: Asia-Pacific Rim hegemony in the twenty-first century /
Randall Doyle.
    p. cm.
  Includes bibliographical references.
  ISBN-13: 978-0-7391-1701-9 (cloth : alk. paper)
  ISBN-10: 0-7391-1701-7 (cloth : alk. paper)
  ISBN-13: 978-0-7391-1702-6 (pbk. : alk. paper)
  ISBN-10: 0-7391-1702-5 (pbk. : alk. paper)
  1. East Asia—Politics and government—21st century. 2. Pacific Area—Politics
and government—21st century. 3. United States—Foreign relations—21st century.
4. China—Foreign relations—21st century. I. Title.
  DS518.1.D69 2007
  327.09182'3—dc22

                                                                    2007016436

Printed in the United States of America

∞™ The paper used in this publication meets the minimum requirements of
American National Standard for Information Sciences—Permanence of Paper
for Printed Library Materials, ANSI/NISO Z39.48-1992.

To Mimi

My Best Friend

Contents

Foreword

Howard Zinn

ASIA-PACIFIC RIM HEGEMONY
IN THE TWENTY-FIRST CENTURY

Professor Randall Doyle is peering into an overlooked corner of U.S. foreign policy—its relations with Australia, Japan, and Korea. It is an important area of study because all three of these nations live in the shadow of the Asian giant, China, which, by its size, its military might, and its swift-growing economy, is the great counter-balance to U.S. hegemony in Asia in the twenty-first century.

We might recall the historical background for the powerful U.S. presence in Asia today. As early as the first decades of the nineteenth century, merchant ships based in New England were engaging in what became known as "the China trade." And, in the early 1850s, became what is known in American schoolbooks as the "opening of Japan," which suggests something peaceful, but, in truth, it actually involved the use of U.S. warships to open Japanese ports to American commerce. In the year 1859, U.S. troops also landed in Shanghai, China to protect American commercial interests there.

By the 1890s, the United States had either annihilated or removed the Indian tribes that stood in the way of expansion to the Pacific Ocean, and there was no longer an "internal" frontier. In the higher circles of the military, of government, of business, there was more and more talk of overseas expansion. Captain A. T. Mahan of the U.S. Navy wrote articles that were read by Theodore Roosevelt and other political leaders. "Americans must now begin to look outward," he wrote.

Another influential propagandist for imperial expansion was Senator Henry Cabot Lodge of Massachusetts, who wrote in a magazine article: " . . . for the sake of our commercial supremacy in the Pacific we should control the Hawaiian islands and maintain our influence in Samoa . . . The great nations are rapidly absorbing for their future expansion and their present defense all the waste places of the earth." It didn't matter that these "waste places" were populated by human beings. It was the same psychology that saw the North American continent as "empty," though Indian tribes had occupied it for thousands of years.

During the 1890s, the search for overseas markets was beginning. Even before his election to the presidency in 1898, William McKinley said: "We want a foreign market for our surplus products." And Senator Albert Beveridge of Indiana declared: "American factories are making more than the American people can use; American soil is producing more than they can consume. Fate has written our policy for us; the trade of the world must and shall be ours."

With the Chinese and Japanese markets beckoning, stepping-stones in the Pacific were needed. Hawaii was, as one American diplomat put it, "a ripe pear waiting to be plucked." Actually, a different kind of fruit was involved, for it was the owners of pineapple plantations who in 1893 called for U.S. warships to support a coup in which Sanford B. Dole was to head a provisional government. However, the Grover Cleveland administration refused to annex Hawaii, and Theodore Roosevelt denounced Cleveland's decision as "a crime against white civilization."

By 1898, however, with William McKinley in the White House, and Theodore Roosevelt appointed assistant secretary of the navy, the time was right. That was the year the United States expelled Spain from Cuba and established its own control over that Caribbean island. And now Hawaii, already dominated by American missionaries and pineapple growers, became the next target. Thirteen rich white businessmen formed a "Committee of Safety," which declared that the Hawaiian queen, Liliuokalani, in adopting a new constitution was endangering "the public safety." The American minister to Hawaii, John Stevens, arranged for a U.S. cruiser, the *Boston*, to land troops in Honolulu, leaving the unarmed Hawaiians helpless to resist. Congress, by joint resolution, annexed Hawaii.

Around the same time, Wake Island, in the Pacific Ocean en route to Japan, was occupied. And Guam, another Spanish possession in the Pacific, and on the way to the Philippines, was taken. In December 1898, a peace treaty was signed with the defeated Spain, in which Guam, Puerto Rico, and the Philippines were given to the United States for a payment of $20 million.

The Filipinos, however, had organized their own movement for independence from Spain and now resisted U.S. occupation. The result was a vicious war which lasted for years, in the course of which the United States Army committed atrocities against the resisters, resulting in the deaths of more than half a million Filipinos. In the Senate, Albert Beveridge spoke, January 9, 1900, for the dominant economic interests: "Mr. President, the times call for candor. The Philippines are ours forever. And just beyond the Philippines are China's illimitable markets. We will not retreat from either . . . The Pacific is our ocean."

With the conquest of Hawaii and the Philippines, the United States was now, unquestionably, a Pacific power. The European imperial powers had long ago, in the early nineteenth century, taken over the "treaty ports" of China to ensure control of the trade with that country. In 1900, the United States declared an "Open Door policy," insisting that it would be treated equally with the other countries in access to Chinese markets. That year, too, the U.S. joined other colonial nations in sending troops to Peking to put down the "Boxer Rebellion." American troops stayed for thirty years.

The Japanese attack on Pearl Harbor, December 7, 1941, needs to be seen in the context of the wider U.S. policy in the Pacific, which was hardly based on humanitarian concerns but on crass economic interests. It was not the cruel Japanese bombing of Chinese cities in 1937 or the massacre at Nanking in 1938 that brought about the declaration of war on Japan, but rather the Japanese assault on Hawaii, a critical link in the Pacific empire of the United States.

With victory over Japan, and the occupation of the Japanese islands (still continuing with the multiple military bases on Okinawa), the United States was thrusting its power even more aggressively into the Pacific. What challenges the United States in China has been not so much the triumph of communism as an ideology, but the existence of a powerful independent nation countering U.S. hegemony in the Pacific.

It is with this historical background that we can read Professor Randall Doyle's impressive and close study of the situation in the Pacific Rim today. The critical issue for the U.S. and other nations may be economic and political hegemony. For the people of the United States, of Japan, of Korea, of Australia, of the other nations in the region—the overriding questions are the prevention of war, the maintenance of human rights, and the prosperity, not just of corporations, but of the ordinary people living within the Pacific Rim.

Howard Zinn,
Professor Emeritus, Boston University
Auburndale, Massachusetts
February 2007

Acknowledgments

This is the section usually completed at the end of a book project where an author feels ethically and morally compelled to acknowledge the significant assistance and contributions of the many individuals who participated in the creation, development, support, and, eventually, publication of an idea, or thesis, that the writer conjured up years ago. In this particular case, that writer is me. And, yes, I have many people to thank in this section of the book. This book was written during my time at Central Michigan University (CMU). Therefore, as expected, many of the individuals mentioned are administrators, professors, or staff personnel at CMU.

To complete a book is often an exhausting experience that convinces many writers to loudly shout, "Never again!" And, for many writers, they indeed keep this promise to themselves. The memory of such a demanding ordeal is simply to be avoided. This is my third book. Obviously, I have not fallen—yet—into this category representing this degree of despair or exhaustion. Partly, because I have found myself in academic environments that promote quality scholarship and provide the proper clerical, financial, and institutional mechanisms that are absolutely necessary for finishing any serious scholarly project. This constructive and supportive environment exists at CMU. Thus, the individuals listed below have played significant roles in the publication of this book.

My gratitude is irrefutable, and my appreciation is boundless.

President Michael Rao is an ardent believer in internationalizing education at Central Michigan University. His leadership and support for my speaking, teaching, and writing on international topics and the global community are invaluable. Thus, Dr. Rao has provided the necessary leadership for the university's mission to expand its educational curriculum and vision for its student body.

The dean of humanities and the social behavioral sciences, Dr. Gary Shapiro, has enthusiastically supported this particular project on Asia-Pacific. Again, a strong supporter of international education, Dr. Shapiro and I first met, in 2005, before I gave a talk on Japan and the atomic bombing of Hiroshima in 1945. I have found him to be a constant supporter of research and teaching on Asia-Pacific.

The chair of the CMU History Department, Dr. Timothy Hall, has provided unstinting support for this project. His vision of creating a history department that offers courses focused upon *all* regions of the world has lifted the department's academic credibility to a new level of respectability.

I also want to recognize the substantial efforts of the history department's executive secretary, Annette Davis. Annette constructed the book's bibliography and she agreed to read the entire manuscript. I wanted a fresh pair of eyes to read it, and to recognize any unintentional errors of prose or presentation. She did a great job on all accounts.

The Office of Research and Sponsored Programs (ORSP) at CMU has been an enormous help. The two primary individuals who have been irreplaceable in terms of assisting me in acquiring the necessary funding for my research trips to Asia are ORSP Executive Secretary JoAnn Gust and Research and Program Officer Deborah Clark. Both of whom have played vital roles in helping me obtain the financial assistance to travel to Australia, China, Japan, and Korea in 2005–2006. JoAnn retired in December 2006, after working for twenty-five years in ORSP. Her vast expertise and knowledge on the maddening contours involved in receiving funding for research will be greatly missed.

Professors Guilan Wang and Patrick Shan are two other individuals that I feel must be recognized for their contributions to my book. Dr. Wang, the director of the Office of International Education, was a great help on two matters: financial assistance and providing me contacts within China. Both of which are vital to the success of any project, particularly for a writer traveling to China for the first time. Dr. Shan, who teaches Chinese history at Grand Valley State University, has been a wonderful colleague and friend over the years. He has provided many insights concerning China, and he also introduced me to Professor Sun Ling Ling, a research associate at the Institute of Japanese Studies at the Chinese Academy of Social Sciences. Professor Sun provided me with additional contacts in Beijing, China. Altogether, they vastly improved my reach and understanding of modern China.

In America, Australia, China, Japan, and South Korea, I want to recognize a number of individuals who graciously provided me an opportunity to interview them, or had conversations with me, or invited me to visit their respective universities or institutions. All these acts of cooperation, generosity, and kindness greatly assisted me in understanding the changes occurring in Asia-Pacific, particularly involving the economic, political, and power relations within the region. They were scholars, politicians, scientists, writers, and representatives of various research institutions. To all, I am deeply grateful. Please forgive me if I have forgotten to mention your name below. Your comments and observations will certainly be recognized within the footnotes and text of the book. The following individuals are noted in no particular order of importance. Thus, *all* those mentioned below were important in the making of this book:

Noam Chomsky, Department of Modern Languages and Linguistics, MIT; Howard Zinn, Professor Emeritus, History Department, Boston University; Alexander Downer, Australian Foreign Minister (1996–present); Bob Hawke, former Australian Prime Minister (1983–1991); Zbigniew Brzezinski, former National Security Advisor, Carter Administration (1977–1981); Christine Milne, Australian Federal Senator, Green Party; Peter Abigail, Major General and former Commander of the Australian Army; Robert Ayson, Australian National University, Strategic and Defense Studies Centre; William Tow, Australian National University, Strategic and Defense Studies Centre; Desmond Ball, Australian National University, Strategic and Defense Studies Centre; Derek McDougall, University of Melbourne, History Department; David Goldsworthy, Monash University, History Department; Alan Oxley, Chairman, the Australian APEC Study Centre, Melbourne, Australia; Jaime Jobson, Executive Manager, the Australian APEC Study Centre, Melbourne, Australia; Jenni Jeremy, Development Librarian, the Bob Hawke Prime Ministerial Library, University of South Australia; Pete Hay, Professor of Environment Studies, University of Tasmania; Richard Flanagan, prominent Australian Writer, Hobart, Tasmania; Ted Lefroy, Director of the Centre for Environment, University of Tasmania; Andrew Wilkie, former Army Officer and current Writer, Hobart, Tasmania; Simon Bevilacqua, Journalist, the *Mercury* newspaper, Hobart, Tasmania; Wayne Crawford, Journalist, the *Mercury* newspaper, Hobart, Tasmania; Zhang Yuping, Associate Professor and Vice Dean of College of Humanities and Law, North China University of Technology; Guo Tao, Dean of the Division of International Cooperation and Exchanges, North China University of Technology, Beijing, China; Guilan Wang, Director of the Office of International Education, Central Michigan University; Sun Ling Ling, Research Associate, Institute of Japanese Studies, Beijing, China; Patrick Fuliang Shan, Professor of Chinese History, Grand Valley State University; Wilhelm Vosse, Director of International Educational Exchange Program, International Christian University, Tokyo, Japan; Shin Chiba, Professor of Political Thought, International Christian University, Tokyo, Japan; Lee Heun-Jae, Deputy Director,

Investment Promotion Division, Gyeonggi Provincial Government, South Korea; Kihong Shim, Asian General Affairs Team, Hyundai, South Korea; Choi Kyung Hwan, Secretary to Kim Dae-jung, Kim Dae-jung Presidental Library, South Korea; Suk-Ho Bang, Professor of Law, Hongik University, Seoul, South Korea; Robert Sutter, Professor, School of Foreign Service, Georgetown University; Don Oberdorfer, former Foreign Correspondent, *Washington Post.*

I want to give special recognition to T. J. MacDuff Stewart. "MacDuff" Stewart is in charge of editorial acquisitions in History and Area Studies at Lexington Books. She believed in this project from the very beginning and was a constant source of support throughout the process. It is our second time working together on a book. MacDuff is a very gifted editor, and she always makes the extra effort to help you produce a quality work beyond your expectations. We have worked well as a team, and I look forward to working with MacDuff in the future.

Finally, I want to thank my wife, Mimi, who is truly my best friend and advisor on so many matters in life. She has always supported my efforts to write this book, including the long trips involved. And I, in return, find great joy in her own success as a teacher and scholar. Mimi's ability to speak and teach several languages never ceases to amaze me. She is indeed a blessing that I never take for granted.

Introduction

The twenty-first century holds great anxiety for America and its dominant position within the Pacific Rim. The emergence of China as a potential economic and military challenger to U.S. leadership within the Pacific Rim, the unending wars in Iraq and Afghanistan, and a volatile financial and political condition domestically could trigger a premature and fundamental restructuring of America's lone superpower status in Asia-Pacific. Hence, how will this recognized potentiality affect America's regional hegemony and security treaties, especially with its key allies—Australia, Japan, and South Korea?

Currently, the well-entrenched post-WWII economic and military regional infrastructures are now being seriously challenged by China's steady rise to power throughout Asia-Pacific. Thus, there is a constant reevaluating process by our key allies of whether their respective regional interests are being respected and supported by the American-based financial and military regional apparatus. When you add into the mix the developing U.S. domestic budgetary crises, such as exploding deficits involving domestic spending and a frightening trade imbalance with the international community, it is not hard to understand why most analysts within the region are questioning America's future staying power. Therefore, the current readjustment of key alliances, and the recognition of serious domestic budgetary and financial issues, will certainly have a sobering effect upon U.S. foreign policy within the Pacific Rim region as the new century unfolds.

Irrefutably, China's dramatic development, economically and militarily, has directly and indirectly initiated a new geopolitical reevaluation of the present relationships between America and its steadfast allies since WWII: Australia, Japan, and South Korea. And China has become noticeably much more important, especially economically, to America's key Pacific Rim partners. Hence, will the United States find itself increasingly marginalized as the twenty-first century progresses? The first part of the book will provide a brief historical post-WWII overview of America's relations with its key allies. The second part will focus more upon a current analysis, concerning the economic and military status of the U.S. and its key allies within the Pacific Rim and how China is making serious diplomatic and economic inroads within all three of them.

The epilogue will examine Asia-Pacific in the twenty-first century, and whether the region will end up becoming a potential Pearl Harbor or, perhaps, represent a historic shift towards a peaceful existence between the two major powers—America and China. My book will shed some light on the significant challenges confronting these two powers and the region during the first century of the new millennium.

Finally, a postscript will be provided which will have significant details, information, observations, and thoughts from my trip to China, Japan, and South Korea taken in May–June 2007. The Asia-Pacific Rim region is changing and evolving so quickly that I felt I had to include a section on my most recent travels to this vitally important area.

In essence, this book will *primarily* focus upon the new dynamics affecting the overall economic and military realities emerging within this critical region for America and its friends. Undeniably, China's economic and military emergence remains *relatively* an undefined factor, though there is an acknowledged uneasiness amongst its Asian neighbors. The world's economic and military axis is turning towards the Pacific Rim. Henceforth, what will emerge from these disparate factors remains *unclear* in the region. What is *clear* is the real possibility that America, Australia, Japan, and South Korea will collectively experience a reshaping and reevaluating of their *respective* relationships and *national* interests within this vital region. Hence, Asia-Pacific, in the twenty-first century, will become the world's new arena of geopolitical intrigue and strategizing—for better or worse.

Finally, I should note a couple of important factors concerning this book. First, I use interchangeably the terms "Asia-Pacific" and "Pacific Rim" throughout this book. Though the Pacific Rim is quite often used to describe the entire Pacific Basin, I use the term to define, identify, or indicate only the *Asian* side of the Pacific. Secondly, the reader should know that, since 1977, I have lived (including military duty), studied, taught, and traveled extensively for the better part of ten years throughout the East Asian hemispheric region—Australia, China, Guam, Japan, Malaysia, New Zealand, Okinawa, Singapore, South Korea, Taiwan, and Thailand. My stints at a few of these destinations were very brief, and others were much longer in duration. Overall, however, during this thirty-year period, I have obtained an enormous appreciation and education on the diversity and uniqueness that each nation, island, or city-state possesses.

Thus, it should be no surprise to the reader that I have had an almost endless number of interesting experiences in all these locations, and the stories connected to these events are often told to my students in my Asian and Pacific Rim history courses at Central Michigan University. It is my hope that one day *all* my students will travel to the Asia-Pacific Rim region, and see for themselves the beauty and grace that exists in this part of the world.

I

POST-WWII ASIA-PACIFIC AND AMERICA

Key Alliances: Australia, Japan, and South Korea

1

The "Yanks" and the "Battlers"

The *real* beginning of this key Pacific Rim "relationship" occurred during one of the darkest periods in Australian history. The Land Down Under found itself dangerously adrift in February 1942. The Japanese Imperial Empire had just overwhelmed British forces at Singapore after only ten days of fighting. As a result, the largest British military outpost in East Asia was no longer a protective barrier between the expanding Japanese militarism, its sphere of conquest, and Australia. The stunning and sudden collapse of Britain, and the loss of its royal naval forces at Singapore, shocked and frightened Australia. It was later learned that 15,000 Australian soldiers were captured at Singapore as well. Their nightmarish internment within Japanese prisoner of war camps was just beginning. In short, Australia found itself at war with Japan and it was simply not ready.[1]

The Australian political leadership, led by Prime Minister John Curtin, immediately recognized their dangerous dilemma. Curtin gave a national radio address where he pronounced that "the fall of Singapore opens the Battle for Australia."[2] The military estimated that a relatively small and well-trained Japanese force—one division—could dominate Australia militarily, and capture the bulk of the continent with relatively little resistance. In fact, a plan to defend the southeastern part of the nation from Adelaide to Brisbane—the "Brisbane Line"—was their best strategy for survival against a probable Japanese invasion.[3] Australia was alone; Great Britain, the mother country, could not protect them from the encroaching Japanese Empire. Henceforth, Australia now looked to America to protect it from a bloody and destructive foreign conquest.

Prime Minister Curtin stated in his end-of-the-year message to the nation, published in the Melbourne newspaper, *Herald*, that "Australia looks to America, free of any pangs as to our traditional links or kinship with the United Kingdom."[4] Indeed, in mid-1942, Australia represented the jumping-off point for American (and Australian) forces at the beginning of their "island-hopping" military campaigns in the South Pacific. Troops from both nations fought ferociously and gallantly. The term and image of the "little diggers" originated from Australia's fateful involvement in WWI, and the tragic trench warfare associated with the "war to end all wars." Again, Australians fought with an unbridled zeal and a nationalistic passion against the Japanese during WWII.[5]

The U.S.-Australia alliance became a major force in the Pacific War, but it had its moments of tension as well. Prime Minister Curtin and U.S. General Douglas MacArthur, commander of U.S. armed forces in the Pacific theater, got along well. However, relations between Australian commander in chief Thomas Blamey and General MacArthur were difficult because Curtin put Australian forces (approximately 446,000) under MacArthur's control (i.e., deployment and strategy).[6] In fact, until late 1943, most of General MacArthur's troops were Australian. There were only a little over 110,000 U.S. forces in Australia at this time.[7]

Cultural differences were also an issue between the Americans and Australians. Though Prime Minister Curtin spoke directly for his support of U.S. troops being in Australia—(they are) "visitors who speak like us, think like us, and fight like us"—nevertheless, the two armies had difficulties—especially over Australian women.[8] Australian troops echoed the British sentiments from WWI concerning U.S. troops being in-country ("over-paid, over-sexed, and over-here"). At the end of WWII, more than 12,000 Australian women married U.S. soldiers. Finally, though not surprisingly, periodic brawls in Brisbane, the site of MacArthur's military headquarters, occurred between U.S. troops and the Australian troops that also included the Brisbane locals as well. Yet, overall, the alliance was extremely successful. Americans were extremely grateful for Australian farmers feeding their army and fighting alongside them at one of the most daunting periods in human history.[9]

Hence, the Yank-Aussie partnership was an extraordinarily successful venture that benefited both sides. The U.S. had used Australia as its primary base for its military operations against the Japanese in the South Pacific, and Australia had a new and powerful protector who had, in geopolitical security terms, replaced their historical colonial masters—Great Britain. By mid-1950, China had already become a Communist nation after a brutal and destructive civil war, the Korean War had just commenced, and there were continued fears of a potential Japanese remilitarization. Considering this trio of daunting potential threats, it is not surprising that Australia continued to look to America as its primary defender in the Pacific Rim region. The "Aussies" were still viewed, quite correctly, by their Asian neighbors as a British outpost within the East Asian hemisphere.

Therefore, due to these irrefutable regional factors and realities, then Australian prime minister, Robert Menzies, observed Asia as potentially hostile but also as a cautious sign of hope for the future. Menzies, prime minister from 1939–1941 and 1949–1966, took a pragmatic view of Australia's precarious geopolitical positioning in Asia-Pacific:

> Situated as we are in the world, washed on our western and northern shores by potentially hostile seas, and numerically incapable—despite intense defense preparations—of defending ourselves for long against all-out attack by a great power without massive aid from our friends, it seems to me to be clear that our foreign policy should be to cultivate friendly relations with our neighbors . . .[10]

AMERICA'S UNCLE SAM: AUSTRALIA'S NEW BIG BROTHER

Australia's most important Asia-Pacific neighbor after WWII, of course, was the United States. The U.S. had the capabilities, economically and militarily, to help Australia immensely in their postwar search for regional security and financial stability. The end result, in September 1951, was the signing of the ANZUS (Australia–New Zealand–United States) Treaty. Menzies, one of the founders of the Australian Liberal Party, wrote in his memoirs that "we (Australians) realized to the full the importance of maintaining and encouraging American interest in our corner of the world."[11] Menzies believed that the U.S. commitment represented not only a degree of security for Australia, but the ANZUS Treaty also showed the world that the U.S. had accepted the responsibility of being a great power:

> Nothing can better demonstrate the role which the United States has accepted since the Second World War, and its willingness to match great responsibilities with great power, than this brief but significant treaty . . . Clearly what Australia and New Zealand could do to assist the United States would be a very small fraction of what the United States could do for Australia and New Zealand. But the Americans made the treaty and ratified it.[12]

Critics, within Australia, pointed out that the treaty did not specify an automatic U.S. involvement if Australia or New Zealand came under attack. They pointed to Article IV of the treaty that spoke of "constitutional processes" taking place (in America) if an attack occurred.[13] In short, it appeared that the Americans had left themselves a potential "out" if they did not want to participate in a war involving Australia and New Zealand. Menzies, in response to skeptical critics, would have none of this quibbling over language and its interpretation. He stated, unequivocally, "It is a contract based on the utmost goodwill, the utmost good faith and unqualified friendship. Each of us will stand by it."[14]

However, technically, it was true that the ANZUS Treaty did not provide an *absolute* guarantee that the U.S. would defend Australia and New Zealand against *all* potential enemies. Yet it was *interpreted* by the Australian foreign policy establishment that America had made a significant commitment toward their collective security and futures in the southern hemisphere of Asia.[15] Richard Casey, Australian external affairs minister in the Menzies government, in 1951, put it bluntly: "The Americans are the only people who can in fact help us in South-East Asia or the Pacific."[16]

This "security union" with the United States was pursued immediately after WWII by the Australian Labor Party. During the war, Australia was primarily led by the Labor government of John Curtin. Curtin, tragically, died in July 1945—just before the end of WWII; his successor, Ben Chifley (1945–1949) sent Dr. H. V. Evatt to America in the late fall of 1945. Having come very close to being invaded by the Japanese Imperial Army and witnessing the humiliation of the British Empire at Singapore, both experienced in early 1942, the Australian government wasted no time in conveying their intentions in getting the U.S. linked to Australia's future.[17]

In November 1945, just three months after the Pacific War ended, Dr. Evatt, the Australian minister of state for external affairs during Chifley's Labor government, spoke at the annual dinner of the New York American Bar Association. Dr. Evatt spoke of a future cooperation between the U.S. and Australia. Though the war had ended and the U.S.-led alliance, including Australia, was victorious, Evatt clearly stated, in a matter-of-fact manner that appeared to be logical for both countries, Australia wanted to continue this battle-tested relationship into the postwar period. Thus, he presented and positioned his argument before this legal audience as a pragmatic inquiry by a loyal friend who is asking about their future relations within this uncharted and undefined new world order:

> If this was possible during the war, why cannot similar cooperation and comradeship endure throughout the postwar period? The machinery already exists. There is an Australian Legation in Washington and a United States Legation in Canberra. Only today I have the pleasant duty of announcing the opening of an Australian Consulate-General in New York City. These are the formal instruments. But the maintenance and development of Australian-American cooperation depends on the will and determination to use those instruments effectively. We must have a peacetime counterpart to our integrated war effort.[18]

Though, the ANZUS Treaty provided an unspoken desire to have a (highly debatable U.S.) nuclear umbrella for Australian security. The Aussies had intended to create a true security partnership and not a master-subordinate role with America after WWII.[19] However, this hope of creating an "equal union" on security objectives was not in the cards. Evatt admitted, without hesitation, that the U.S. was to provide the *leadership* in the post-WWII world.[20] Therefore, as the Cold War began to heat up between the West and the East, Australia's *real* role, or *perceived* role, in global affairs became a lightning rod within Australian politics.

From 1946 onward, Liberal Party leaders Robert Menzies and Percy Spender harshly criticized the Curtin-Chifley Labor governments, especially Dr. Evatt, for committing four fundamental errors in defining Australian foreign policy:

1. Labor broke the continuity in Australia's foreign policy
2. Labor "meddled" in international affairs—instead of obeying the dictates of "real power"
3. Labor appointed a new class of managers who interfered with the normal processes of foreign policy
4. Finally, and most fundamentally, Labor disturbed the organic ideal of the Empire/Commonwealth and Australia's role therein[21]

Dr. Evatt was an unrepentant and fervent believer in the United Nations and the potential it represented to all nations in creating a more stable and peaceful world. And, according to Evatt, Australia was going to play a major role in the creation of a new world, and the international legal parameters in which it would operate, not just in the Pacific but throughout the world—

> . . . the work done at San Francisco is only a beginning. Australia has a vital stake in world peace and in progressively improved standards of living. Much more can be done as Australian leaders receive the steady backing of all Australians. For this purpose an active, energetic and progressive Australian foreign policy has to be pursued. While such a policy will, of course, negate isolationism, it cannot be limited even to Pacific matters; for Australia as a British country cannot possibly contract out of Europe, nonetheless, Australia has a very vital interest in the future of the Pacific.[22]

However, it was Evatt's staunch belief that a better world could emerge from such international institutions, such as the United Nations, and that Australia's participation in world affairs was a must. Though this proactive internationalist position sounded great at international forums and gatherings at home, in Australia, it left the Labor Party vulnerable to charges from its political opponents that their grand vision for the country's future was unrealistic, if not foolish, about the cold-blooded nature of global power politics. It is important to remember, the debris and smoke had not been completely removed from WWII: approximately 60 million people died, from 1939 to 1945, on four different continents. Needless to say, Evatt was targeted by a vociferous Liberal opposition as being dangerously naïve about how the world really worked.

Menzies and Spender, the latter becoming the minister of external affairs in Menzies' government from 1949 to 1951, called the United Nations an "experimental" organization, and said that it represented just another attempt to create a fantasy world based upon untested precepts concerning the behavior of nations. The Liberals believed that Labor's new reforms constituted a revolution in the nation's foreign policy, according to Australian historian David Lowe, by attempting to move Australia away from its traditional role of representing the British Empire in Southeast Asia. However, Professor Lowe also writes that Labor's new positions were not as revolutionary as the Liberals suggested, but they did redefine, to some degree, Labor's prior policy positions on the nature of the nation's external affairs.[23]

Though the U.S. had helped Australia survive WWII intact, and had prevented a Japanese invasion of the mainland in 1942, Menzies and the Liberal Party still perceived Australia as an appendage of the British Empire. Even after signing the ANZUS Treaty, in 1951, and acknowledging that it was the "keystone" of Australia's Pacific security, Menzies wrote that it had equal importance with the country's "ancient and largely unwritten ties with Great Britain and the Commonwealth . . ."[24] Therefore, in the end, talking about Australia playing a key or major role in reconstituting global affairs was simply high-minded and wishful thinking. Australia was a small power, and its real influence, though important at times, was really marginal at best in the grand scheme of power politics—as it is practiced in the real world.

Finally, from 1945 to 1951, the specter of communism dominated the political dialogue and debate in Australian politics. After a ferocious debate and an acrimonious campaign, the Liberal Party was returned to power, in 1949, after an eight-year hiatus. Robert Menzies proved to be very effective in tapping into the nation's historical roots, and in identifying its real influence and role in global affairs. He *loved* Britain and all things British, but he and Australia *depended* on America for its survival against the Soviet Union and the global threat of communism during the Cold War years. Menzies played both cards with unusual skill and shamelessness.

John Pilger, a globally renowned Australian investigative reporter who lives in London, wrote, "Menzies's return to power ended the hope and ambiguity of the 'New World' years. Evatt's commitment to internationalism had remained at odds with a perceived need to maintain a 'special relationship' with the United States, the great power that had 'saved' Australia."[25] Pilger points to the Korean elections held after WWII as an example of Australia kowtowing to U.S. demands. The Australian Labor Party had spoken out against the widespread torture and murder of political dissidents, and against the proposition (an American idea) of separate elections being held, in South Korea. Pilger, however, explained the new dynamics of U.S.-Australian relations: "Under Menzies the policy was now clear: the goal of assisting small countries like Korea was to come a poor second to unqualified support for the policies of the United States."[26]

As the U.S. (and Soviet Union) demanded, separate elections were held in North and South Korea, and the country remains divided to the present day—even after a terribly destructive civil war from 1950 to 1953. And Menzies remained in power until 1966, and the Liberal Party retained power until 1972. Obviously, Australians, at least an electoral majority, supported Menzies and the Liberal Party's U.S.-based foreign policy throughout the first decades of the Cold War.

BOOM TIMES DOWN UNDER

Highly respected and an award-winning Australian historian, David Day wrote,

> Despite the threatening horizon, Australians enjoyed unparalleled prosperity during the 1950s as full employment and easy credit allowed for the purchase of consumer and other goods. Car ownership tripled during the 1950s as savings accumulated during the war, as well as from the prosperous postwar years, were spent on locally produced Holden cars.[27]

In retrospect, a *strong* argument can be made for Australia tying its future security and economic interests to the American global agenda. During and after WWII, the U.S. initiated and then implemented global economic institutions such as the Marshall Plan, GATT, the World Bank, and the International Monetary Fund. Australia benefited greatly from these ideas from 1952 to 1965; Australia's economic growth was very solid. The nation's gross domestic product (GDP) averaged around 5 percent annually during this period. Though not seen as spectacular when compared to West Germany and Japan's economic growth figures, nevertheless, it created a very solid and functioning economy of one of America's key allies during the Cold War.[28]

Another key factor that contributed to Australia's economic growth was the creation of an aggressive immigration policy during the postwar period. By 1961, Australia's population grew to 10.5 million—from 7 million at the end of WWII.[29] From 1952 to 1963, over 2 million immigrants made their way to Australian shores—most were from Europe.[30] In 1959, Sir MacFarlane Burnet, a prominent Australian medical researcher, came out with a somewhat shocking new policy toward interracial marriage. He stated that interracial marriage should be encouraged because "the best characteristics of each parent (will be) inherited by their children."[31] Though government policy toward producing children from interracial marriages may have softened, the fact is that only 2,000 Asians, from 1940 to 1960, were granted permanent residence status.[32] Colonial and racial vestiges based upon an imperial age are hard to shake.

Though U.S. military power replaced the British Empire as Australia's primary guarantor and source contributing toward its relative security in the Asia-Pacific region, Great Britain remained its biggest trading partner and domestic investor until 1961. By 1966, America's direct investment into Australia equaled Britain's contribution—approximately 40 percent apiece.[33] However, Great Britain remained one of Australia's primary trading partners and domestic investors until the late-1970s.[34]

Australian exports grew steadily during the 1950s and 1960s, particularly those commodities from the rural regions of Australia, such as iron ore, coal, and wool. These items and the demand for many others provided prosperity and a healthy export market for Australian businesses and workers alike.[35] Conversely, though economic prosperity came, to a significant degree, from the "outback" regions of Australia, the overall rural population base was shrinking during these boom times. In fact, the nation's rural population fell from 20.31 percent (1954) to 17.86 percent (1961), and this substantial decrease occurred despite concerted efforts by the Australian government to provide solid employment for those who lived outside their major cities.[36]

For instance, the Snowy Mountain Authority, a huge public works program that was inaugurated in 1949, was designed to create new electrical power for cities, such as Sydney and Melbourne, but it was also intended to be used as a springboard to create inland cities—with new factories—populated by people who moved to the interior away from the already crowded Australian cities. In the end, though, the urban migration trend continued unabated, and the rural regions remained sparsely populated.[37]

Nevertheless, Australia, overall, experienced a solid progression of economic growth that provided the country with a sense of confidence and purpose. America and Great Britain, however, reminded Australia that there were "no free lunches" in this world. In the 1950s and 1960s, Britain and the U.S. were intensely involved in trying to maintain their postwar empires in Asia. Their considerable investments in Australia came with a price— a geopolitical price. Communism was an ever-present specter in Asia, especially after China fell in 1949. Thus, unsurprisingly, when the British and American colonial empires ran into turbulence, they looked to Australia, without hesitation, for assistance.

AMERICA'S ASCENDANT EMPIRE
AND BRITAIN'S LAST STAND IN EAST ASIA

After WWII—particularly the Pacific campaign—Australia needed a new benefactor to ensure their future existence in what they perceived as a hostile region. Australians, from the moment of federation in 1901, never attempted to embraced or understand their Asian neighbors. The "Asian peril" was very much real and unnerving in their minds. The mere thought of millions of "yellow people" ascending upon their British Eden caused many Australians to experience sleepless nights. Thus, the "White Australia" policy that existed, if not always as official policy, certainly in spirit, until the early 1970s, was a result of racism, isolationism, and a "cringing" sense of inadequacy to protect their own.

The post-WWII global landscape was quickly and radically altered. Great Britain withdrew from India (1947) and Burma (1948). In the year 1949, China fell to Mao Zedong's Communist forces, the Dutch were removed from power in Indonesia, and the Soviet Union stunned the West with the detonation of their first atomic bomb. Needless to say, these events, and the specter of Asian communism, struck the Australian government as a "grave threat."[38] Hence, the immediate recognition of geopolitical realities, the enhancement of the national defense, and immediate population development were pursued with nationalistic vigor.

In 1950, a formal peace treaty with the former Japanese Imperial Empire had not been signed by the Australian government. The eventual construction of the San Francisco Peace Treaty (1951) was interpreted to be too "soft" for many Australians who fought tenaciously against the Japanese in the jungles of southeastern Asia. Spender, Prime Minister Menzies' external affairs minister, expressed his misgivings about the perception of the treaty itself, and the dual threats represented by a Communist China and a potentially resurgent Japan. Therefore, Australia's signature on the peace treaty would be contingent upon whether the U.S. could provide a substantive commitment to protect them from potential communist or military adversaries.[39]

By 1954, Australia had obtained and signed two qualified and substantive defense treaties with the United States. First, the ANZUS Treaty, in 1951, involving Australia, New Zealand, and the United States—dubbed by some critics as the "White Man's Club"; New Zealand and Australia had insisted that *only* they, and America, sign the treaty. Three years later, SEATO (South-East Treaty Organization) evolved—which was a collective security agreement for the region. The U.S., Britain, France, Australia, and New Zealand agreed to provide security to the Philippines, Thailand, and Pakistan.[40] These two agreements brought a large degree of relief to the Australian establishment. Though, as part of the price for great-power protection, Australia found itself sending their young men to fight in various regional military conflicts—Malaya, Korea, Vietnam—during the next twenty years.

Australia's involvement was consistent and faithful. Soldiers were sent to the Vietnam War and they fought well. There were sizable casualties—475 killed/4,307 wounded.[41] However, Australian participation did not have the same intensity as exhibited in WWI and WWII. Nevertheless, their commitment and loyalty were unquestioned. The Vietnam War was not terribly

popular back in Australia, and the Aussie soldiers were somewhat questioning of the Americans as jungle fighters. Yet Menzies and the other Liberal Party leaders justified Australia's military presence in Southeast Asia because of the infamous "domino theory." The generally accepted premise for
this theory was simply stopping expansionist powers (i.e., China and the
Soviet Union) from overwhelming their weaker neighbors.[42]

The theory sounded rational and understandable to the average Australian citizen, but unfortunately the nuances and complexities that are always part of war were not so explicable. In 1972, the newly elected Labor
Party prime minister, Gough Whitlam, immediately pulled the plug on Australia's involvement in Vietnam and brought the troops home. Whitlam
also quickly established new relations with China and North Vietnam. The
U.S., initially, was not pleased with these independent regional readjust-
ments of Australian foreign policy.

However, America soon discovered that the Whitlam government wasn't
quite finished with its new agenda concerning external affairs. The new
prime minister also signaled that there were going to be some significant
changes in the U.S.-Australian relationship as well. Needless to say, these
developments did not go down well in the halls of power within the American government.

In 1975, Whitlam was removed from power by an in-house constitutional coup. It was fully supported by the U.S. intelligence community, due
to the prime minister's thinly veiled threats about not signing new leases for
the highly sensitive, strategic, and vital satellite bases located in Australia's
outback. Though these bases were technically called joint U.S.-Australian
communication facilities, the truth was that America shared very little of its
intelligence information with its Australian mates.

I know this to be an absolute fact, because I worked at one of these *vital*
facilities at an area called the Northwest Cape in Western Australia, for two
years (1977–1978). This relatively isolated joint communication facility
was called Naval Communications Station Harold E. Holt. It primarily dealt
with assisting and providing communications for the surface ships and submarines in the Indian Ocean region. The base itself was located near a small
town called Exmouth. It was a town of approximately 5,000 people—
mostly U.S. military personnel and family members. I can count on one
hand all the times that I took communications information to our Australian allies—who had their own communications facilities at the base. In
my opinion, to say that NCS Harold E. Holt was a *joint communication* facility was a bit of an overstatement.

It was this reality, in late 1975, which drove Whitlam to demand that the
Americans become more forthcoming by sharing vital intelligence, gathered
at these bases, with the Australian government. It didn't happen, and Whitlam's government was dispatched without a shot being fired. Australia's

Governor-General John Kerr, appointed by Whitlam himself, liquidated Whitlam's government on 11 November 1975.

Though there were huge rallies demanding Whitlam's reinstatement, the newly unelected Prime Minister Malcolm Fraser moved into power with relative ease. A short time later a perfunctory election was held to legitimize Fraser's power. The Australian governing elite and the American intelligence community fully backed the coup. However, even today, there are still millions of Australians who still feel the effects of what became known as "The Dismissal," and these individuals remain bitter about America's stealth involvement.[43]

Nevertheless, Australia did not participate in another U.S.-lead military expedition until Gulf War I, in 1991, involving the removal of Saddam Hussein's Iraqi forces from Kuwait. Later on, in 2003, the Aussies showed up for the sequel Gulf War II (involving Afghanistan and Iraq) to establish democracy in the Middle East, and to find weapons of mass destruction. Neither has occurred at the time of this writing. Nevertheless, the events of 9/11 shook America out of its self-induced complacency, and terrorism became the new –*ism* that threatened the free world. However, the economic dynamics and geopolitical relations in Asia-Pacific are in a state of transition. China's economic and military emergence, particularly in the last five years, has caused the Australian government to reevaluate their defense policies in relation to their commitment to the U.S. in the region.

If called upon to fight China over Taiwan, within an American-led coalition, former Labor Party Prime Minister Bob Hawke stated in an interview that Australia's involvement in such a military conflict involving Taiwan could have a catastrophic effect for everyone in the region. Therefore, the United States should not take for granted that Australia would blindly follow them into such a conflict.[44] These same sentiments were also expressed recently by the current Liberal Party government and its foreign minister, Alexander Downer.[45] These recent declarations are not isolated cases of discontent.

The Lowy Institute located in Sydney, in 2005, surveyed Australians about their feelings toward China and America. The results should give those in Washington pause and a sense of trepidation concerning their overall policies for Asia-Pacific. Sixty-nine percent had "positive feelings" for China; only 58 percent had "positive feelings" for the U.S.; and 72 percent agreed with Hawke and Downer—no blind commitment toward a China-U.S. war.[46] In 2006, the Lowy Institute produced another survey showing that 69 percent of Australians believe that the U.S. has too much influence in their country's foreign policy decisions. Yet 70 percent of these very same people surveyed believe that the U.S. remains important for Australia's security. Needless to say, these results are a bit disconcerting and contradictory for the U.S., especially, when you consider that Australia is one of America's most loyal allies in Asia-Pacific and in global affairs. Hence, what does this *mean* for the future viability of the U.S.-Australian alliance?

> It doesn't matter whether the cat is black or white, as long as it catches the mice.

> —Deng Xiaoping

Chairman Deng Xiaoping's declaration in defending capitalism in the People's Republic of China, in the late 1970s, can also, to some degree, relate to Australia's shifting economic priorities. The only island continent in the world had remained comfortably within the realm of the British Commonwealth. This dual existence and psychological dependency continued in Australia until the British joined the European Market in 1973. The loss of British markets, due to the rules and regulations within the framework of the European Market, initiated an aggressive search by the Australian government for new markets for Australian exports. They found them quickly. The new markets existed in their own backyard—Asia.

In the 1970s, Australia took significant steps toward restructuring their relationships with several Asian nations. During this decade, there was a development boom in Asia, particularly in Japan and South Korea. The Japanese and Koreans were desperately in need of significant amounts of natural resources for their burgeoning manufacturing sectors. Australia supplied, in abundance, large amounts of various natural resources that kept their factories running nonstop. Trade with China, Singapore, and Taiwan also grew as well.[47]

As expected, Australia has profited handsomely from these new resource-based export business arrangements. Australia also sent a strong message to its Asian neighbors that a new foreign policy was also emerging within the political establishment. These new and extremely profitable business deals indicated that Australia's economic future was indeed within the Pacific Rim, and away from its British/European colonial past. Geoffrey Bolton, a widely respected historian at Edith Cowan University in Western Australia, wrote,

> The old British Commonwealth connection based on investment and migrations was yielding to the compulsions of geography. Australia was becoming part of the Pacific economy. Trade conquered ideology in Australia's quest for markets.[48]

However, it was two other events that cemented Australia's new regional approach in the minds of Asian skeptics. As mentioned earlier in this chapter, in 1972, new relations with China were initiated during the Australian prime ministership of Gough Whitlam (1972–1975). This dramatic shift in regional policy caught their primary ally, the U.S., by surprise. And, in the same year, Whitlam called home the remaining Australian troops stationed in Vietnam. Thus, even the casual observer noted that Australia was indeed moving upon a fundamentally new path in its foreign policy. Despite the U.S's initial unhappiness with Australia's sudden and unilateral foreign policy decisions, trade with the U.S. continued unabated.

Hence, during the 1970s, East Asia witnessed a new geopolitical evolvement and identification process occurring in Australia. Economically and militarily, the Australian global axis was turning steadily away from Great Britain (and the European continent), and toward the U.S.-dominated Pacific Rim region with the ascending economies of Japan, Singapore, South Korea, and Taiwan. In 1978, China began its revolutionary economic "reforms," due to its embracement and incorporation of free market principles—after Deng Xiaoping had solidified his power base within the Chinese Communist Party.

Today, Australia's primary trading partners in the Pacific Rim region are China, Japan, South Korea, and America. This vital "Asian connection" is now widely recognized and accepted by the average Australian citizen. Though, there remain the occasional anti-Asian outbursts from ultra-conservative populists, such as the former leader of One Nation, Pauline Hanson, during the mid-1990s. Hanson, a former fish n' chips operator in Queensland, and her die-hard followers made headlines in newspapers throughout Asia, because of their strident (and racist) statements concerning Asian immigration into Australia.

In truth, most Australians look upon Asia with varying degrees of acceptance; Hanson and One Nation represented a vociferous minority who resented, bitterly at times, the presence of foreigners on their shores.[49] The recent conflagration between white native-born Aussies and Lebanese immigrants at a beach close to Sydney, the worst race riots in recent Australian history, indicates that One Nation–type xenophobic sentiments remain very near the surface of Australian politics.[50]

However, the longtime and nationally prominent Australian historian Geoffrey Blainey writes of a new Australia emerging in the Asia-Pacific region:

> In the last quarter of a century Australia has multiplied its links with Asia, primarily East Asia. Today the majority of Australian exports go to Asia. . . . The teaching of Asian languages far exceeds that of European languages in Australian schools. . . . Defense links with Asian nations, especially Indonesia, are probably stronger than with Europe. . . . This is a remarkable swing, and certainly was predicted by nobody 40 years ago. That Australia sits more easily with its (Asian) neighbors, its understanding of the diverse Asian cultures is greater, that its links with them are quickening and widening: all this is welcome.[51]

Though Australia's relations with its Asian neighbors are being transformed on several levels, the dynamics of the Asia-Pacific region are changing—change is an ever-present element in all phases of international relations. To be more succinct, China is becoming increasingly important to Australia in terms of trade and security, but for diametrically different reasons. The trade factor is interpreted as a very positive factor, but the security issue represents a growing foreboding in the nation's capital, Canberra. China's emerging military power concerns many policymakers and regional analysts in the Australian establishment. The potential clash of interests in the region, between China and Australia's primary benefactor, the U.S., has many uneasy at the beginning of the twenty-first century. In short, the Pacific Rim has become more complicated, and dangerous, for all the nations in the region.

Australia's economic relations with its key trading partners in the Pacific Rim, including China, represent its future prosperity. However, its security is also hinged upon its Asian neighbors as well. To be direct on this matter, it is imperative for Australia to maintain its access to Asian markets. A recent Australian governmental foreign and trade policy white paper shows irrefutably how important Asia has become for this nation of 20 million antipodeans:

1. Asian countries account for seven of Australia's ten largest export markets.
2. Southeast Asia is Australia's front line in the war against terrorism.
3. Australia sends a greater proportion of its exports to Asia than any non-Asian country in the world.
4. Australia signed an agreement on cooperation to combat international terrorism with Malaysia—a country with a large Muslim population.
5. Australia ranks number one in attracting international investment funds amongst Asia-Pacific capital markets (excluding Japan), according to the Morgan Stanley Capital International index.
6. Nearly 25 percent of Australia's current population of 19.6 million were born overseas, and almost 5 percent of all Australians were born in Asia. Also, tens of thousands of Australians live and work throughout Asia.
7. The Asia-Pacific region is home to eight of the world's ten largest armies, and this region has two of the most dangerous existing situations: North Korea's nuclear program and Taiwan's movement toward independence.[52]

Australia has experienced steady growth and economic prosperity. Its purchasing power parity income is approximately $27,000—Australia ranks sixteenth in the world.[53] Their financial house is so solid that the tumultuous Asian financial meltdown in 1997–1998 barely registered within Australian money markets. In fact, Australian exports to their primary Asian trading partners have steadily increased during the past decade. In 2002, Japan, China, South Korea, Singapore, Hong Kong, and Indonesia ranked as the second, third, sixth, seventh, ninth, and tenth largest trading partners of Australian commerce. All these countries have acquired a larger percentage of trade with Australia since 1991. Though America remains Australia's number one trading partner, their bilateral trade represents slightly less than 15 percent of Aussie global trade.[54]

In short, Australia's financial situation, in terms of domestic and international growth, is reasonably sound and functioning well. Unemployment is low (5.75 percent) and the value of the Australian dollar is up significantly (31 percent) in 2003 against the U.S. dollar.[55] Prime Minister John Howard was rewarded by the Australian electorate with a fourth straight election victory in October 2004. Though Howard's support for the U.S. intervention in Iraq continues to be very unpopular with many Australians, the nation's economic growth and stability has diluted the intensity of the political backlash associated with his policies concerning the Middle East.

Yet there remains an emerging anxiety concerning U.S.-China relations. Australia, without hesitation or reservation, has stood shoulder-to-shoulder with the U.S. military since WWII. America's wars in East Asia, primarily in Korea and Vietnam, were evidence of an unquestioned Yank-Aussie alliance against the encroachment of communism in Asia during the Cold War. But the Cold War is over. The new source of discomfort for Australia and the U.S. is the emergence of China. The recent tensions between the U.S. and China have created a newfound concern over the future of the Pacific Rim region.

Currently, there are no wars occurring in the region, and economic growth continues at a healthy clip throughout much of Asia-Pacific. Obviously, maintaining the stable and profitable status quo is to Australia's benefit. Yet the Aussies' close relationship with the Yanks puts them in a precarious, if not a potentially dangerous, position. What will Australia do if the U.S.-China situation deteriorates over sensitive issues such as Taiwan, North Korea, unbalanced trade, or regional hegemonic positioning?

Former Australian Prime Minister Bob Hawke (1983–1991), in 2004, warned that the U.S. cannot count on Australia's complete and unswerving support, as they have in the past, especially if America initiates military action against China, in the near future. Hawke believes that Australia reserves the right to determine whether, or not, they have their own national interests at stake.[56]

This nationalistic declaration, by the former Australian prime minister, comes from an individual who also acknowledges that the U.S. must remain in the Pacific theater to maintain regional stability.[57] However, Mr. Hawke's analysis and concerns reflect the new geopolitical realities emerging within and amongst Pacific Rim nations. Clearly, the statistics provided

earlier indicate that Australia's future economic vitality is irrefutably tied to
East Asia, particularly China, Japan, and South Korea.

In terms of regional and national security, however, the Cold War having
officially ended in 1991, a new chapter in Australian and global history is
now being written. Two of its primary topics are most likely to be the emergence of the *Asian Century* and the continued "war on terror." How that
chapter unfolds in the twenty-first century may indeed provide an indicator
for the future sustainability of U.S.-Australian relations. Will America recognize and respect the real and understood national interests of Australia?
Or will the U.S. continue to be somewhat indifferent to Australia's financial
and security necessities within the Pacific region, and demand (and expect)
the same degree of loyalty shown by this former British colonial outpost
since their victorious alliance during WWII?

NOTES

1. Geoffrey Bolton, *The Oxford History of Australia—Vol. 5* (Melbourne: Oxford
University Press, 1996), p. 7.

2. Ibid.

3. Ibid., p. 8.

4. John Molony, *History of Australia: The Story of 200 Years* (Victoria: Penguin
Books of Australia, 1987), p. 285.

5. Ibid., pp. 289–90.

6. John H. Chambers, *A Traveller's History of Australia* (New York: Interlink
Books, 2002), p. 235.

7. Ibid.

8. Ibid.

9. Ibid., p. 236.

10. Sir Robert Gordon Menzies, *The Measure of the Years* (Victoria: Cassell Australia LTD, 1970), p. 44.

11. Ibid., p. 50.

12. Ibid., pp. 52–53.

13. Ibid., p. 53.

14. Ibid., p. 54.

15. David Day, *Claiming a Continent: A New History of Australia* (Sydney: Harper-
Collins Publishers, 2001), pp. 256–57.

16. Ibid., p. 257.

17. H. V. Evatt, *Australia in World Affairs* (Sydney: Angus & Robertson, 1946), pp.
114–16. This footnote comes from an Evatt speech titled, "The Future in the Pacific."

18. Ibid., p. 85. The speech was titled, "Australian-American Co-Operation."

19. Ibid., p. 86.

20. Ibid.

21. David Lee and Christopher Waters, Editors, *Evatt to Evans: The Labor Tradition in
Australian Foreign Policy* (Australian National University: Allen & Unwin, 1997), p. 63.

22. Evatt, *Australia in World Affairs*, p. 39.

23. Lee and Waters, *Evatt to Evans*, p. 74.

24. Menzies, *The Measure of the Years*, p. 52.

25. John Pilger, *A Secret Country* (Victoria: Vintage Books, 1992), p. 163.

26. Ibid., pp. 154–63.

27. Day, *Claiming a Continent*, p. 258.

28. Bolton, *The Oxford History of Australia*, p. 90.

29. Day, *Claiming a Continent*, p. 269.

30. Ibid., p. 267.

31. Ibid., p. 269.

32. Ibid., p. 268.

33. Bolton, *The Oxford History of Australia*, p. 90.

34. Ibid., pp. 90–91.

35. Ibid., p. 91.

36. Day, *Claiming a Continent*, p. 261.

37. Ibid.

38. Ibid., p. 255.

39. Ibid., p. 256.

40. Ibid., p. 256–57.

41. Bolton, *The Oxford History of Australia*, p. 166.

42. Ibid.

43. Pilger, *A Secret Country*, chapter 5 "The Coup"

44. Interview with Bob Hawke, 4 June 2004, Sydney, Australia. I have interviewed the former Australian prime minister on four different occasions.

45. David Shambaugh, "Rising Dragon and the American Eagle—Part 1," *Yale-Global* online, 20 April 2005.

46. Ibid.

47. Bolton, *The Oxford History of Australia*, p. 183.

48. Ibid.

49. Paul Kelly, "Hanson, a Symptom of a Deeper Problem," *Paradise Divided: The Changes, the Challenges, the Choices for Australia* (Australia: Allen & Unwin, 2000), pp. 142–53.

50. Mahir Ali, "Fight Them on the Beaches? Australia's Identity Crisis and the Sydney Riots," *ZNet/Australia*, 20 December 2005, pp. 1–3.

51. Geoffrey Blainey, *In Our Time: The Issues and the People of Our Century* (Melbourne: Information Australia, 1999), p. 184.

52. Commonwealth of Australia, "Advancing the National Interest," *Australia's Foreign Affairs and Trade Policy White Paper*, 2003. (Chapter 1)

53. Bruce Vaughn, "Australia: Background and U.S. Relations," *CRS Report for Congress* (Updated 14 July 2004). Vaughn is an analyst in Asian Affairs, Foreign Affairs, Defense and Trade Division.

54. Commonwealth of Australia, *Australia's Foreign Affairs and Trade Policy White Paper* (Appendix 2).

55. Vaughn, "Australia."

56. Hawke interview, June 2004.

57. Ibid.

2

The Return of the Rising Sun

America's war with Japan, from 1941 to 1945, was a vicious collision between two distinct civilizations that fought over the future hegemony of
Asia-Pacific. The war between these two expansionist and powerful nations officially began with Japan's massive and well-coordinated naval
aerial sneak attack upon Pearl Harbor—the largest U.S. naval facility in
the Pacific region—on 7 December 1941, and ended with the first and
only ever military use of atomic weaponry, at Hiroshima and Nagasaki in
early August 1945. The war continues to shape U.S. foreign policy within
the Pacific Rim.

In retrospect, according to Walter LaFeber, professor of History at Cornell
University, the Pacific War represented the culmination of tense relations
between Japan and the U.S. since Commodore Matthew Perry's uninvited
and unwanted arrival upon Japanese shores in 1853.[1] Japan's aggressive
military actions toward China, Korea, Taiwan, and Southeast Asia from the
1890s onward meant that they were charting a territorial expansionist
course of action. Eventually, Japan's own version of "manifest destiny" in
Asia-Pacific collided with American and European interests in the region.
Professor LaFeber writes about two nations, America and Japan, with similar regional agendas for Asia-Pacific, but, tragically, they really didn't know
or understand one another:

> Each people had too often seen the other through the distorted lenses of
> racism and parochial national interests. But on the central issue, each under-
> stood the other quite well. For their part, Japanese officials were determined to
> protect their society's traditional values by breaking its long dependence on the

West (and increasingly on the United States) through the creation of a "new order" in Asia that centered on China and was defined and controlled by Japan.[2]

JAPAN: IMPERIALISM, WAR, AND DESTRUCTION

Japan's hunger for territorial conquest was quite transparent—much like the
Europeans themselves. Their aggression against China in 1895—coveting
Manchuria and Korea—eventually led to the creation of America's Open
Door policy in 1899. U.S. Secretary of State John Hay designed this stratagem to maintain the "status quo" amongst the great powers in relation to
having "equal opportunity" to exploit China's natural resources and cheap
labor.[3] It was also created toward avoiding potential military conflicts—
especially with the Japanese—within and outside the respective treaty ports
of the great powers situated in China.

However, Japanese aggression, in 1904, reappeared at the coastal treaty
port called Port Arthur, located in southern Manchuria. This particular port
was acknowledged as a Russian treaty port. It became quite apparent, early
on, that the Russian navy was no match for Japan's modern and powerful
naval forces. In the end, the Japanese humiliated the Russians, and gave no-
tice to the other European powers that an Asian power was in ascendance.
Though Japan suffered a sizable amount of casualties in its war with Russia,
it was still seen as a shocking victory, and it certainly got the attention of the
United States as well.

In 1905, a negotiated settlement was completed with the help of U.S.
President Theodore Roosevelt—who received the Nobel Peace Prize for his
efforts. Interestingly, Roosevelt's original agreement was rejected by the
Japanese government. The first ever anti-American riots erupted in Japan.
Eventually, an acceptable agreement was constructed. In 1908, the U.S. and
Japan recognized each other's economic and military positions ("status
quo") in Asia-Pacific with the signing of the Root-Takahira Agreement in
1908.[4] This agreement confirmed Japan's standing as a major power in the
Pacific, but it also contributed to an anti-Japanese backlash within America
at the beginning of the twentieth century.

In 1906, the San Francisco Board of Education sent a controversial direc-
tive to the city's school principals that they were to send "all Chinese, Japanese and Korean children to the Oriental School."[5] President Roosevelt
harshly criticized the San Francisco Board of Education for its actions, and
he also wanted to avoid a potentially nasty confrontation with Japan.[6] The
Japanese government protested vigorously about this overt discriminatory
measure. In 1907, the California legislature debated and eventually passed,
in 1913, a bill that denied landownership to Japanese immigrants.[7] Finally,

in 1908, President Roosevelt negotiated a Gentlemen's Agreement with the Japanese government to limit Japanese immigration.[8] These are just three examples of a growing anti-Japanese sentiment within the U.S., and they contributed to the racist suspicions that the Japanese held toward America. Conversely, the Japanese saw themselves as special and unique within the Pacific region. Like Americans, the Japanese perceived themselves as a people of (manifest?) destiny.

In the 1920s, Thomas Burkman, a professor of history at the State University of New York at Albany, wrote that Shidehara Kijuro, the primary foreign minister of Japan throughout most of the 1920s, came to symbolize the position of Japanese international accommodation during this decade. "Shidehara diplomacy" came to be seen as a strategy seeking cooperation and stability with the major global powers, and a policy of nonaggression toward China.[9] However, this historical perspective did not represent the attitudes or beliefs of everyone who lived in America during the 1920s.

Billy Mitchell, an officer in the U.S. Air Service, predicted in 1925, that Japan and America would eventually go to war, because both countries wanted to dominate the Pacific region. In fact, Colonel Mitchell predicted that Pearl Harbor and the Philippines would be attacked by Japan in the near future. Needless to say, his comments caused an immediate uproar. U.S. politicians and the American military ridiculed, or simply ignored, his concerns and observations about future relations with Japan.[10] Mitchell died in 1936, five years before Japan's assault upon Pearl Harbor and the Philippines, but he was awarded a special medal posthumously by President Harry Truman, in 1946, for his "outstanding pioneer service and foresight in the field of American military aviation."[11]

In 1931, the tide of internationalism began to recede within the Japanese government due to an incident in Manchuria. An explosion on the South Manchurian Railway, near Mukden, began a diplomatic downward spiral for Japan and the global community. Highly respected Nitobe Inazo, the former undersecretary-general of the League of Nations (1920–1926) and, in the 1930s, the chairman of the Japanese Council of the Institute of Pacific Relations, traveled to the U.S. to explain Japan's interventionist actions in Manchuria. The trip proved to be a rude awakening for Inazo and the Japanese government. Japan's primary argument was with concern for its self-preservation; thus, they sought an independent Manchuria to enhance their security. This point of view fell upon deaf ears in Washington. Angered, but not really surprised by the U.S. response, the Japanese believed that America's counter-arguments represented the tiresome but typical Western hypocrisy toward Asia. The U.S. had previously made similar interventionist arguments concerning Central America and the primacy of their own security. Yet, when these same principles were applied by Japan with concern to Manchuria, they were rejected outright. Afterwards, the Japanese became so disillusioned by this double standard that they quit the League of Nations in 1933.[12]

In 1939, Japan began to take steps toward becoming the dominate power in East Asia. In fact, the overall objective was named the East Asia "Co-Prosperity Sphere," which represented their overall stratagem for the region. The plan called for European influences throughout East Asia to be removed and replaced by Asian power. However, Japan represented the vanguard of Asian power. Thus, the paternalistic control of Asian resources, in their hands, was the *real* objective for Japan, and not *just* the removal of the European presence in East Asia.[13] Japan's growing strength in the Pacific region began to be viewed by the U.S. as an irrefutable danger to their positioning in East Asia, especially in the Philippines. By the end of the 1930s, Japan dominated large parts of eastern China, and had total control of Formosa, Korea, and Manchuria. It now cast its eyes upon Southeast Asia, and its valuable natural resources. In 1940, the prior incendiary and provocative statements made by Colonel Mitchell, in 1925, did not appear to be so hysterical or irrational in retrospect.

Historian Howard Zinn writes in *A People's History of the United States* that America's entry into WWII was due to the bombing of Pearl Harbor on 7 December 1941, and not because of the carnage and death that occurred at Nanjing, China, in 1937. Zinn states, "It was the Japanese attack on a link in the American Pacific Empire that did it."[14] Thus, the war began, and when it ended it represented one of the most vicious struggles in human history. John Dower, author of *Embracing Defeat*, quantifies Japan's defeat—2.7 million servicemen and civilians killed, equal to approximately 4 percent of Japan's overall population, and millions injured or malnourished due to the war.[15] Also, sixty-six cities, including Hiroshima and Nagasaki, were seriously damaged from massive bombings, 30 percent of the population was homeless, and 40 percent of urban Japan was destroyed.[16] Thus, in the post-WWII aftermath, Japan was confronted with the mind-boggling challenge of rebuilding a shattered nation.

The final acts of the Pacific campaign were the dropping of atomic bombs upon Hiroshima and Nagasaki. Though, it was recognized by most leaders and policymakers within the U.S. military and government, respectively, in August 1945, that the Pacific War was nearing its end. President Truman, nevertheless, ordered these weapons dropped upon a clearly defeated enemy. Truman *believed*, and stated continuously afterwards, that he did it to spare the lives of hundreds of thousands of American troops. In short, the U.S. did not have to invade the Japanese mainland as a consequence of the bombings. Thus, *the decision*, to this day, remains politically controversial and historically complicated for both nations.

I taught a history seminar on the dropping of the atomic bomb on Hiroshima while teaching for the University of Maryland–Asian Division at Kadena Air Base, which was situated upon the Japanese island prefecture of Okinawa. I found myself torn between the immorality of the act and the recognition that this horrendous act (and the Nagasaki atomic bombing) did end the war, and probably saved thousands of lives as Truman continually stated throughout his postpresidency. Like the American civilian and military leadership, in August 1945, the decision to drop the atomic bombs on Japan remains an open wound in my intellectual and spiritual consciousness. Though, to be perfectly honest, if I was on a transport ship headed toward the Japanese home island of Kyushu, in August 1945, to invade it and to know absolutely that massive casualties would occur, I would have supported the dropping of this monster weapon for reasons based upon nothing more than self-preservation.

In 1995, the Smithsonian Institute, in Washington, DC, attempted to commemorate the fiftieth anniversary of the Hiroshima and Nagasaki bombings, when all hell broke loose. Historical interpretations and ideological perspectives collided in the nation's capital, causing a national firestorm unseen since the days of protest concerning another Asian war—Vietnam. In the end, the Smithsonian Institute finally decided to present a watered-down mediocre display telling of the event. Needless to say, the Hiroshima and Nagasaki bombings remain too sensitive, and current, for an honest reevaluation within America. Perhaps, when the WWII-generation finally fades into the pages of history, maybe, just maybe, Americans might be able to finally have an honest discussion concerning the ramifications of this monumental decision that not only ended a war, but changed the course of human history.

In Japan, these bombings are presented as proof that *they* were the real victims of WWII. However, Japan's wartime behavior, particularly in China, Korea, and Southeast Asia, has been glossed over by the country's educational and political institutions. I know this from my personal experiences teaching various U.S. history and american government courses in Japan and Okinawa for four years. Many of my Japanese students were quite often confused or mystified by my statements concerning WWII (the Pacific War) and the Hiroshima and Nagasaki bombings. After class, they explained to me that their Japanese teachers simply never addressed the issues concerning the war directly.

This admission of ignorance by my Japanese students is easily understandable. There were good reasons for their teachers' (and their government's) omissions concerning Japanese behavior during WWII. Brian MacArthur's book, *Surviving the Sword*, tells of the brutality visited upon Allied soldiers who were tragically encamped at a Japanese P.O.W. facility in

East Asia during WWII. They were referred to as *Fepows*—Far East prisoners of war. During the first five months of the war, approximately 133,000 British, Dutch, Australians, and Americans were captured by Japanese forces. It is estimated that about 27 percent died in these camps (compared to 4 percent of Germans in Allied camps). About one-third of the dead met their fate while building the Burma-Thailand railroad, later immortalized in the movie, *The Bridge on the River Kwai*.[17] (Note: I have visited this specific site, and the graveyards occupied by fallen Allied soldiers. It was very hot and humid that day—I could quite clearly understand why and how Allied soldiers, who survived this brutal treatment, often weighed less than 100 pounds upon their release, and why many of these survivors never forgave the Japanese for their wartime behavior.)

Professor MacArthur, a visiting scholar in the Asia/Pacific/American Studies Program at New York University, described in unsparing detail the inhumane realities and treatment that confronted the Allied *Fepows*: starvation, disease, slave labor conditions, constant beatings with bamboo and wire, and lit cigarettes put into their noses and ears. And, unsurprisingly, other creative means of torture were also used against the Allied prisoners. All together, the images that one conjures up concerning a Japanese P.O.W. camp can be accurately described as being dark, terrifying, ugly, and satanic. Though some men attempted to survive this nightmare, others became cowards, collaborators, and thieves in response to the Japanese unending panoply of inhumane behavior.[18]

In retrospect, it is not hard to understand the blind rage and deeply felt bitterness of many WWII Allied veterans, who encountered, fought, and/or were taken as a P.O.W. by the Japanese, during the Pacific War, and why the Japanese establishment avoids this *conversation* with the children born in the postwar era.

THE AMERICAN OCCUPATION (1945–1952)

After the Pacific War, America occupied Japan until 1952. It was the signing of the San Francisco Peace Treaty (1951) that finally put the Pacific War to rest between the U.S. and Japan. Like in the American South, after the American Civil War—the bloodiest and most destructive war to ever take place upon American soil—the U.S. government embarked upon an awesome reform project to restructure Japanese society. In hindsight, as a result of the American occupation, all phases of Japanese life were affected to some degree or another. U.S. Army General Douglas MacArthur, the supreme commander of Allied Powers (SCAP), was essentially given the authority to reform a militaristic and rigid hierarchical society into one directed toward peace, social mobility, and stability.

Though General MacArthur publicly declared himself a possessor of "the Asian mind," in truth, the Asian (including the Japanese) mentality continued to baffle him despite having lived in the region for decades.[19] In reality, General MacArthur *was* the U.S. government for all intents and purposes during his tenure in Japan. To accomplish the nation-building task of molding and reforming Japanese society to the satisfaction of the U.S. government, General MacArthur was provided with 400,000 American troops to provide the security framework to get the job done.[20] The proposed agenda was certainly broad, intense, and sweeping. In retrospect, this task was probably perceived as daunting and intimidating, at first, for MacArthur and his occupation troops. However, in the end, fundamental reforms did occur at the civic, economic, and political levels within Japanese society.

The political changes were truly revolutionary—the *sovereignty* rested with the *people*, not with the emperor. The emperor became a useful *symbol* of Japanese unity and culture—but he had no *real* power under the new constitution. The *primary* political institution, in Japan, was now the popularly elected national parliament (the Diet). And the once formidable Japanese Imperial military forces that had only recently conquered large swaths of East Asia were irrevocably dismantled and abolished. In their place, Article 9 of the new constitution, written partly by MacArthur himself but mostly by his legal staff, *forbade* Japan to maintain an army, and to *ever* go to war again.

The economic changes were equally significant. Land reform was very important in the minds of the American government toward creating a democratic Japanese society—Thomas Jefferson's *Notes on the State of Virginia*[21] comes to mind. Before the war, the average size farm in Japan was approximately an acre. The Owner-Farmer Establishment Law (1946) bought approximately 4 million acres and sold it cheaply to 2 million farmers throughout Japan. The existence of land tenants dropped to 8 percent, and the newly empowered farmers have remained a political force in Japanese politics to the present day.[22] Common workers also received the right to unionize—a touch of the New Dealism that still existed within the U.S. government. Between December 1945 and March 1947, three laws were passed by the Diet that gave Japanese workers the right to organize unions if they wished. Independent labor unions had been dismantled during WWII. However, with these new labor laws supporting the rights of workers, union membership in Japan grew dramatically to 6.75 million by 1948.[23]

Finally, the infamous but powerful *zaibatsu* (the intra-connected Japanese family-based business community) was confronted by General MacArthur in 1947. Unfortunately, the anti-*zaibatsu* measures supported by MacArthur, and U.S.-designed antitrust legislation, fell far short of expectations. Hence, the efforts to legally and realistically separate Japanese business conglomerates from Japanese financial institutions unequivocally failed. Professor LaFeber mentions the opinion of one expert concerning Japan's business-financial partnership, "Unless the business and financial structure in Japan is radically transformed, all other changes will be rendered nugatory."[24]

By 1949, with the collapse of China's nationalists' government, the plan for radically restructuring Japan's economy appeared risky, if not dangerous for U.S. interests in the region. Japan, in the end, was allowed to control its own development. It was determined by the Truman administration that Japan's economic recovery was the second most important priority—only second to U.S. security interests overall. Therefore, the United States focused upon a few fundamental goals for Japan's economy:

1. Remove existing obstacles to the revival of Japanese foreign trade
2. Accelerate private enterprise
3. Raise production and maintain high export levels through hard work
4. Attack high inflation through balanced budgets[25]

It is important to note, according to Herbert Bix, a Pulitzer Prize–winning historian and a prominent professor of Japanese history, "compared to military occupations of other countries by other armies, the occupation of Japan had been mild and correct; now the peace treaty was extremely generous and non-punitive . . . the only reparations that Japan would ever have to pay—approximately 1.02 billion worth of goods and services—were to the Philippines, Indonesia, Burma, and (later) South Vietnam."[26]

Though, it should be acknowledged that American troops have remained in Japan over sixty years since the surrender terms were agreed upon and signed by the U.S. and their allies on the U.S.S. *Missouri* in Tokyo Bay. And Japan, especially Okinawa, as prominent historian of modern Japan, Chalmers Johnson, believes has become an essential and irreplaceable part of the American empire in the twenty-first century.[27]

ECONOMIC MIRACLE: JAPAN'S BOOM YEARS, 1950–1975

Professor Rhoads Murphey writes, "The growth of production and income in Japan from 1950 to 1975 was faster than has been measured in any country at any time; in those twenty-five years, output and incomes roughly tripled."[28] Murphey, a professor of Asian history at the University of Michigan, points out that during this *period of time* "Japanese goods became the best in the world market, notably cars, camera, sound reproduction equipment, optics and many electronics."[29]

Professor Chalmers Johnson, professor emeritus at the University of California, San Diego and now president of the Japan Policy Research Institute, confirms Murphey's analysis, by writing, "From approximately 1950 to 1975, the United States treated Japan as a beloved ward, indulging its every economic need and proudly patronizing it as a star capitalist pupil. The United States sponsored Japan's entry into many international institutions, like the United Nations and the Organization of Economic Cooperation and Development, well before a post-WWII global consensus in favor of Japan had developed."[30]

From 1945 until 1992, Japan's economy grew impressively, resulting in the country becoming the second largest, in terms of gross national product (GNP), economic power in the world. This achievement is even more astounding, when you take into consideration that Japan imports almost all of its basic resource necessities (99.8 percent of its iron, 99.6 percent of its oil, 86.7 percent of its coal) which are desperately needed to create and maintain its economic prowess.[31]

However, since the early 1990s, Japan has endured a harsh economic recession. The primary reasons for its economic doldrums were its overvalued real estate market collapsing and numerous banking failures resulting from bad loans provided to various risky business ventures. Since 1991, according to research done by the Real Estate Economic Institute and Credit Suisse First Boston, the average value of Japanese residential land fell 33 percent. And, in six large cities, including Tokyo, the decline in residential land averaged 65 percent, and the value of commercial land collapsed 87 percent.[32]

Nevertheless, in 2006, Japan's economy remains the second largest in the world and it has recently shown signs of recovering, and there is optimism that has been missing since the early 1990s. Martin Fackler, a reporter for the *New York Times*, wrote in December 2005, from Tokyo,

> College graduates face the best job market in a decade, and wages are rising again. The lead stock market index has doubled in value in two years. Corporate profits are the highest in recent memory. And for the first time since 1990, land prices in Tokyo are up . . . Could it be that Japan, long the sick man among major global economies, has finally recovered?[33]

This optimism is not based upon false data. Japan's GDP (gross domestic product) has shown an average of 2 percent real growth per year from 2003 to 2005. Full-time employment has increased since 2003. Average dividend yield for Japanese nonfinancial listed companies has steadily grown since 2002. And, finally, a major reason for Japan's reemergence has been its deepening economic integration with its Asian neighbors, particularly with China since 1998.[34]

However, despite recent signs that Japan's economy is slowly emerging from a decade plus of decline or stagnation, the Japanese have certainly learned some hard lessons from the economic slump experienced since the early 1990s. Provincial towns and rural areas suffered greatly; suicides and crime rose dramatically—according to Japanese standards. Tragically, suicides increased by 50 percent since 1990; they paralleled the rising level of poverty and store closings in local communities throughout Japan.[35] Obviously, the golden days of economic prosperity associated with the 1980s have faded from memory. What was badly needed was an infusion of new ideas and rules to stimulate the business community within Japan.

The beginning of this turnaround occurred in the 1990s and has continued to the present time. The following areas were focused upon to reform, or stimulate, in order for businesses in Japan to move forward:

1. The law and regulatory system needed to be overhauled. The protective role of banks and cross-shareholdings were no longer strong enough for Japanese industry.
2. The use of subsidiaries to hide problems, such as surplus staff and disguised risky business adventures, were costly and no longer viable options as profits fell.
3. A new law, in 2000, gave companies the right to sell "noncore" business units (divisions or subsidiaries) that were underperforming. Also, the capital requirements to create a new limited company was reduced by 66 percent to 1 million yen.
4. The role of shareholders has been enhanced. They have voted against management on a number of occasions. "Poison pill" resolutions to fend off mergers have also been voted down.
5. James Abegglen, a veteran consultant and scholar in Tokyo, wrote about the mergers that have consolidated several industries with Japan. During this process, thousands of subsidiaries have been closed or traded by the parent companies.[36]

It is these economic reforms and new legal parameters that have jump-started the Japanese economy during the past few years. Overall, these changes have resonated positively throughout Japanese society, and especially within the business community.

However, the most important economic relationship for Japan is the one they enjoy with the United States. According to a Congressional Research Service White Paper created by William H. Cooper, a specialist in international trade and finance within the Foreign Affairs, Defense and Trade Division,

The U.S.-Japan economic relationship is very strong and mutually advantageous . . . The *relative* significance of Japan and the United States as each other's economic partner has diminished somewhat with the rise of China as an economic power . . . Nevertheless, analyses of trade and other economic date suggest that the bilateral relationship remains important, and policy leaders of both countries face the challenge of how to manage it . . . The U.S. and Japanese economies remain closely intertwined through trade and capital flows.[37]

Cooper's analysis also informs readers that the U.S. and Japan, combined, represent over 40 percent of global domestic production of goods and services. Thus, their financial clout is enormous, which makes them vital actors on the world's economic stage. Yet they also need one another to sustain their precarious global standing amongst the developed nations. For instance, Japan is the most significant source of capital needed to finance the burgeoning U.S. debt, and both countries provide absolutely necessary foreign direct investment (FDI) into each other's economies, which ensures their continued growth and development. Finally, they both possess large markets for their respective goods—exports and imports—and their economic systems are deeply integrated and dependent upon one another. Cooper states within this extensive report, without ambiguity or hesitation, "(The) U.S.-Japan economic relationship is important to U.S. national interests and to the U.S. Congress . . . Economic conditions in the United States and Japan have a significant impact on the rest of the world."[38]

Though the economic realm is recognized and greatly respected by the U.S. and Japan, their views on foreign policy, particularly toward China and North Korea, have created tensions within this special alliance. There is a growing segment within Japan's foreign policy establishment who are publicly stating it's time for Japan to restructure its foreign policy to match its economic prowess, and support the nation's vital interests.

In short, there is a strong sentiment within the country to become a "normal country" in terms of creating an independent foreign policy, or at the very least to exercise a bit more autonomy with concern to U.S. regional policies. This populist trend represents a direct threat to America's ability and capacity to remain the hegemonic power within the Pacific Rim. The primary reason for these stimuli within the Japanese foreign policy establishment is primarily the dramatic rise of China—economically and militarily—and, secondarily, North Korea's progress, and unanswered questions, concerning its nuclear weapons program, and its future behavior in Northeast Asia.

Both developments are of great concern to Japan and its future status in the Pacific region. To be specific, China's hegemonic potential and North Korea's intransigence on the nuclear issue threaten Japan's future influence, stature, and security in Asia-Pacific. It's a dilemma of great concern to both the U.S. and Japan. The region's balance of power and future stability are at stake. In essence, the region and the world are entering a new phase of global power politics. America's overall stature is incrementally declining, especially due to the twin failures in Afghanistan and Iraq, but also due to China's incredible economic growth rates over the past twenty-five years, and its double-digit military expenditures. When you throw in the unpredictable rogue states of North Korea and Iran, the tinderbox of Taiwanese calls for (potential) independence, and the growing competition for natural resources to keep Asian economies humming along, no wonder many regional analysts are suffering from acid indigestion!

Therefore, let's examine briefly, and with a bit more depth, the volatile relationship between the two most powerful countries in East Asia, China and Japan. And, perhaps, we can understand why this relationship is the *key* to future prosperity and stability throughout the region. If achieving *harmony* is beyond the capabilities of these two major powers during the twenty-first century, then the U.S. will certainly be dragged into any conflagration that occurs between the two. If this tragic scenario plays itself out, then it will mean with absolute certainty that the comprehensive and regionally integrated post-WWII economic and security structure designed by the United States will be dismantled. Two major factors will dramatically affect the U.S. economy: First, Chinese money to pay for our growing national debt will disappear. Secondly, the Asian markets for U.S. goods will disappear. It's hard to see any winners in a military confrontation.

Therefore, key questions abound in Asia-Pacific, but particularly with China and Japan. First, when, or can, China and Japan bury the hatchet, like France and Germany did after WWII? Can the U.S. mediate such an event? It's becoming increasingly obvious to the U.S., China, and Japan, and their neighbors throughout Asia-Pacific, that the future would be infinitely more secure and prosperous if these two Northeast Asian behemoths finally dropped their swords aimed toward each other, and worked together to construct a new Asian paradigm. But, in 2007, we appear to be a long way from that moment in history. Therefore, can the U.S. become the "honest broker" needed to bring a common understanding between these two nations who have had a deadly and poisonous recent past? The roots of the present-day poison (and potential death) rest within the soil of China—planted there in 1895.

China, a country that has experienced abuse, colonization (Manchuria), imperialism (treaty ports), occupation, and military devastation—much of it at the hands of the Japanese (and Europe too!)—is reestablishing itself as the "Middle Kingdom" in East Asia. Historically, and geographically, China has evolved into a unified entity for the first time since the 1840s. Only Taiwan remains outside the fold, in terms of total political control. Ironically, since the 1980s, China and Japan have established prosperous and robust trade relations, and their respective governments continue ongoing negotiations concerning their future economic evolvement into the twenty-first century. Unsurprisingly, though, Japan has also interpreted the reemergence of China with a certain degree of anxiety and wariness. Why?

The terrible physical and psychological wounds suffered by China at the hands of Japan, and its wartime leaders Emperor Hirohito and Hideki Tojo, since the early 1930s, have not fully healed. In truth, Japan has had great difficulty owning up to its ruthless treatment of China since 1895, which includes the conquests of Taiwan (1895), Korea (1905), and Manchuria (1931), the rape of Nanjing (1937), and the gruesome and irrefutable truth that they literally killed millions of Chinese civilians from 1895 until 1945. Japan's dysfunctional (delusional?) postwar behavior of war crime denials, and shameless acts of nationalism, such as former Japanese Prime Minister Koizumi Junichiro's visits to the Yasukuni War Memorial, where convicted Class A war criminals are buried, have caused a high degree of angst, anxiety, hysteria, and pain amongst many Asian nations. Renowned historian, Herbert Bix, a professor in the Graduate School of Social Sciences at Hitotsubashi University in Tokyo, believes the key to long-term stability in the region is to teach Asian students about WWII in an honest manner, or

> the possibility exists that neo-nationalist currents will feed off one another. Peace groups everywhere need to understand the politics of the Northeast Asian nations and work to prevent that from happening. Never has the need for historical reflection on World War II in Asia been greater.[39]

In February 2006, Japan's two major newspapers, *Yomiuri* and *Asahi*, and their respective editors, Watanabe Tsuneo and Yoshibumi Wakamiya, took a bold step and jointly called for a new National War Memorial to replace the Yasukuni War Memorial. Essentially, the Yasukuni War Memorial is simply too inflammatory within Asia, and it represents a historical and psychological diplomatic barrier between Japan and East Asia, but particularly with China and Korea.[40]

Hence, China's relatively recent economic and military reemergence, in Asia-Pacific, presents a serious dilemma for Japan's future—Is China their economic competitor or their future enemy? If Japan is truly interested in regional stability then why does it constantly provoke the Chinese leadership with constant insulting acts and references to WWII, which spark emotional outbursts of nationalism throughout China?[41] Does the Japanese leadership realize (or care?) that this type of public relations is unsettling, and potentially dangerous, between two countries that were mortal enemies only seventy years ago?[42]

These China questions, concerning Japan's bizarre and disturbing behavior toward the Chinese, are extraordinarily important because they are also directly relevant to the U.S.-Japan alliance. Thus, it is appropriate to ask, is this the *proper* moment for Japan to begin an evolutionary process of developing its own foreign policy, and minimizing its commitment to the U.S.? Or should Japan *recommit* itself to its American ally and participate in what some regional observers have called the "soft containment" of China as the twenty-first century unfolds?

In the last few years, Japan has pushed very hard to become a permanent member of the U.N. Security Council—a move that China is dead-set against. Yet the Japanese have broad support from other nations, including WWII adversaries America and Australia, who think it is time for the world and the U.N. to move on from its WWII origins, and restructure the institute's most important council to reflect the new geopolitical realities in the world. Nevertheless, there remains some apprehension among some U.N. members, particularly China and South Korea, that Japan has not properly atoned for its brutal and barbaric behavior during WWII.

Thus, China, being one of the five permanent members of the U.N. Security Council, has veto power over any enlargement initiative concerning the future construction of the Security Council. The primary countries mentioned most often for permanent membership on the U.N. Security Council are Brazil, India, Germany, and Japan—sometimes referred to as the "Group of Four" (G4). To avoid, or deny, permanent membership for these four major global powers puts the future credibility of the U.N. Security Council at risk. In the end, due to pressing global pressures, Japan might achieve its ultimate goal—permanent membership on the U.N. Security Council. However, according to Emily Bruemmer, "its (Japan's) strong commitments to the goals of the United Nations, which include peacekeeping operations, have demonstrated the country's (positive) capabilities. It must now convince its neighbors and the world that this potential can become a global reality."[43]

Stay tuned, the return of the Rising Sun is certainly going to have ramifications in Asia-Pacific and globally. I believe the key factor in Japan's reemergence as a trusted member of the global community is whether America can convince China that the Japanese represent no threat to their future status in the region. President George H. W. Bush was able to convince the leaders of the former Soviet Union, Mikhail Gorbachev and Boris Yeltsin, that German unification, in 1990, would not be a threat to Russian security. In the first decade of the twenty-first century, China is seeking the same kind of assurances from the U.S. concerning its most important ally in Asia—Japan.

The endgame for this delicate and dangerous situation in Northeast Asia is the following: Do the Chinese trust the U.S. to keep Japan on a short leash, especially militarily, and ensure that China's current economic development will not be derailed by the remilitarization of the Rising Sun? Paul Bracken, a professor of political science at Yale University, author of *Fire in the East*, believes that America must play a key role in preventing an arms race from occurring in Asia:

Engagement may be the only sensible diplomatic solution for dealing with countries with nuclear weapons and missiles. . . . The problem is that the United States isn't thinking about what it will be like to live in a world where five to ten Asian countries are nuclear powers . . . All these countries will have a much greater ability to ignore any embargo of Western technology or arms control roadblocks meant to slow them down. This is the new political reality the West will face in the next century (twenty-first), and major challenges to U.S. national security and international order will result from it.[44]

To put things succinctly, the key factor in preventing a dangerous situation from evolving into a destructive military confrontation between China and Japan is for both nations to find enough common ground to coexist and prevent a conflagration that will take down the entire region, economically and militarily, including America's post-WWII regional infrastructures that have kept the (relative) peace for over sixty years.

NOTES

1. Walter LaFeber, *The Clash: U.S.-Japanese Relations throughout History* (New York: W.W. Norton & Company, 1997), p. 213.

2. Ibid., p. 214.

3. Herbert P. Bix, *Hirohito and the Making of Modern Japan* (New York: Harper-Collins Publishers, 2000), p. 147.

4. Bruce W. Jentleson, *American Foreign Policy: The Dynamics of Choice in the 21st Century* (New York: W.W. Norton & Company, 2004), pp. 95–96.

5. Ronald Takaki, *Strangers from a Different Shore: A History of Asian Americans* (New York: Little, Brown and Company, 1998), p. 201.

6. Ibid.

7. Ibid., p. 203.

8. Ibid.

9. Thomas W. Burkman, "Japan and the League of Nations: An Asian Power Encounters the European Club," *Wilson and the League of Nations, Part 2.* (www.24hourscholar.com).

10. C. V. Glines, "Billy Mitchell: Air Power Visionary," *Aviation History*, September 1997.

11. Ibid.

12. Burkman, "Japan and the League of Nations."

13. LaFeber, *The Clash*, p. 191.

14. Howard Zinn, *A People's History of the United States, 1492–Present* (New York: HarperCollins Publishers, 1999), p. 410.

15. John W. Dower, *Embracing Defeat: Japan in the Wake of World War II* (New York: W.W. Norton & Company/The New Press, 1999), p. 45.

16. Ibid.

17. Robert Asahina's book review, "All the Enemy's Mercy, in Asia . . . ," *The Washington Post*, 24 July 2005, concerning the book, *Surviving the Sword: Prisoners of the Japanese in the Far East, 1942–1945* (New York: Random House, 2005).

18. Ibid.

19. Ibid., p. 261.

20. Ibid.

21. Thomas Jefferson Papers (an electronic archive), The Massachusetts Historical Society.

22. LaFeber, *The Clash*, p. 265.

23. Ibid., p. 264.

24. Ibid., p. 269.

25. Ibid., p. 274.

26. Bix, *Hirohito*, pp. 650–51.

27. Chalmers Johnson, *The Sorrows of Empire: Militarism, Secrecy, and the End of the Republic* (New York: Henry Holt and Company, 2004), pp. 199–202.

28. Rhoads Murphey, *East Asia: A New History* (New York: Pearson/Longman, 2004), p. 419.

29. Ibid.

30. Chalmers Johnson, *Blowback: The Costs and Consequences of American Empire* (New York: Henry Holt and Company, 2000), p. 177.

31. Dean W. Collinwood, *Japan and the Pacific Rim* (Dubuque, IA: McGraw-Hill/Dushkin, 2006), p. 32.

32. David Turner, "Tokyo Home Prices Start to Rise for First Time in 13 Years," *Financial Times*, 2 August 2005, p. 5.

33. Martin Fackler, "New Optimism about the Japanese Economy after a Bleak Decade," *The New York Times*, 7 December 2005.

34. *The Economist*, "The Sun Also Rises: A Special Issue on Japan's Economic Revival," 8–14 October 2005, pp. 4, 5, 9.

35. Ibid., p. 6.

36. Ibid., pp. 8–9.

37. William H. Cooper, Specialist in International Trade and Finance, Foreign Affairs, Defense and Trade Division, "U.S.-Japan Economic Relations: Significance, Prospects, and Policy Options," *Congressional Research Service*, updated 28 February 2005.

38. Ibid.

39. Herbert P. Bix, "Hirohito and History: Japanese and American Perspectives on the Emperor and World War II in Asia," *ZNet/Activism*, 30 July 2005.

40. Yoshibumi Wakamiya and Tsuneo Watanabe, "Yomiuri and Asahi Editors Call for a National Memorial to Replace Yasukuni," www.zmag.org, 19 February 2006.

41. Jim Frederick, "Why Japan Keeps Provoking China," *Time* (Web Exclusive), 10 December 2005.

42. Ibid.

43. Emily Bruemmer, "Join the Club: Japan's Security Council Bid," *Harvard International Review*, Summer 2006.

44. Paul Bracken, *Fire in the East: The Rise of Asian Military Power and the Second Nuclear Age* (New York: HarperCollins Publishers, 1999), p. xiii.

3

Korea: Nationalism and the Hermit Kingdom

America's relations with Korea, like Australia, were forged during WWII, though, for entirely different reasons, and under different circumstances. Korea, nor the Korean peninsula, was considered an important ally, or a key strategic area, respectively. It was almost an afterthought for the U.S. postwar planners, who were completely focused upon defeating and then restructuring Japan's society after its surrender. The war's termination was due to the atomic bombings of Hiroshima and Nagasaki in early August 1945.

However, Korea's sudden emergence as a geopolitical issue was due to the actions of one of America's most important allies in WWII—the Soviet Union. The Russians had positioned troops in the northern part of Korea in their pursuit of the Japanese Imperial Army. There was no American troop presence on the peninsula at the end of the Pacific campaign. Yet the U.S. government did not want the Soviet Union to have controlling interest over the entire country because of its military implications for East Asia. Yale University historian Richard Whelan wrote, "The U.S. government would probably have been happiest if Korea simply had not existed."[1]

Though America did not have any visible military, or strategic political leverage, to exert influence on this matter, the Russians readily agreed to divide the Korean peninsula into two spheres. Unbeknownst to the American military and governmental officials in charge of creating a plan concerning the future division of Korea, their idea of separating the country at the thirty-eighth parallel was previously discussed by the Japanese and Russians almost fifty years earlier.[2]

Dean Rusk, then a lieutenant colonel in WWII and, later on, the U.S. secretary of state in the Kennedy and Johnson administrations (1961–1969), and Charles Bonesteel, also a lieutenant colonel and later named the U.S. military commander in South Korea (1966–1969), were simply ignorant of the historical irony that the Japanese and Russians had chosen the thirty-eighth parallel as a potential dividing line for the Korean peninsula at the beginning of the twentieth century. No Korean experts participated in this expedited process to divide Korea during the frantic days just after the end of the Pacific War. Several years later, Rusk stated, "Had we known that, we almost surely would have chosen another line of demarcation."[3]

For Koreans, the presence of the Americans and Russians, instead of the Japanese, after WWII, did not matter. The new occupiers were just practicing the same old game—imperialism. Therefore, it can be said that America's eventual dominance of South Korea, beginning in 1945, was a result of a poorly planned geopolitical shotgun wedding—between the U.S. and the Soviet Union. It wasn't sophisticated, or part of any grand global scheme per se, but simply emblematic of the post-WWII territorial occupation and political pragmatism exhibited by the two remaining superpowers, who were soon to part ways over the destiny of East Asia.

Korea was not surprised, nor stunned, to discover during the post-WWII period that their country had been divided without a national plebiscite taking place, or by consultation of any kind. The history of the twentieth century had not been respectful to the integrity of Korea, and, unsurprisingly, they now had two new imperial *masters*—none of which were requested nor wanted. David Kang, a professor of government at Dartmouth College, writes, "In 1945, the Soviets and the United States divided the Korean peninsula as a way of disarming the Japanese."[4] Thus, Korea's actual importance was secondary to the Allies' real goal of neutralizing Japan as an enemy. Unfortunately, this reality of having a foreign presence upon Korean soil is not uncommon in the nation's volatile and, at times, violent history. In short, Koreans have vast experience in enduring harsh and brutal occupiers due to foreign invasions, imperialistic occupations, or wars.

In 1948, the dividing of the Korean peninsula became a permanent feature within the context of the Cold War. This new phase of international conflict became quite profound for Koreans. Their homeland, though quite often ignored by policymakers in the halls of power in Washington, DC, irrevocably became a primary factor within the U.S. foreign policy establishment due to the attempted "war of unification" by North Korean leader Kim Il-sung in June 1950. Bruce Cumings, a distinguished professor of Asian history at the University of Chicago, writes, "The crucible of the period of national division and opposing states that still exists in Korea was the years from 1943 to 1953. Nothing about the politics of contemporary Korea can be understood without comprehending the events of this decade . . . "[5]

Both Korean leaders, Syngman Rhee (South) and Kim Il-sung (North), disliked the externally enforced division of Korea. Professor Cumings, the author of a critically acclaimed two-volume history of the Korean War, believes that the primary responsibility of dividing Korea along the thirty-eighth parallel lies with the U.S. and the Soviet Union. Cumings commented that "there was no historical justification for Korea's division: if any East Asian country should have been divided it was Japan. Instead Korea, China, and Vietnam were all divided in the aftermath of World War II. There was no internal pretext for dividing Korea . . ."[6]

Though the Americans and Russians had divided Korea, many Koreans continued to see themselves, and their country, as a unified whole. Thus, the Korean War from 1950 to 1953, between the Communist North and non-Communist South, in retrospect, could be credibly interpreted as a case where *both* sides attempted and failed to unify the nation. Yet even that analysis is a bit simplistic because the Korean War can be described as a conflict of great reluctance on the part of both superpowers—America and Russia. Neither side, for their own particular reasons, wanted to waste their resources on this backward and strategically questionable country in Northeast Asia. And, more importantly, both superpowers were *determined* to avoid direct military contact with each other during the early stages of the Cold War.

Against China, however, U.S. General Douglas MacArthur advocated for invasion and for the potential use of nuclear weapons in the winter of 1950–1951. These ideas were presented to the Truman administration due to China's massive intervention (approximately 300,000 troops) into North Korea, in December 1950, which deterred Western forces from potentially crossing the Yalu River into the People's Republic of China. In retrospect, Mao Zedong's military initiative had definitively derailed MacArthur's dangerous and delusional idea of aggressively seeking regime change within China. Mao had warned the U.S. repeatedly that China would not tolerate U.S.-U.N. forces near its territory. General MacArthur ignored these warnings and situated his forces too close to the Yalu River—the recognized border between China and Korea. As a result, the American-led army found themselves swamped by Chinese troops. The U.S.-U.N.'s hasty withdrawal down the peninsula into South Korea represented an absolute military fiasco and humiliation for MacArthur.

When General MacArthur, after publicly criticizing President Truman's policies concerning the Korean War, demanded that stronger measures be taken against China, President Harry Truman, in April 1951, fired the legendary military icon for insubordination. Initially, President Truman was vilified in the conservative press, and in some quarters of the American government. Yet the president and his close advisors, such as U.S. Secretary of State Dean Acheson and U.S. Army Generals Omar Bradley and George Marshall, wanted the U.S. to avoid starting World War III in Asia.

George F. Kennan, the famed architect of the "containment policy," created in 1946, which represented the philosophical core of U.S. foreign policy during the Cold War, questioned the wisdom of committing U.S. resources to fight for a country with ambiguous value to America's overall security strategy for East Asia:

> A period of Russian domination (of Korea) while undesirable, is preferable to continued U.S. involvement in the unhappy area, as long as the means chosen to assert Soviet influence are not, as was the case with those resorted to in June (1950), ones calculated to throw panic and terror into other Asian peoples and thus to achieve for the Kremlin important successes going far beyond the Korean area.[7]

Kennan's analysis of Korea's actual importance to America's overall East Asian security framework, in October 1950, five months into the Korean War, stunned his boss, Secretary of State Dean Acheson. Secretary Acheson responded to Kennan's evaluation of Korea's limited worth to America's regional agenda with stunned incredulity by stating that Kennan's views were "flatly unrealistic and irrelevant to the crisis at hand."[8]

Put simply, it was not an accident that Acheson and Kennan viewed the conflict in Korea from entirely different foreign policy prisms. Kennan, who spent approximately three decades in the U.S. Foreign Service as a Russian specialist, was an unyielding realist who evaluated global situations in a blunt and cold-eyed manner that quickly discerned the utilitarian advantages and costs of a particular foreign policy crisis or initiative. Acheson, conversely, was a brilliant corporate lawyer who served in various capacities within the U.S. State Department during WWII. In 1950, he was the U.S. secretary of state, but that meant he was also a presidential appointee. Thus, Acheson was a politician and a statesman, simultaneously, who served at the pleasure of President Truman. During the Korean War, he was criticized and scrutinized relentlessly by a mistrustful and skeptical Congress, and from within an anxiety-filled international community during the Cold War.

Therefore, Acheson's unrelenting domestic and international responsibilities often prevented him from making the grand and sweeping analysis, or the dogmatic responses, often heard from those in positions of less responsibility and stature. Kennan, on the other hand, had the unique opportunity to evaluate difficult global situations within the narrow confines of an abstract geopolitical theory, from inside the quiet confines of the U.S. State Department. Acheson never functioned within such a cloistered existence during his tenure as secretary of state. There were simply too many political fires to put out or contain on a daily basis. In short, these two men existed and operated in different worlds within the same government.

As expected, Kennan's working relationship with Acheson quickly deteriorated and he left government service to spend the bulk of his post–Foreign Service career at the Institute of Advanced Studies at Princeton University. He never again held a high government post, though he did have brief stints as a U.S. ambassador in the Soviet Union (1953) and Yugoslavia (1961–1963). Henceforth, it was Kennan's award-winning books, the periodic (though controversial at times) public lecture, or the occasional (though controversial at times) congressional testimony that kept his strong beliefs and unorthodox ideas inside the political arena. In retrospect, Kennan simply never quit fighting for a pragmatic and realistic U.S. foreign policy throughout the Cold War.[9]

The Korean War lasted from 1950 to 1953, and its effect upon Korea, and the nations who contributed soldiers to the fight, was horrifically destructive and quite deadly. I know from my own experiences living in South Korea during a very hot summer and cold winter in 1994, and from traveling in the country, the weather and topography were indeed difficult obstacles for all the soldiers during the Korean War.

Though North Korea initially appeared to be winning the war against South Korea and the U.S., eventually the tide turned against them. America was able to quickly put together a U.N. multinational force to repel the Communist attack. North Korean leader Kim Il-sung later wrote, "The U.S. imperialists, who occupied South Korea in place of Japanese imperialism, whipped together reactionary forces and maneuvered in every way to frustrate our people's struggle to build a democratic, independent, and sovereign state."[10]

The total carnage—estimated to be 3 million dead—was widespread and significant. Eighteen countries contributed troops to the Korean War. Both Pyongyang and Seoul were leveled, and like WWII, the majority of deaths were civilians.[11] In the end, an unsatisfactory armistice was signed between the North and South in 1953. Yet Kennan's initial assessment continued to haunt policymakers for years. His skeptical and penetrating questions concerning Korea's *real* geopolitical value for the U.S., and its Pacific defense structure within East Asia, remained valid in many people's minds long after the war was over. Essentially, *was* the Korean War worth the American blood and national treasure spent to keep Korea from being unified and/or Communist? The total devastation associated with the Korean War was truly shocking—especially when you consider that neither America nor Russia thought very highly of Korea in geostrategic terms.

A good example of Korea's perceived lack of stature, within the American foreign policy establishment, occurred on 12 January 1950. Secretary of State Acheson gave a speech titled, "Crisis in China: An Examination of United States Policy," at the National Press Club in Washington, DC, concerning the American defense perimeter and priorities in East Asia.[12] During his talk, Acheson spoke of the importance of the China situation, the role of Japan, and other vital elements to U.S. strategy in East Asia.

However, he neglected to mention South Korea and its future role in the region. Many analysts and observers understood this to mean that South Korea was not important to America's overall plan for East Asia. In truth, though, Acheson did recommend a $150 million aid package to South Korea, while U.S. troops were to be withdrawn. Thus, South Korea was not forgotten but Congress dragged its feet in passing this legislation. Eventually, they passed the bill containing $100 million for 1951.[13]

In his published memoirs, in 1969, Secretary Acheson vehemently claimed that the perceived slight of the Korean peninsula was completely unintended. He wrote,

> Throughout our history the attitude of Americans toward the peoples of Asia had been an interest in them not as pawns in the strategy of power or as subjects for economic exploitation, but simply as people.[14]

Acheson also proclaimed that the American people's own interests were "parallel and not contrary to the interest of the peoples of Asia."[15]

Nevertheless, Acheson's speech was later interpreted by many Asians and Asian experts, in January 1950, to be an indication of America's slow retreat from the East Asian mainland. University of Alabama historian Howard Jones wrote, "He (Acheson) defined the 'defense perimeter' of the United States in Asia as a line enveloping the Aleutians, Japan, the Ryukyus, and the Philippines . . ."[16] Professor Jones believed that Acheson's overview of Asia was based on political autonomy, freedom, and self-preservation being sought by those oppressed. And the U.S. would provide economic and administrative assistance, rather than military, to achieve those goals. Yet Jones writes, "Observers were convinced that Acheson had removed both South Korea and Formosa from the U.S. defense system."[17]

Whether Acheson's remarks triggered a incremental process, within Kim Il-sung's North Korean government, to seek support from China and the Soviet Union to eventually attack the South remains debatable. However, what is certainly irrefutable is that the North Korean military came storming across the thirty-eighth parallel, in June 1950, and they encountered a shockingly low level of resistance from U.S. and South Korean forces, and almost captured the entire peninsula within the first few months. Initially, the U.S. government saw this attack as the beginning of a series of "coordinated actions on (the) part of (the) Soviets."[18]

Eventually, after three years of bitter fighting, the U.S. and its U.N. coalition were able to stave off a North Korean victory, but the destruction and death on the Korean peninsula left the entire country economically, politically, and socially moribund until the early-1960s.

The final conditions and numbers concerning the Korean War are sobering:

- An estimated 3 million Koreans dead from causes related to the war
- 900,000 Chinese dead and wounded
- 33,000 Americans dead, 1,000 British dead, 4,000 other nationalities dead
- 129,000 civilians in the South killed—during the North's occupation of the South
- 84,000 kidnapped
- 200,000 South Koreans press-ganged into the northern territory
- Economies on both sides destroyed
- South Korea: 5 million homeless; 300,000 women widowed; 100,000 children orphaned
- Millions of families separated; tens of thousands of schools and other buildings destroyed
- $3 billion in damages, 43 percent of manufacturing facilities destroyed, 50 percent of mines wrecked
- Inflation skyrocketed: currency in circulation—1949 (71, 383 million won); 1953 (650, 153 million won)[19]

I have often commented to my students that Korea is the "Poland" of Asia. Poland, of course, remains sandwiched between Germany and Russia in eastern Europe. Presently, Korea finds itself caught within a geographical triangular web of great powers—China, Japan, and Russia—and is currently the home (occupied?) of approximately 37,000 U.S. troops, and over 100 American military facilities, since the end of the Korean War (1950–1953).[20] Upon hindsight, Michigan State University historian Warren Cohen wrote, "The Korean War was a momentous turning point in the Cold War. An almost inevitable civil war among a people, Communist and non-Communist, determined to unite their country, became an international war and a catalyst for a terrifying arms race."[21] It remains astounding, to current analysts and historians, how a war-torn and poverty-stricken nation, in the northeastern region of Asia, has had such a profound effect upon the international order since 1945.

In 1954, the U.S. signed a Mutual Defense Treaty with South Korea. Syngman Rhee, the American-supported seventy-year-old Korean puppet leader put in charge of South Korea after the official creation of the Republic of Korea (ROK) in August 1948, despised the armistice agreement, and refused to sign it in 1953. He also continually threatened to "march north," though he didn't have the military power to back up such a plan. Yet, for many years, South Koreans kept waiting for Rhee to initiate this "unification march" to the north.[22] This promise to unify the Korean peninsula was not empty talk, according to Don Oberdorfer, a longtime

Washington Post reporter and author of *The Two Koreas*. Oberdorfer writes that "Rhee had a messianic belief that he was destined to reunite Korea under an anticommunist banner."[23] Obviously, this type of megalomania behavior unnerved the U.S. government.

Unsurprisingly, in an interesting bit of diplomatic jujitsu, President Rhee, who sought the destruction of the Korean armistice, also wanted to remain in power. Thus, the American government found itself uncomfortably supporting a crafty and dangerous authoritarian. In truth, there were no other legitimate alternatives, in South Korea, at the end of the Korean War. According to John Lewis Gaddis, the preeminent Cold War scholar at Yale University,

> (Syngman) Rhee got a bilateral security treaty, together with a commitment from Washington to keep American troops in South Korea for as long as they were needed to ensure that country's safety. This meant that the United States was defending an authoritarian regime, because Rhee had little patience with, or interest in, democratic procedures. South Korea was what he, not the Americans, wanted it to be, and to get his way, Rhee devised a compelling form of Cold War backmail: if you push me too hard, my government will fall, and you'll be sorry.[24]

As the Korean War statistics indicate, *both* Koreas were savaged by the war, and, with bitter irony, *both* countries ended up with repressive regimes. In South Korea, the U.S. had ensured the existence of an authoritarian regime for the foreseeable future, and, in the North, the signing of the armistice guaranteed a tyrannical form of communism—morphing into a cult-based society. In short, in the 1950s the Korean peninsula was not a pretty place to be in any capacity. Professor Cumings commented that Rhee had no *real* or definable grassroots support amongst the Korean people; his power was solidified and maintained due to the presence of the American military.[25] The U.S. had few options in terms of leadership for South Korea. The choices were either Korean collaborators—who conspired with the Japanese before WWII—or the new Korean collaborators—who were now working with the Americans after WWII.[26] Either way, the roots of imperialism, of some sort, became a way of life on the Korean peninsula that continues into the twenty-first century.

In 1961, a bloodless coup occurred in South Korea, led by General Park Chung Hee, who initiated a new era in Korean politics, and the implementation of an ego-driven vision of economic development that represented a historical epoch for the nation. Park's politics had a top-down military-type of orientation throughout his reign in office (1961–1979) that did not tolerate dissent or questioning of his actions. Professor Cumings wrote, "Korea had long prided itself on civilian leadership, but it now had the military in the saddle . . . "[27]

In 1963, Park was elected president, though the election results were "fiddled," as future elections were as well, to ensure the intended outcome.[28] President Park stated that South Korea was ready for an "administrative democracy," but not a Western parliamentary-style democracy found in western Europe, until an industrial revolution had occurred. He further commented that his regime represented only a "transition period"—a transition that lasted eighteen years![29] Obviously, the tides of history had produced a different and difficult course for South Koreans. The country's citizenry endured this form of military-directed governance until 1993.

Yet most Koreans today do *not* see this historical "transitional period" as representing a dark and repressive era. In fact, in March 1995, a daily newspaper based in Seoul took a national poll that indicated President Park was the nation's greatest president by a 66 percent majority.[30] Why? Well, it's rather simple. Follow the money—as the Hal Holbrook character stated in the movie, *All the President's Men*. President Park's successful economic policies had lifted South Korea from abject poverty to respectability in East Asia. It was a stature that Koreans desperately sought, in a region where they historically were quite often dominated by their powerful neighbors (China, Japan, and Russia). I noticed on my last trip to South Korea, in June 2005, how confident the country felt to me. I asked a few people who know Korea quite well, at an international conference commemorating the fifth anniversary of the South-North Joint Declaration, which met at the Shilla Hotel in Seoul, if perhaps, I had misinterpreted the situation. They quickly agreed with my analysis. In short, the recent rise in South Korean confidence parallels its economic growth, and its political maturity as a democracy—which I will talk more about at the end of this chapter.

In 1962, Park initiated his first five-year plan for economic development. The results were stunning. South Korea experienced an 8.3 percent GNP annual growth during this period. It was followed with a second five-year plan that produced an annual growth rate of 11.4 percent. Overall, the prosperity had an enormous effect upon the people and the peninsula. North Korea refused to believe their southern neighbor's new wealth and success.[31] The economic success in South Korea was quite visible to the public at large; new office buildings were constructed, local roads and a national highway were built, and factories and new apartment complexes sprang up everywhere. The evidence was overwhelming to regional and international observers—South Korea was booming.

Economic ideas and policy implementation rested strictly within President Park's domain. He took a direct hands-on attitude to ensure that his beliefs and national vision were constructed according to his specifications. Though, Park's political leadership was seen by many observers as inflexible and totalitarian, yet it remains difficult to denigrate or refute the net results. Park's presence bespoke of a man who had a serious commitment to developing his country, and his willingness to exercise power, at times ruthlessly, got the job done. He also used American economists within his governmental agencies to advise and guide his national projects.[32] President Park, according to Professor Oberdorfer, a former *Washington Post* reporter, created an "economic situation room next to his office in the Blue House to monitor the implementation of the plans . . . "[33]

The economic numbers and accomplishments, achieved from 1961 to 1979, are stunning, upon retrospect:

1. Poverty (households) was over 40 percent in 1965 and below 10 percent in 1980
2. Per capita income: $87 (1962); $9,511 (1997); $10,000+ (2006)
3. South Korean economy (GNP) grew almost 9 percent annually for over three decades
4. South Korean GNP: $2.3 billion (1962); $442 billion (1997)
5. Automobiles: 30,800 (1962); 10,413,427 (1997)
6. By the 1990s, South Korea had the eleventh largest economy in the world, was the thirteenth largest trading nation in the world, and was a major producer of ships, cars, electronics, and steel[34]

In 2006, the International Monetary Fund (IMF) indicated that South Korea was now the tenth largest economy in the world, according to their statistics.[35] No matter how you evaluate South Korea's economic development since WWII, whether in economic or political terms, the old saying "the numbers don't lie" certainly pertains to their miraculous growth. Though, it should be noted that the "Korean Miracle" was founded upon hard work, perseverance, sacrifice, and undaunted leadership during the heart of the Cold War.

Before moving on to surveying present-day South Korea, I think I should mention three important events that occurred in 1973, 1979, and 1980. All three of these episodes involved directly, or indirectly, democracy advocate Kim Dae-jung. These historical epochs changed the fundamental dynamics and nature of South Korean politics that eventuated in the country becoming a real and functioning democracy. Conversely, these actions, in the end, reduced the overall influence of the U.S. on the Korean peninsula. Thus, the effects of these events are still profoundly felt throughout South Korea, and continue to resonate within the halls of power in Washington, DC.

First, there was the last-minute saving of Kim Dae-jung's life by the U.S. government, in 1973, after he was abducted from a Tokyo Hotel by the Korean Central Intelligence Agency (KCIA). Only the decisive intervention by the American CIA, due to frantic calls from Kim's friends and supporters, saved Kim's life.[36] Kim Byong-kuk, however, a former professor and president of the Seoul Institute of International Economics in South Korea, claims in his book that Kim's life was spared due to divine intervention.[37] The CIA and God, indeed, are a potent combination.

Though the origins of the intervention that saved Kim's life remain somewhat elusive, there is no doubt in my mind, from a present-day perspective, that Korean history is greatly different today because a future president and Nobel Peace Prize winner (2000), wrapped in chains, did not die in the dark and murky Sea of Japan. I first met the former president in 1994, and then again at the fifth anniversary of the South-North Joint Declaration in Seoul in June 2005. The media that once shunned him, or condemned him for his harsh criticism of Korea's dictatorial and military junta leaders, now surrounded and fawned over him like a rock star because of his brilliant and prescient "Sunshine policies" promoting Korean unification.[38]

Second, the assassination of President Park Chung Hee, on 26 October 1979, by the head of the KCIA, Kim Jae Kyu, brought about a military coup in South Korea led by Korean Army General Chun Doo-hwan. The dimensions of the coup had seriously destabilized the security of the country. General Chun had troops defending the border against North Korean forces transported to Seoul to ensure the success of his military-led coup. The American military command was stunned by such an audacious and reckless action by the Korean military. U.S. Army General John Wickham, who was in charge of operational control of U.S. and Republic of Korea (ROK) forces, later claimed to be "shock(ed) and dismay(ed)" by the series of events. General Chun, and his supporters within the military, made their move on 12 December 1979—better known as "12/12" the night of the generals.[39]

President Jimmy Carter convened an emergency National Security Council meeting approximately two hours after President Park's death was confirmed. The security of South Korea and the U.S. troops stationed there were the president's first priorities. However, the president also wanted to prevent any potential "external attempt to exploit the situation" from occurring, especially by North Korea.[40] President Carter tried to convince Prime Minister Choi Kyu Ha to assert more constitutional authority in South Korea, but these urgings went unheeded. The military was now in charge.

U.S. Ambassador William Gleysteen believed the U.S. had to be very cautious because the people of South Korea might perceive the U.S. playing a major role in the creation of this military junta. Ambassador Gleysteen wrote to Washington, in January 1980, "Few of them (critics) realize that our influence is limited in large part by the fact that we could not pull our powerful security and economic levers without risk of destroying the ROK's stability."[41]

Nevertheless, the stigma and presence of an oppressive and rigid military rule, symbolized by Generals Chun Doo-hwan and Roh Tae-woo, initiated the stirrings of a grassroots movement that grew in intensity, throughout the 1980s and 1990s, toward creating a democratic South Korean society. Kim Dae-jung was at the forefront of this democratic movement demanding that Koreans, not Americans or the Korean military, should determine the country's destiny. The culmination of these prodemocratic efforts, strongly supported nationwide, was the popular election of Kim Young-sam, in December 1992. However, Professor Cumings points out that Kim's presidency was always in a precarious position, because critics continually pointed to the fact that he received only slightly more than 40 percent of the overall vote. Thus, during difficult moments in Kim's presidency, there were "persistent rumors" that a "group" might stage another coup to supplant the civilian-elected leadership.[42]

Finally, there was the Kwangju Masscre in May 1980. This attack upon civilians in the city of Kwangju killed an estimated 4,900.[43] Other estimates had the death toll over 5,500.[44] As late as 1997, a full and in-depth government investigation of this massacre had not occurred; nevertheless, this horrific incident had enormous ramifications for President Chun Doo-hwan, and the U.S.'s military presence, and reputation, in South Korea. Henceforth, to many Korean observers, the Kwangju Massacre, though an act of cold-blooded murder initiated by General Chun and carried out by obedient ROK soldiers, subsequently had a huge role in pushing Korea toward becoming a democratic nation—demanded by the people—in 1987. Well-known Korean novelist Hwang Sok-yong states, "The Kwangju Uprising lit the fuse of the dynamite stick of democracy. It was the birth of citizenship. It was the beginning of a western-style civil society—and Korean modernity."[45]

I spoke to a Catholic priest while teaching a course at Kunsan Air Base in southern South Korea in the fall of 1994. I flew down to Kunsan every Friday night to teach a three-hour course on American history on Saturday, and then I would return to Seoul on Saturday night or Sunday morning depending on seat availability on Korean Air. The father and I found ourselves living in the base's officers' quarters for job-related reasons. Eventually, we had a chat about why both of us were in Korea. Needless to say, his story was much more interesting than my own. I was fascinated and shocked to hear his story concerning the Kwangju Massacre. Simply put, he had been there during the *event*. He spoke of the carnage everywhere he looked. He could not provide me with an exact number of the dead after the military siege of the town, but he quickly stated that the government's public statements were false and misleading. Obviously, my recalling of this conversation indicates its impact upon my own interpretation and perception of Korea during my stay.

U.S. culpability in this nightmarish tragedy remains inescapable. According to Professor Cumings, the U.S. had operational control, under the United States–South Korean Combined Forces Command, throughout the country. Thus, "the release of frontline troops (along the North Korean border) made hash of Carter's human rights policies—the United States paid dearly for both in Korean attitudes thereafter."[46]

I spoke to a young army veteran who was also a student in my history course, on a neighborhood street during a power outage in Uijonbu, South Korea. It was a large town with a population of approximately 100,000 located north of Seoul—geographically close to the demilitarized zone (DMZ). I was assigned to teach American history at Camp Red Cloud— located in Uijonbu. It was my first teaching assignment for the University of Maryland–Asian Division.

This particular soldier hoped to become a highway patrolman in his home state of Virginia after retiring from the army. We spoke, on a dreadfully hot summer night, about the U.S. military presence in South Korea. He told me that Korean attitudes had changed dramatically toward U.S. soldiers during the 1980s. He had been in Korea on a previous tour of duty in the 1980s, and was now finishing up his army career with one last tour in Korea. He said that Koreans used to offer free food or beer, occasionally, to American soldiers and thank them for serving in Korea. However, in 1994, this was no longer the case. In fact, he said several Koreans had respectfully told him that it was time for the U.S. to leave Korea.[47]

After the Korean military got the Kwangju protests under control, Kim Dae-jung was soon arrested and convicted, by a "kangaroo court" type of legal proceedings, and sentenced to die. Why? Kim was considered one of the primary ringleaders of the Kwangju uprising.[48] Once again, as in 1973, the U.S. government stepped into this vacuum of illegitimacy, and pressured General Chun to commute Kim's sentence to life in prison.[49] It appeared that Kim had escaped the executioner, once more, due to American intervention on his behalf.

However, before General Chun commuted his death sentence, Kim confronted his impending death with sorrow and great uncertainty in a prison letter titled, "Impending Death and Faith in the Resurrection of Jesus," dated 21 November 1980:

> I had until now thought of myself as one who possessed considerable religious fiber, and yet, standing at the very [edge] of the precipice looking out on imminent death, I feel my religious faith, as it concerns my existence, grow weaker each day. Hope and despair, joy and fear, the anguished conflict over resolution and doubt—all of these assail me daily, and I am not able to free myself from their recurrence.[50]

Kim Dae-jung survived the beatings, death threats, and imprisonment by those who feared his influence, and was miraculously elected president in 1997. In 2000, he won the Nobel Peace Prize for his efforts to unify the

Korean peninsula. In retirement, Kim continues to push an increasingly independent course for South Korea.

The current president, Roh Moo-hyun, a protégé of Kim Dae-jung, continues to support his predecessor's dream of Korean unification. Hence, South Korea is cautiously creating and determining its own course at the beginning of the twenty-first century. What will this mean for Northeast Asia, the Pacific Rim, or its future relations with America? No one really knows. Yet Koreans do acknowledge that they live in a dangerous neighborhood—surrounded by erstwhile friends who have their own agendas within the region. These "neighbors" see South Korea's economic and political development with a mixture of acute interest and fearful uncertainty as to what it all means for them.

Paradoxically, South Korea remains a nation *externally* surrounded by several major powers, and *internally* occupied by a foreign army representing the strongest power in the world. Finally, it is a country *sensing*, at best, only lukewarm support from these very *same* powers on the issue of unification. In my opinion, present-day South Korea finds itself confronting its past and future simultaneously, which is another way of saying the past is mere prologue to the future of this divided peninsula. Put specifically, Koreans find themselves stuck between a rock and a hard place in the modern geopolitical configuration of Northeast Asia.

This uncomfortable geographical positioning has been a tragic dilemma for Koreans in the twentieth century. From 1895 to 1945, Korea was brutally dominated by Japan, indirectly or directly, until the end of WWII. Japan had formally colonized Korea in 1910.[51] Japan's physical and psychological occupation was demeaning and spiritually devastating to a proud and hardworking people. If you've recently been to South Korea, then my prior sentence does not represent baseless hyperbole or mush platitudes.

Nevertheless, the aftereffects of Japan's colonization and occupation still scar the Korean psyche.[52] In 1948, South Korea was one of the poorest countries in Asia. In 2007, South Korea has clearly risen like a phoenix from the ashes of a wasteland, dominated by poverty, death, and humiliation, to become a major economic and military force in East Asia.

The Koreans are not considered a major power, but they are certainly a *significant* power in Asian affairs. However, the difficult challenge confronting South Korea today is steering an economic and military course between the increasingly intense relations between the U.S., China, Japan, North Korea, and the wary Russians. Unexpectedly, South Koreans find themselves in a hard-fought position to shape their own future to a degree unimaginable to past generations. Yet this historic "moment of opportunity" is fraught with danger.

Upon closer scrutiny, today, the Korean peninsula is still not, unfortunately, far removed from the Cold War identification and configuration of

East Asia established over sixty years ago. In essence, the Korean peninsula still finds itself trapped inside an awkward time warp. Sadly, South Korea, though recognized by the international community as a functional and thriving democracy, remains a hostage within the Cold War paradigm.

Therefore, to the present day, the peninsula remains divided along the artificially created thirty-eighth parallel—which was arbitrarily decided upon by the U.S. and the Soviet Union after WWII. Its buffered border—symbolized by the DMZ—between North Korea and South Korea remains one of the most heavily armed regions in the world. However, in 2007, even this potentially apocalyptic Cold War anachronism is clearly beginning to recede in importance militarily, and in terms of ideological symbolism.

In mid-June 2000, South Korean President Kim Dae-jung and North Korean ("Dear") leader Kim Jong-il met at Pyongyang (North Korean capital) International Airport and they began the first public dialogue between the leaders of these two nations since the partitioning of the peninsula after WWII. In 2000, President Kim became convinced that North Korea did not completely oppose the existence of U.S. troops upon the Korean peninsula. Conversely, they simply wanted America to constructively "engage" them in policy talks instead of constantly threatening them with military action or regime change.[53] Later that year, at the Sydney Olympics, North and South Korean athletes marched together under one flag—it was the first public presentation of a unified Korea since 1945.[54]

The initial reactions in both Koreas, concerning the historic "Kim Meeting" in North Korea and the "unified" Olympic presence in Australia, were met with guarded optimism and cautious expectations. Koreans have learned, quite well, from recent history that their collective fates rest, irrefutably, outside their control. The U.S. government remains indifferent toward Korean unification. Since 2000, America has continued to show very little diplomatic interest in President Kim's fateful peace mission, which reflected his visionary and dynamic "Sunshine policies" developed in the late 1990s.[55]

In mid-June 2005, I was invited to attend the fifth anniversary of the South-North Joint Declaration at the Shilla Hotel in Seoul, South Korea. During this highly publicized international conference, I had the opportunity to meet the former president, and the 2000 Nobel Peace Prize winner, Kim Dae-jung for a second time. He provided the keynote address, and then listened to the current president, Roh Moo-hyun, who made an unannounced appearance, give a speech strongly supportive of future efforts to bring unity and peace to the Korean peninsula.[56]

The speeches supporting unification and the event itself were unthinkable ten years ago. Put succinctly, Korea has experienced a seismic and fundamental shift in its economic and foreign policies, especially since the election of George W. Bush. The Bush administration remains hostile toward the "Sunshine" policies created by former President Kim. Nevertheless, the South Koreans have continued to work with the North Koreans in seeking an enlargement of common ground. Trade and investment continue between the two nations, and, perhaps, in the near future, a real breakthrough will occur in diminishing the military threat that continues to hang over the peninsula like a dark cloud. Though, Kim's ideas are continually criticized and scrutinized, yet they appear to be viewed as a quasi-blueprint for potentially unifying the peninsula.[57] Such unification would enormously assist, or eliminate, some of the most pressing and serious issues involving North Korea and South Korea.

A prime example of an unresolved and serious issue is the nuclear threat on the Korean peninsula. In 2007, the six-party talks produced a significant result: The North Koreans agreed to abandon their nuclear weapons program. The participants, which included China, the U.S., Japan, South Korea, and Russia, agreed in principle to provide North Korea with humanitarian aid and oil, and they also promised not to seek regime change in the future. South Korea, along with China, strongly supported this agreement. America, bogged down in Afghanistan and Iraq, had no choice but to go along with the final agreement, even though President Bush had identified North Korea as being one of the "axis of evil" in his 2002 State of the Union address.

The Bush administration also, grudgingly, thanked China for its diplomatic leadership on the North Korean nuclear crisis. This short-term achievement represents evidence of China's rising influence in East Asia. Former diplomatic correspondent for the *Washington Post* and longtime observer of Asia, Don Oberdorfer, stated that "China played a major role in the six-party talks with concern to North Korea's nuclear weapons program. This is the first time that China is on the world stage since 1949. Its actions, so far, have been positive."[58] Thus, quite subtly, a new geopolitical dynamic is taking shape within the Asia-Pacific Rim. China represents a new and powerful factor in the regional equation. What this shift in power and influence means for the U.S. within the region is presently consuming many analysts' energies and minds in America.

In 2005, three telltale but profound events took place in South Korea, one affecting the nation's military relations with the U.S., the second indicating future economic relations, and the last representing an educational trend. First, it was announced that overall U.S. forces in South Korea will be reduced from 32,500 to approximately 20,000 during the next three years. The Yongsan Army Garrison, located in the heart of Seoul, will no longer be the U.S. military headquarters by 2008. The troops and new operational facilities will be reconstituted at Pyongtaek, approximately forty miles south of Seoul.[59]

In late 2006, Oberdorfer, now distinguished journalist in residence and adjunct professor of international relations at Johns Hopkins University's

Nitze School of Advanced International Studies (SAIS) said, "The move out of Yongsan U.S. Army facilities (located in Seoul) is long overdue. Though, the move itself is not important, and the eventual troop reduction to 25,000 is not surprising either. Twenty-five thousand troops is still a hell of a lot of troops."[60] Oberdorfer, the author of an award-winning book on the present-day situation in Korea, also mentioned that "most South Koreans want the U.S. to maintain a presence in their country until things (i.e., North Korea's nuclear weapons program) with North Korean leader Kim Jong-il are settled."[61] His final assessment of Korea and its future is one of cautious optimism: "Korean unification will occur, but only after the departure of Kim Jong-il from the scene. Kim Dae-jung's bold and dynamic 'Sunshine policies' will not be dismantled by future governments in South Korea, but they will be temporarily reduced in importance."[62]

Secondly, in 2005, it was announced that China had replaced the U.S. as South Korea's number one trading partner, and, finally, that China had now become the primary destination of Korean college students studying overseas.[63] All three of these events and trends are significant for South Korea, and the future role of the U.S. on the Korean peninsula. Historically, Korea has always been seen as a significant tributary of the "Middle Kingdom." This time-honored relationship was disconnected during the past century due to colonialism, imperialism, and various forms of occupation—primarily by the Japanese and Americans. However, as the old saying goes, "time stops for no man or nation." In short, fate and history have taken a new course upon the Korean peninsula, and change is in the wind. America's enormous power is increasingly neutralized by growing nationalism in South Korea and East Asia as well. Yet South Korea and North Korea face some uncomfortable challenges and truths as the twenty-first century unfolds.

Perhaps, the lightening of America's footprint within South Korea is indicative of the changing geopolitical realities in Northeast Asia, and China becoming the North and South's primary trading partner can be justified due to their common heritage and historical roots. Yet, this writer chafes uncomfortably for various reasons when evaluating the future progress and volatility of the Korean peninsula:

1. The North Korean nuclear situation has not been definitively resolved. North Korean leader Kim Jong-il remains an unpredictable source of anxiety in the region. A transparent and crystal-clear agreement—concessions made by *all* sides—must be designed and approved by all the major parties concerned.[64] Knowledgeable observers of Korea believe this moment in time represents a "rare opportunity" to finally end the proliferation of nuclear weapons in Northeast Asia.[65]
2. Japan is steadily becoming a significant military power again. Its military spending ranks fourth in the world.[66] The potential of a remilitarized

Japan would trigger shockwaves and severe anxiety throughout East Asia, but especially within China and the Koreas. Therefore, Japan's future intentions must be crystal clear, and an American military presence remains a must within Japan.

3. China's recent reemergence as a growing economic and military power is not completely welcomed by Koreans. Yes, historical roots exist, and China's market does represent a large degree of economic prosperity for both Koreas. However, it must be noted that Korea is historically seen as the "younger brother" to China's "elder brother" status. This author believes that Koreans, in the twenty-first century, want a much more autonomous and independent relationship with the resurgent "Middle Kingdom." In essence, Koreans, justifiably, are quite proud of their recent accomplishments, especially in becoming a flourishing democracy. Henceforth, they don't want to live in anyone's shadow ever again—whether it be Japan, America, or China!

Nevertheless, South Korea's movement toward China's sphere of influence is not so much due to a fundamental change of their attitude toward America, but an unstoppable reassertion of history. Yet the intrusion of history upon a volatile region—like Northeast Asia—represents a mixed blessing. The potentially bright future for East Asia can go terribly wrong if the tragic lessons of the past are not avoided, thus triggering again the self-immolation of one of the oldest civilizations on earth. Tragically, Korea continues to be one of the most dangerous and volatile pieces of real estate in the world.

Yet, according to Ban Ki-Moon, the former South Korean foreign minister, in 2006, there is real hope for the Korean peninsula in the twenty-first century: "Beyond the remnants of the Cold War and the North Korean nuclear challenge, the most important preconditions for achieving permanent peace on the Korean peninsula and in Northeast Asia are a coherent strategic vision and the willingness of regional members to work together through a multilateral framework."[67] It appears that good fortune has smiled upon Mr. Ban because he will have a golden opportunity to create that new strategic vision for Northeast Asia, including the Korean peninsula. In late 2006, he was chosen to be the next secretary-general of the United Nations. In January 2007, he became the first Asian to hold this vaunted position in thirty-five years, and his appointment, in the minds of many, could not have come at a better time because East Asia is steadily becoming the axis and fulcrum of power in the twenty-first century.[68]

Journalist Michael Fullilove writes that though the U.N. intervened in the Korean War in the early 1950s, and helped to relocate 3 million Indo-Chinese refugees in the 1970s, the institution itself has been perceived, within the region, with a strong degree of suspicion since its inception. This perception was due to issues concerning state sovereignty, the region's colonial history—which continues to haunt the region—and a healthy mistrust of international institutions such as the IMF, due to their decisions and policies implemented during the 1997–1998 financial meltdown. However, with the end of the Cold War, and the emergence of new security threats (disease, resource scarcity, and environmental catastrophes) within the region, Fullilove writes, ". . . these interconnected security threats in the region have demonstrated the advantages of international cooperation. As these threats escalate, so will the work of the U.N. and its agencies."[69]

Kim Dae-jung, sometimes referred to as the "Nelson Mandela of Asia," has spent his adult life working toward bringing democracy to Korea. In June 2000, he courageously stepped forward to begin a new dialogue with North Korea and its leader, Chairman Kim Jong-il. Kim Dae-jung's irrepressible democratic spirit has undeniably altered the course of contemporary history upon this Asian peninsula. Now the question becomes increasingly self-evident for observers of this troubled land—who will be the next Korean leader to take a bold and defining step toward achieving a higher degree of integration and unification between North and South Korea in the twenty-first century? When that *leader* emerges and that *moment* arrives, the "Hermit Kingdom" will no longer be seen as an outdated artifact of the Cold War, but as a country that has finally come of age. And the geopolitical impact of a unified Korea will undoubtedly be felt throughout the Asia-Pacific Rim.

NOTES

1. Don Oberdorfer, *The Two Koreas: A Contemporary History* (New York: Basic Books, 2001), p. 6.

2. Ibid.

3. Ibid.

4. Muthiah Alagappa, Editor, *Asian Security Order: Instrumental and Normative Features* (Stanford: Stanford University Press, 2003); David Kang, "Acute Conflicts in Asia after the Cold War: Kashmir, Taiwan and Korea," p. 353.

5. Bruce Cumings, *Korea's Place in the Sun: A Modern History* (New York: W.W. Norton, 1997), p. 185.

6. Ibid., p. 186.

7. Randall Doyle, "The Reluctant Heretic: George F. Kennan and the Vietnam War, 1950–1968," *Grand Valley Review*, Volume 27, Spring 2004.

8. Ibid.

9. Ibid.

10. Kim Il-sung, *On the Building of the People's Government* (Pyongyang, Korea: Foreign Languages Publishing House, 1978), p. 279.

11. Niall Ferguson, *The War of the World: Twentieth-Century Conflict and the Descent of the West* (New York: The Penguin Press, 2006), p. 595.

12. Dean Acheson, *Present at the Creation: My Years in the State Department* (New York: W.W. Norton & Company, 1969), p. 355.

13. James Chace, *Acheson: The Secretary of State Who Created the American World* (New York: Simon & Schuster, 1998), p. 269.

14. Acheson, *Present at the Creation*, p. 355.

15. Ibid., p. 356.

16. Howard Jones, *Crucible of Power: A History of U.S. Foreign Relations since 1897* (Lanham, MD: S.R. Books, 2001), p. 268.

17. Ibid.

18. Ibid., p. 268–70.

19. Michael Breen, *The Koreans: Who They Are, What They Want, Where Their Future Lies* (New York: St. Martin's Griffin, 2004), p. 124.

20. David Ross, interview of Chalmers Johnson, "Fickle, Bitter, and Dangerous," 1 April 2004, *ZNet/Activism*.

21. Warren I. Cohen, *The Cambridge History of American Foreign Relations—Volume IV: America in the Age of SOVIET Power*, 1945–1991 (New York: Cambridge University Press, 1993), p. 79.

22. Breen, *The Koreans*, p. 199.

23. Oberdorfer, *The Two Koreas*, p. 8.

24. John Lewis Gaddis, *The Cold War: A New History* (New York: The Penguin Press, 2005), p. 130.

25. Tae-Hyo Kim and Brad Glosserman, editors, *The Future of U.S.-Korea-Japan Relations: Balancing Values and Interests* (Washington, DC: Center of Strategic and International Studies, 2004), p. 107.

26. Ibid.

27. Cumings, *Korea's Place in the Sun*, p. 349.

28. Breen, *The Koreans*, p. 202.

29. Ibid.

30. Oberdorfer, *The Two Koreas*, p. 33.

31. Breen, *The Koreans*, pp. 136–37.

32. Oberdorfer, *The Two Koreas*, pp. 33–35.

33. Ibid.

34. Breen, *The Koreans*, p. 134. Oberdorfer, *The Two Koreas*, p. 37.

35. International Monetary Fund, http://en.wikipedia.org/wiki/Lst_of_countries_by_GDP_(nominal).

36. Breen, *The Koreans*, p. 204.

37. Kim Byong-Kuk, *Kim Dae-Jung: Hero of the Masses, Conscience in Action* (Seoul: Ilweolseogak Publishing Company, 1992), p. 95.

38. I attended the press conference, taking photos and watching the proceedings, at the Shilla Hotel in Seoul on 15 June 2005. Though I cannot speak Korean, there was absolute reverence and respect directed toward the one-time democracy advocate who has lived long enough to see South Korea become a democracy. And, at the age of eighty-one, he might just witness the unification of Korea.

39. Oberdorfer, *The Two Koreas*, pp. 118–19.

40. Ibid., p. 111.

41. Ibid., p. 123–24.

42. Cumings, *Korea's Place in the Sun*, p. 391.

43. Ibid., p. 378.

44. Kim Byong-Kuk, *Kim Dae-Jung*, p. 143.

45. Becky Branford, "Lingering Legacy of Korean Massacre," *BBC News Online*, 18 May 2005.

46. Cumings, *Korea's Place in the Sun*, pp. 377–78.

47. I remember this story because I knew nothing about Korea—its culture, history, or politics—when I arrived at Osan Air Base in May 1994. I also remember that someone told me that the summer of 1994 was the hottest in thirty years. I never received an absolute confirmation on this fact, but it sure felt like it.

48. Cumings, *Korea's Place in the Sun*, p. 378.

49. Ibid.

50. Kim Dae-jung, *Prison Writings* (Berkeley: University of California Press, 1987), p. 1.

51. Dean W. Collinwood, *Japan and the Pacific Rim* (Dubuque, IA: McGraw-Hill/Dushkin, 2006), p. 110–12.

52. Kate McGeown, "Raking Over South Korea's Colonial Past," *BBC News Online*, 19 August 2004.

53. Cumings, *Korea's Place in the Sun*, p. 503.

54. Oberdorfer, *The Two Koreas*, p. 434.

55. Ibid., p. 424, 427–28.

56. Kim Dae-jung and Yonsei University (Organizers), "From Stalemate to New Progress for Peace in Korea," International Conference to Commemorate the 5th Anniversary of the 15 June South-North Joint Declaration, June 2005. I listened very intently to President Roh's speech and later read accounts in the press and their reaction to it. Overall, very positive.

57. Chung-in Moon and David I. Steinberg, Editors, *Kim Dae-jung Government and Sunshine Policy: Promises and Challenges* (Seoul: Yonsei University Press, 1999).

58. Interview with Don Oberdorfer, 28 December 2006.

59. Eric Talmadge, "U.S. Troops in Asia Undergo Transformation," *Associated Press*, 16 November 2005.

60. Interview with Orberdorfer, 28 December 2006.

61. Ibid.

62. Ibid.

63. Charles K. Armstrong, "South Korea and the United States: Is the Love Affair Over?," 6 June 2005, http://hnn.us/articles/12241.html.

64. Selig S. Harrison, *Korean Endgame: A Strategy for Reunification and U.S. Disengagement* (Princeton: Princeton University Press, 2002), pp. 278–83.

65. Donald Gregg and Don Oberdorfer, "A Moment to Seize with North Korea," *The Washington Post*, 22 June 2005, p. A21.

66. Charles Recknagel, "World: Global Spending on Military Tops $1 Trillion, Nears Cold War Peak," *Radio Free Europe/Radio Liberty*, 8 June 2005.

67. Ban Ki-Moon, "For Permanent Peace: Beyond the Nuclear Challenge and the Cold War," *Harvard International Review*, Summer 2006.

68. Michael Fullilove, "Ban's Debut Is Chance for Asia to Step into Spotlight," *Financial Times*, 19 December 2006, p. 11.

69. Ibid.

II

POST-9/11 ASIA-PACIFIC AND AMERICA

A New Regional Order

4

Zhongguo: The Wild Card in Asia-Pacific

Most Asia-Pacific Rim observers and scholars appear to agree that China (Zhongguo) represents the *key* factor as to whether the region continues to evolve in relative peace and prosperity, or plummets into the traditional angst and tensions associated with hegemonic power politics. Presently, the primary topic concerning China's future role is raging within various associations, institutions, think tanks, and universities throughout America and Asia. There is no established consensus on this topic—right now. But the intensity of the debate will heighten as China's *economic* and *military* development translates into possessing stronger influence within Asia-Pacific. Some analysts believe that China has already reached this stage; others are more cautious in their determinations concerning the current and future status of the "Middle Kingdom." Former U.S. Secretary of State Henry Kissinger wrote in an article for the *Australian*, in June 2005,

> The rise of China, and of Asia, will, over the next decades, bring about a substantial reordering of the international system. The centre of gravity of world affairs is shifting from the Atlantic, where it was lodged for the past three centuries to the Pacific. The most rapidly developing countries are located in Asia, with a growing means to vindicate their perception of the national interest.[1]

Hence, the hyper-verbosity and voluminous writings related to China's future have shifted into overdrive within America and Asia-Pacific. This chapter will provide a number of economic and political observations and geopolitical views toward answering questions concerning the future relevance of China in the twenty-first century: First, specifically, will China become America's geopolitical adversary, strategic competitor, or regional partner in Asia-

Pacific? Second, how will the world react to the continuing growth of the Chinese economic juggernaut as the twenty-first century unfolds, and will China's financial prowess be ultimately directed toward global dominance? Third, can China avoid a domestic implosion from significant, if not staggering, challenges, such as unemployment, pollution, corruption, and ever-widening wealth disparities? Finally, what will be the comprehensive effect of China's rise to power throughout Asia-Pacific? This chapter will address these vital questions and present recent evidence that China is already emerging as a regional and global power. However, its long-term prospects as an emerging superpower and challenger to U.S. global hegemony remain clouded with uncertainty.

CHINA: ADVERSARY, COMPETITOR, OR PARTNER?

The current argument of whether China should be considered a geopolitical adversary, a strategic competitor, or a regional partner concerning the U.S. in Asia-Pacific, during the twenty-first century, will be the focus of debate amongst experts for the next twenty years. Yet what *is* surprising to many observers of the region is the accelerating speed with which the geopolitical dynamics have begun to change. Yet no one expects, or desires, the United States to withdraw from Asia-Pacific, including China. Nevertheless, the irrefutable swiftness in which the East Asian hemispheric landscape has been altered by recent economic trends, and, perhaps, will be by future military encounters, once again reinforces the historical perspective concerning the unpredictability of human affairs. Jonathan Spence, noted Yale University historian and eminent China chronicler, puts this debate and its inherent complexities, I believe, in their proper perspective:

> The prospect of China's rise has become a source of endless speculation and debate. To speak of China's "rise" is to suggest its reemergence. It can also imply a recovery from some kind of slump or period of quietude. But "rise" can also mean that a change is being made at someone else's expense. Must a fall always accompany a rise? If so, then a conflict will occur almost by definition. These are difficult questions made all the more so by the fact that a country as vast and complex as China makes up at least half of the equation.[2]

David Shambaugh, director of the China Policy Program at the Elliot School of International Affairs at George Washington University, agrees with Professor Spence's overall observation concerning China's current status in Asia. In January 2006, Shambaugh spoke at the Chicago Council on World Affairs. His topic was "The Changing Nature of the Regional Systems in Asia-Pacific."[3] Professor Shambaugh emphasized that China represents a complex challenge for the U.S. and the Pacific region. China's recent economic and military growth is a bit disconcerting for its regional neighbors, yet over 70 percent of China's foreign direct investment (FDI) originates in Asia-Pacific.[4] As a result, China has emerged as the economic engine for the region's steady growth, and the world's as well. Shambaugh makes a subtle but important point when he analyzes China's current intentions for itself and the region: "China is not attempting to dominate *ASEAN* (Association of Southeast Asian Nations) or *APEC* (Asia-Pacific Economic Cooperative), the region's two most important organizations at the present time, but how much longer will China allow itself to be a 'backseat' partner?"[5] That is the question that many in the region want answered, but it is an answer some fear with equal trepidation.

Natalia Rigol, an associate editor for the *Harvard International Review*, believes there is little cause for alarm, right now, for those who fear a U.S.-China showdown in the near future.[6] Rigol presents a rational and well-thought-out argument on the current nature of relations between these two global powers. Hence, I will mention a few of her major observations below that most accurately reflect her analysis concerning the U.S. and China situation. First, from a geopolitical standpoint, China, presently, accepts the *status quo* condition of U.S. hegemonic power in Asia-Pacific. And there is currently no major issue, or primary reason, for China to challenge the U.S. position. Secondly, within the Asia-Pacific region, the Chinese have not *directly* challenged American leadership, or any of its key alliances.[7]

However, China has sought to establish itself as a power in Asia and around the world by further integrating itself into the international business community. Merle Goldman, history professor emeritus at Boston University, stated, "China has integrated itself into the world system by becoming a member of such global institutions such as the WTO, IMF and the United Nations. Thus, the economic transformation of China has occurred very fast."[8]

This aggressive economic behavior can be described as the Chinese version of "dollar diplomacy" that was energetically pursued and imposed by the American government and its business clients upon its quasi-colonial outposts in the Caribbean region, and in Central and South America, beginning in the early decades of the twentieth century. This philosophy remains functional and powerfully served in these regions today. In short, it is focused upon using intimidating economic incentives, and, at critical times, military intervention, to obtain the kind of business agreements desired by powerful American corporations. The U.S. Congress has often played the role of a well-bribed midwife in this unholy process.[9]

In the case of China, this strategy is once again paying off handsomely. Yet the Chinese are aware and sensitive to the irrefutable fact that not all their regional neighbors are enjoying the near double-digit growth that is transforming the Middle Kingdom. According to recent global trade figures,

China now represents over 13 percent of total world trade—second only to the U.S. Therefore, to avoid what Rigol calls "sociopolitical instability" in the region, China has negotiated beneficial economic partnerships with most of them.[10] In short, China's diplomatic efforts to date have been subtle and *under the radar* in terms of acquiring and projecting influence throughout Asia-Pacific. Nevertheless, almost everyone acknowledges that China and the region's status and stature will change dramatically in the coming years.

Of course, the ultimate outcome in the Asia-Pacific region will greatly depend on the U.S. response to China's economic and military rise in the twenty-first century. If mishandled (i.e., war), the entire economic and security artifice built within the region during the post-WWII period would suffer irreparable harm. This type of regional catastrophe would most certainly stunt the Pacific Basin's development and growth for decades to come. Thus, the omnipresent question of America and China's *coexisting* in this vitally important area of Asia is not a rhetorical exercise based upon vacuous or mundane academic doublespeak, but rather one of profound international importance. And what results will occur due to the expected stress and strains associated with financial, military, and technologically-driven change remain speculative at best, and certainly unnerving and unsettling for many in the region. It is a given that the collateral damage from a failed U.S.-China collaborative effort to coexist in Asia-Pacific will be significant and far-reaching throughout the world as well.

Eric Heginbotham and Christopher Twomey believe America is exercising an Asian policy that is poorly designed for the realities confronting the region and the interests of the U.S. in the twenty-first century. They believe U.S. President George W. Bush is currently exercising the realpolitik philosophy utilized in the late 1800s by German Chancellor Otto von Bismarck. Yet, unfortunately, they also think that this particular policy is ill suited for the challenges and demands confronting the U.S. in Asia, at this point in time. First, this Bismarckian (i.e., "realist") approach dilutes America's ability to shape and define Asia's security framework, and, secondly, its implementation will result in increased nationalist sentiments that will trigger regional tensions—leading to unrest and unpredictable results.[11]

Their antidote to this *policy* predicament is for the U.S. to create a more balanced and nuanced approach to the region, and not see it as an opportunity to exercise raw power—economic and military—to achieve its goals. Thus, America should support Asia's multilateral institutions, such as ASEAN, APEC, ASEAN Regional Forum, and, perhaps, a formalized version of the Northeast Asian Cooperation Dialogue. This path, in their opinion, would go a long way toward stabilizing the region and enhancing America's voice in regional affairs. Secondly, the U.S. should support the development of democracy and its relevant institutions, but not support "nationalist agitation" because the outcome is almost always unpredictable, and the perceived potential of U.S. intervention could lead to an unwanted war.[12] Death and destruction are not the kind of factors that usually lead a nation, or a people, toward democracy.

Perhaps, the implementation of "soft power," as defined by Harvard University government professor Joseph Nye can be much more advantageous and influential for the U.S. in Asia than the use of overwhelming military power to achieve its goals. American culture, consisting of our schools, music, books, movies, and way of life remains a powerful force and extremely influential for hundreds of millions of global citizens seeking a better existence. In short, Professor Nye believes that soft power is a very attractive alternative for individuals and governments who desire to transform their respective societies, and enhance their ability to bring new ideas to challenging problems.[13]

Therefore, Heginbotham and Twomey believe that Bismarckian philosophy should be left where it originated, in the nineteenth century. America, instead, should seek a more enlightened and constructive approach to a region that will have an enormous effect upon itself and the world in the twenty-first century.[14]

Finally, the recently updated analysis of China-U.S. relations by the Congressional Research Service uses the word "competition" to describe the present-day relationship between the two major powers in Asia-Pacific. Kerry Dumbaugh, specialist in Asian Affairs within the Congressional Services' Foreign Affairs, Defense and Trade Division, writes that both nations are in "competition for resources, power, and influence around the world."[15] Dumbaugh points out that China's relations with its regional neighbors have improved significantly since the mid-1990s. Issues such as "territorial disputes, diplomatic deadlocks, and deep ASEAN concerns about China's military ambitions and its regional economic competitiveness" represented a plethora of troubles for the Chinese government within the region.[16]

However, this sense of foreboding and mistrust of China has receded over the past decade. The Chinese have reached out to the members of ASEAN— with the signing of a Free Trade Agreement in 2004. In the same year, the Chinese signed major trade deals purchasing iron ore and energy from Australia (a key U.S. ally). And, in 2005, China initiated a "strategic dialogue" with India (another U.S. ally) concerning terrorism, resource competition, and America's role in Asia.[17]

Though America's role in Asia continues to consume many Chinese officials, and the definition of U.S.-China relations remains frustratingly elusive, there are scholars and observers of U.S.-China relations who feel both countries need each other to create regional and global stability. Professor Patrick Shan, born and raised in China, who currently teaches Chinese history at Grand Valley State University, stated matter-of-factly that "China and the U.S. will not go to war because they need each other to stabilize the global economy."[18] Professor Shan also mentioned, "I simply do not believe that China will ever attempt a preemptive attack on America. And China has worked very hard during the past decade to improve its relations with its neighbors."[19]

Perhaps, the best example of China reaching out to its neighbors, and attempting to be seen as a constructive leader and stabilizing force in the northeastern region of Asia, is their founding, in June 2001, of the Shanghai Cooperation Organization (SCO). The primary focus of the SCO is to establish economic and security agreements with Russia and the Central Asian nations formerly of the Soviet Union. Within this dual-policy framework, there is a consensus to build gas/oil pipelines, initiate rail-link development, and participate in joint military activities. The activities of the SCO have certainly caught the attention of policymakers in the U.S. and Asia. However, no one is interpreting this relatively new organization as a direct threat to America's dominant position in Asia-Pacific.[20]

In short, the anxiety and tensions experienced in the mid-1990s have been replaced, thus far, by a constructively engaged China. However, the Middle Kingdom and its variable actions are being closely monitored by its Asian and Pacific neighbors to ensure that its rise remains within the realm of constructive and nonthreatening (i.e., military) competition for its legitimate place in Asian affairs, and not as a precursor for regional, if not global, dominance.

As expected, it is not hard to find informed opinions or voices of alarm in America or Asia-Pacific that interpret China's emergence as a *real* power in the region as a threatening development—that will *probably* lead to some level of military conflict. The most candid of these voices is University of Chicago Professor John Mearsheimer, who states unequivocally, "If China continues its impressive economic growth over the next few decades that the U.S. and China are likely to engage in an intense security competition with considerable potential for war."[21] Professor Mearsheimer, a self-described great-power realist, also believes that if China becomes a threatening force in Asia, America's key allies and friends in the region will join the U.S. in containing China's hegemonic intentions.[22]

However, there are skeptics who believe that the anti-China mentality gripping the Bush administration in 2007 is a by-product of the neoconservative elements within the policymaking structures of the U.S. government. Professor Michael Klare points to the Defense Planning Guidance (DPG) for fiscal years 1994–1999 as the "master blueprint for U.S. dominance in the post-Cold War era."[23] Professor Klare, director of the Five College Program in Peace and World Security Studies at Hampshire College, identified three events, in 2005, that reflected a new (manufactured?) hostility toward China: First, in February 2005, the announcement came that the U.S.-Japan alliance was to be strengthened even though the U.S. knew that China would react in a hostile manner to this new agenda; second, Secretary of Defense Donald Rumsfeld's speech at a strategic conference held in Singapore, in June 2005, singled out the Chinese and its military buildup as a real threat to stability in East Asia; and third, in July 2005, the Pentagon released a report, *The Military Power of the People's Republic of China*, that once again focused upon the potential danger of China's military development. Klare writes, "The main thrust of the report is that China is expanding its capacity to fight wars beyond its own territory and that this effort constitutes a dangerous challenge to global order."[24] He continues on to say conservative policymakers in America, since the early 1990s, after the Cold War was acknowledged to have ended due to the complete dissolution of the Soviet Union in December 1991, have sought a complete and total dominance of military affairs throughout the world.[25]

Amongst our allies in Asia-Pacific, there seems to be a strong disagreement about the nature of the Chinese threat to the region. Two Australian writers and longtime observers of China's development since the 1960s, Gregory Clark and Ross Terrill, perceive China's emergence in Asia, and the world, through different prisms of interpretation. Clark, vice president of Akita International University and a former Australian diplomat, sees the "bogeyman" thesis, once again, being applied to China by its detractors.[26] Terrill, an associate researcher at Harvard University's John K. Fairbank Center, interprets China as a country in transition and burdened with indecision by whether to become a fully functional nation-state, or a new Chinese empire. This dual internal struggle has reached a midpoint, and China's final determination of its future will have tremendous regional and global ramifications, according to Professor Terrill, the author of *The New Chinese Empire*.[27]

Yet Clark believes the current hysteria over China's dramatic economic and military growth is a manifestation of the "China Threat" lobby, which has been constantly in motion since the Korean War, 1950–1953. *Every* political or military struggle in East Asia is always traced back to some subliminal plot hatched up by the Chinese government. In both Australia and America, the "China threat" crowd is constantly linking China with any, if not all, events in Asia that are considered a threat to the Yank-Aussie interests in the region.[28] Clark sees all this nonsense as smoke and mirrors to protect the real interests involved in these contrived moments of frantic Chinese xenophobia—the military-industrial-intelligence complex. This hydra-headed bureaucratic monstrosity needs threats to justify its budgets and expenditures (and activities), and it counts on dubious academics and other commentators in the media to sell the public on this new threat to freedom. Afterwards, Clark states, "when it is all over and the alleged threat has proved to be quite imaginary, the threat merchants move on to find another target. But not before billions have been spent. And millions have died."[29]

Professor Terrill, on the other hand, sees a more savvy, ambitious, and dangerous Chinese empire emerging in the twenty-first century. By contrast, the American empire is seen by the author as a tripod of global interests: technology and investment, popular culture, and a nonimperialistic military that intervenes and then leaves. In short, America represents a soft empire in its overt handling of international affairs. However, Terrill believes that the Chinese see themselves, and their *new* empire, in a very different light. China's leaders perceive themselves as the "guardians of truth."[30] Therefore, any compromises or decisions that the Chinese leadership makes are done with the understanding that these are just *tactical* decisions. Thus, their decisions do not represent any moral comparability between China and the rest of the world.[31] Nevertheless, according to Professor Terrill, the new Chinese empire does indeed represent a *real* threat to America's global preeminence and its hegemonic system—both of which are based upon its economic, political, and social values:

> The new Chinese empire is different. At once more modest and more arrogant, it is an empire of theater and presumption. It is a construct both of domestic repression and of international aspiration. Its arsenal of weapons includes secrecy, deception, and a sense of history that enables it to take a long view of China's interests and ambitions.[32]

Though, critics of the anti-China faction have made solid arguments concerning their dismay at the level of hysteria directed toward China. However, there exists *equally* persuasive evidence that China is indeed building up its military capabilities at an alarming rate. And this modernization of their military, overall, has caught the attention of their neighbors and the United States. When you look at the raw numbers, the Chinese are indeed putting together a rather formidable force that appears to have the potential to project Chinese power well beyond their shores. In an increasingly transparent world, any nation's military buildup does not go unnoticed— especially by America. However, it is the issue of *transparency* that is most troubling to the U.S. government. Therefore, the lack of clarity on the issue of military expenditures by the Chinese government is emerging as an unsettling issue between the U.S. and China.

This thesis, concerning the potentiality of a China threat and the lack of (complete) information on their overall military spending, are detailed in the Department of Defense's (DoD) annual report (mentioned earlier in the chapter) to the U.S. Congress from the Office of the Secretary of Defense titled, *The Military Power of the People's Republic of China*. This well-structured report contained numerical figures representing China's troop levels, budgetary and expenditure figures, missile capabilities and present military priorities and strengths within the East Asian theatre, and what it will mean for future U.S. military strategists and regional policymakers.[33]

One of the primary focuses of the report was its analysis of China's capabilities in dealing with Taiwan, and with those nations who might potentially come to the island's defense, if a military conflagration erupted between them. It is not a secret to U.S. regional analysts that the most important regional matter for China is to reassimilate Taiwan into the Chinese nation-state family. This is a *red-button* issue for the People's Republic of China's (PRC) leadership in Beijing. The DoD's report also provides credible evidence that China's massive remodernization of its military also represents the potential capability of disturbing the power balance, or status quo, within East Asia.[34] This disturbing fact has certainly caught the attention of China's neighbors, who are increasingly unsettled about such a development. Here are some of the basic figures presented in the DoD report on China's *overall* military situation:

Ground Troops: 1.6 million
Tanks: 6,500
Artillery Pieces: 11,000
Air Force: 1,500 fighters; 780 bombers
Naval Forces: Destroyers/Frigates: 64; Landing Ships: 43; Submarines: 57
Ballistic Missile Capability: Short Range: 650–730; Medium Range: 29–37; Intermediate Range: 14–18; Intercontinental Range: 20–24 (5,500 km), 20 (8,500 km); Submarine Launched: 20–24

It is these precise figures (and growing) that have unnerved many in the U.S. government and in national governments throughout East Asia. Initially, China responded angrily to the DoD's report and its analysis concerning the threatening situation involving China and Taiwan. In a fit of nationalistic frustration, Zhu Chenghu, a PLA (People's Liberation Army) major general and professor at China's National Defense University, stated that China might have to resort to using nuclear weapons against America, if the U.S. interfered on the behalf of Taiwan during a war with China. This remark certainly caught the attention of the Bush administration and the Pentagon. However, the Beijing government dismissed the remark as an individual making a "personal opinion" about a sensitive matter. Interestingly, General Zhu was not reprimanded publicly for his impolitic and provocative comment.[35]

Many China-watchers were not surprised by the lack of zeal shown by Beijing to denounce General Zhu's inflammatory remark. Many believe that Zhu's position is widely supported within the upper ranks of the PLA. Therefore, the CCP (Chinese Communist Party) is reluctant to rebuke the general publicly. Jing Huang, a foreign policy analyst at the Brookings Institution, believes, "Mr. Zhu would never have been able to make such comments unless he was backed by powerful forces within the PLA."[36]

So what is the future outcome, economically and militarily, between these two Pacific powers—America and China? In an attempt not to be ambiguous or evasive on this serious question, the *actual* consensus concerning U.S.-China relations remains deeply divided. Robert Kaplan and Richard Haass are perfect examples of the intellectual division existing in American policy circles today. Both are greatly respected and have done excellent work on global issues, especially concerning U.S. security matters. Kaplan, a renowned global analyst, whose writings have focused upon the future condition of various parts of the world, interprets the American position in the Pacific as the defining element that will determine the U.S.'s future role as a global power in the twenty-first century.

According to Kaplan, the keys to America's future hegemonic presence in the Pacific will be its capacity to project naval power (re: Alfred T. Mahan's famous 1890 thesis[37]), and to possess the technological capabilities to match similar advances made by China in its land-based missile systems, and within its naval surface and submarine fleets as well. Kaplan writes, "In the coming decades, China will play an asymmetric back-and-forth game with us in the Pacific, taking advantage not only of its vast coastline but also of its rear base—stretching far back into Central Asia—from which it may eventually be able to lob missiles accurately at moving ships in the Pacific."[38] At the end of his article, Kaplan states that the U.S. Navy must redefine itself to meet the military challenges represented by China, and take special note of the significant geographical factors confronting our regional strategists with concern to China and East Asia.[39]

Haass, currently the president of the Council on Foreign Affairs, America's most prestigious foreign policy organization, states that both America and China simply can not let things get out of control in East Asia, because both nations have too much to lose—economically, militarily, and in terms of global influence. However, he also emphatically believes it's futile to attempt to control, or manage, the overall development of any nation-state:

> The rise and fall of countries (like China) is largely beyond the ability of the United States or any other outsider to control. The performance of states is mostly the result of demographics, culture, natural resources, educational systems, economic policy, political stability, and foreign policy.[40]

Haass admits that a great deal of history is determined by relations between and amongst the great powers, at any particular point in time, and the key relationship that demands watching in the twenty-first century is the one between China and the U.S. Presently, the recent rise of Chinese nationalism presents a degree of difficulty for America and China to reach an understanding on many significant issues.[41] However, Haass asserts with absolute certainty that "a U.S.-China cold war would be costly, dangerous, and distracting, robbing attention and resources from pressing internal and global challenges. Both countries have a stake in avoiding this outcome."[42]

On that note of rational introspection, I think it is appropriate and proper to end this section of the chapter with a survey that was completed by David Rothkopf, a visiting scholar at the Carnegie Endowment for International Peace and a widely respected national security analyst. In 2005, Rothkopf conducted an extensive survey at the Carnegie Endowment for International Peace on a number of issues, priorities, and topics concerning U.S. foreign policy.

Overall, almost 180 individuals participated in answering Rothkopf's multiple questions. I will only focus on a few of the answers obtained by Rothkopf and his team of researchers. These experts were asked twice a two-fold question: The first was which countries and/or entities are most likely to be important allies or friends, or otherwise important to the support of U.S. initiatives over the next five and the next twenty years. The second question was the flip side of the first question. Which countries and/or entities would most likely be America's potential adversaries, rivals, or challengers to our interests in the world over the next five years and the next twenty years? The answer for all four categories was China.[43]

It is not an understatement to say that the American foreign policy establishment is quite divided over the *proper* response to China's rise in global affairs. Therefore, should we be surprised that our inconsistent national policies and positions emanating from the White House and the U.S. Congress toward China are simply a mirrored reflection of the multitude of opinions within the ranks of academia, journalists, think tanks, and other policymakers within the U.S. government? This intellectual scrum, though vibrant and combative, does represent a distressing element involving the construction of American foreign policy. Almost all the "experts" mentioned in this chapter basically agree that the moment of truth is coming relatively soon for America and China. Yet we are not even close to having achieved a consensus concerning the development of a coherent and operational strategy concerning the rise of China, and East Asia, in the twenty-first century. Put directly, this lack of a functional, proper, and, perhaps, visionary strategic framework for this vital region of the world is simply not healthy or reassuring for the collective global interests at large.

THE CHINA ECONOMIC JUGGERNAUT

Napoleon is alleged to have stated, "When China wakes up, it will shake the world."[44] This famous and prophetic quote remains shrouded by a degree of doubt concerning its authenticity, but its essential truth has come to pass in the twenty-first century. However, what is not in doubt is the present-day rumblings emanating from China's dynamic and evolving economy. Indeed, the world's focus is shifting irrefutably toward the Asia-Pacific Rim. Specifically, it is the steadily growing Asian economies, with China performing as the region's locomotive that is turning the global economic crankshaft away from a North Atlantic (i.e., America and the European Union) perspective to one now comprising the United States and the East Asian hemisphere.

Henceforth, this specific section of the chapter will focus on two primary topics of vital concern: first, an overview of China's current and future economic prowess and the ramifications for America, East Asia, and the world. As China's economic presence looms ever larger amongst the advanced economies, particularly for those workers in the West, how soon will it be before the voices of nationalism bend their respective governments' policies toward greater protectionism? And influence their respective societies to finally distance themselves from the perils of globalization? In truth, most workers see this economic paradigm as the main reason for the massive layoffs, especially within the manufacturing sector, resulting in the physical relocation of friends, and themselves.

Secondly, the potential for conflict in East Asia exists over the issue of retaining access to the natural resources within the global marketplace, especially oil and gas. Specifically, if the advanced economies of the world continue their pace of growth and the volume of natural resources begins to diminish, who gets the resources? When the music stops, who is left without the necessary commodities to ensure economic expansion and prosperity? This is the *key* question that demands an answer from the major economic powers in the very near future.

According to Gilbert Achcar, professor of politics and international relations at the University of Paris–VIII, "China plays a key role in the world capitalist market, and the more this market becomes dependent on the state of the Chinese economy, the more global capitalism will have a stake in the stability of China."[45] In short, China's economic growth has created a mutual need between itself and the outside world. Neither can prosper without the other. It's an international version of a shotgun wedding— East and West brought together despite misgivings by both partners. For example, America needs the Chinese to purchase billions of dollars of U.S. Treasury notes to pay for our skyrocketing national deficits (i.e., America's domestic budget and international trade), and China needs access to our domestic market to sell their exports—which in turn keeps the economic engines running in the Middle Kingdom and helps to maintain employment for millions.

The West, though, is finding out that this new economic gambit called globalization has a serious downside. In America and Australia, their respective automobile industries are increasingly confronting unrelenting Asian competition, primarily from Japan and South Korea. The production of cars and steel represents middle-class wages and it also provides a certain degree of self-respect for workers in these industries. In short, making automobiles and steel personifies a certain dignity and strength reflected by its owners and workers in their local communities and countries.

This sector of the American economy is under threat, and its painful transition due to international competition is tearing communities apart— as witnessed in my adopted home state of Michigan. General Motors (GM), once the kingpin of American automakers, is now in freefall in terms of its U.S. market share in North America. Conversely, this American corporate icon now possesses the largest market share (11.2 percent)—for a foreign automaker—*in* China. It now possesses a workforce of over 15,000 in the "Middle Kingdom." In the meantime, its U.S. market share (26.2 percent) continues to slump, falling another 1.3 percent during 2005. Ironically, though a difficult reality for most GM autoworkers to accept, GM's highly profitable auto plants in China are now paying the bills in its ever-shrinking North American operations and market share.[46] It should be noted that, in January 2007, GM publicly announced that it had achieved record car sales in China. Its overall sales in the Chinese market improved 32 percent during 2006. Overall, GM sold 876,747 vehicles in China in 2006.[47] Many of them were assembled at GM's production plants that are now situated in China, not Michigan.

Yet GM's surge in profits in China was a distant second place to Ford's own eye-popping 89 percent increase in car sales (155,404) in China for 2006.[48] GM and Ford's increased profitability in China has meant the end of the line for thousands of U.S. autoworkers. Both Michigan-based car companies have drastically reduced their hourly and salaried workforces in their North American operations over the past few years. In 2007, no one really knows when the U.S. auto industry will hit rock bottom. However, most industry observers recognize that it will probably experience and suffer the same fate as the American steel industry in the 1980s. In the end, approximately 75 percent of the industry's employment was terminated due to the production of high-quality steel by a much lower-paid workforce, within more efficient steel mills in East Asia, primarily in Japan and South Korea.

In short, in 2007, the cold-blooded realities of the modern-day marketplace, and the raw power of globalization, possess an irrefutable omnipresence throughout the automotive industry in America. It appears, for now, only a fraction of the U.S. auto industry will survive and remain profitable and viable during the twenty-first century.

Yet this profitable situation for GM in China appears to be a short-term panacea, because Chinese automakers are now in the process of building cars for their own domestic market, and for the international market as well. The Lifan Group, led by visionary Yin Mingshan, is planning to export cars to Europe and America by 2009. In 2006, the Lifan Group took a bold step in this direction by purchasing one of the world's most sophisticated engine plants in Brazil from the DaimlerChrysler and BMW auto company. They will dismantle it and transport it 8,300 miles to Chongqing in western China. In the end, the Lifan Group wants to produce a competitive sedan with leather seats, dual air bags, and a DVD system for only $9,700.[49]

America and Europe are not the only targeted markets for these Chinese autos in the near future. Australia is now being seriously considered as a new market for their cars. Of course, the (much) less costly Chinese models will completely undermine the price structure for cars in the Land Down Under. If allowed to penetrate the Australian market with any degree of significance, the Aussie auto companies will almost certainly become noncompetitive and perish from their local communities, because they will almost certainly be forced out of business due to a price war they can't win.

Australian Greens Federal Senator Christine Milne stated, "If China obtains total access to Australia's car market, the nation's auto plants will soon be closed. It would be suicidal for the Australian car industry to give China a full-go at its domestic market."[50] John Wormald, a senior analyst for Autopolis, a major automotive consultancy firm, confirms Senator Milne's assertion that Australia's car industry would be drastically damaged by unrestricted trade: "The effect of Chinese carmakers entering the Australian market would be dramatic. The effect will be to pull the whole price structure (for cars) down. Even if the local industry isn't directly competing against Chinese vehicles the effect of their coming will be severe."[51]

This same scenario is repeating itself in industry after industry in America, Australia, and the rest of the industrialized world. Growing market shares, trade surpluses, and an ever-expanding Chinese economy is indeed shaking the economic foundation of the world. Therefore, again, not unexpectedly, demands for government intervention on behalf of struggling industries in America are becoming a common occurrence in Washington, DC. Nucor's CEO, Daniel R. DiMicco, in charge of the largest steelmaking facility in America (in Charlotte, North Carolina), is concerned about the future ability of the U.S. to produce competitive steel in a global market being shaped by Chinese industrial policies. DiMicco states that China is exporting steel despite absorbing most of it for domestic use. He claims more steel mills are being built in China, and they are "massively subsidized" by government-supported interest-free loans, an undervalued currency, and generous export tax breaks.[52] Thus, according to the embattled Nucor CEO, "if China decides to export significant amounts of steel, there will be no such thing as competition."[53] The American and Australian auto industries and the U.S. steel industries are concrete examples of the degree of market penetration associated with China's new economic presence in terms of global production and trade.

Already, China has a dominating global production presence in several categories involving labor-intensive goods, such as toys (70 percent), bicycles (60 percent), shoes (50 percent), and luggage (33 percent).[54] The Chinese are now making serious and successful global inroads in product production requiring low-tech capabilities, such as microwave ovens (50 percent), television sets and air conditioners (33 percent), and refrigerators (20 percent).[55] Oded Shenkar, author of *The Chinese Century*, writes that as China "moves up the ladder" in terms of product sophistication and technology, unlike Japan and Korea before them, they are not allowing these lower rung economic production systems to be moved (outsourced) to other countries. The profits from these low-level manufacturing sources of production continue to finance China's move toward "knowledge-intensive areas" such as products associated with the information age.[56] The primary reason for China's reluctance to outsource these lower-tech positions is because the Chinese government must maintain stable levels of employment for its 1.3 billion citizens. This challenge is unrelenting for the Communist leadership in Beijing.

The only reasons keeping China from even further domination of the products mentioned above, and gaining an even larger market share in the West, are the agreed upon quotas and tariffs which are insisted upon by the national governments throughout the developed world (i.e., the U.S., Japan, Australia, and the European Union). There is a good reason for these economic protections for America—massive job losses. Scott Robert, a researcher at the Economic Policy Institute in Washington, DC, provided disturbing and frightening evidence concerning the employment ramifications of America's trade policies with China since 1992. Robert's analysis determined that almost 700,000 jobs were lost between 1992 and 1999. And he projects even greater job losses (almost 900,000) for the American economy in the near future, if trade policies and trends remain the same with China.[57] In short, if everything remains the same in terms of trade policies and economic trends between the U.S. and China, the potential job losses for America's economy will be approximately 1.6 million.[58]

Though the U.S. economy will gain some jobs during this period of global readjustment and transition, the message remains quite clear and disturbing. Presently, and during the next decade or so, China will represent a monumental threat to those who earn their livings in the manufacturing sector of the American economy. Again, Robert indicates that states in the upper Midwest and the Mid-Atlantic like Michigan, Wisconsin, Minnesota,

Ohio, Indiana, Pennsylvania, New Jersey, and New York, have been, and will continue to be, hit hard by the Chinese economic juggernaut.[59]

China's voracious appetite for the world's natural resources has grown almost exponentially, thus causing global prices for various commodities (oil, gas, iron ore, copper, cement mix, etc.) to rise dramatically as a result. In terms of global distribution, the diminishing volume and/or availability of various resources represents a real danger concerning future global stability. It is a threat with many foreboding dimensions: economic, political, social, and military.

An editorial in the *Asian Times* declared that China now possesses the fourth largest economy in the world—having catapulted themselves over Great Britain, France, and Italy in 2005. Economist Jim O'Neill at Goldman Sachs, in London, stated about China's immense growth during 2005—without a revised gross domestic product (GDP) completed— "China could squeak in ahead of Britain even without a revision. It just goes to show how much it's contributing to the world economy."[60]

Lester Brown, founder of World Watch Institute in 1974, and currently president of the Earth Policy Institute, wrote, in spring 2005, "Although the United States has long consumed the lion's share of the world's resources, this situation is changing fast as the Chinese economy surges ahead, overtaking the U.S. in the consumption of one resource after another."[61] Brown points to China's importation of grain, meat, coal, and steel as examples of the Middle Kingdom surpassing American levels of consumption—except for oil.[62] However, in his latest book, *Plan B 2.0*, Brown states unequivocally, that "the inevitable conclusion to be drawn from these projections (concerning China's future resource needs) is that there are not enough resources for China to reach U.S. consumption levels."[63] China, from the standpoint of consuming the earth's resources, is increasingly interpreted by its neighbors and global competitors as a threatening element to their own survival in the twenty-first century.

Though I have focused primarily on the effects upon the American economy, the same scenario is playing out in national economies around the world. Therefore, the question that is increasingly asked amongst the *developed* world, *developing* nations, and even amongst *Third World* countries is, How does a nation maintain its competitiveness against an economic Goliath who possesses an immense workforce and an extremely low-wage economy? Will Hutton, the former editor of the *London Observer* and economic editor of the *Guardian*, utilizes within his book, *The Writing on the Wall*, the research of Suzanne Berger at MIT, and her team of researchers, who interviewed 500 companies in America, Europe, and Asia. Their collective efforts produced an irrefutable conclusion concerning the variables of globalization, and that was "wage costs are not the be-all and end-all of economics."[64]

However, Berger's own book, *How We Compete*, indicates that a Chinese worker earns only 4 percent of the wage of an American worker, though she quickly points out that the Chinese worker is only 4 percent as productive as an American worker.[65] Hutton, presently the chief executive of the Work Foundation, again, uses Berger's work to provide evidence, and dilute the ever-growing myth, that not all the low-skilled and low-paying jobs will disappear from Western economies and Japan. Berger's research showed that companies often found it necessary, physically and culturally, to have production facilities close to their respective markets.[66]

Nevertheless, the recent outsourcing of millions of jobs from the U.S., and from other developed economies in the world, has accelerated without question. Indeed, it certainly appears that hiring Chinese workers, at a fraction of the labor costs encountered in developed economies, has proven extremely tempting and profitable for hydra-headed multinationals.

THE DRAGON'S ACHILLES' HEEL

Presently, the much-feared Chinese "economic tsunami" appears to be on the verge of permanently altering, if not reshaping, the global marketplace due to its sheer size and breath of existence—both of which are growing on a daily basis. Though there is concern over China's staggering economic presence and potential, it has not yet evolved into an irrational panic within the global community. Why?

Well, it is becoming increasingly evident to many keen observers of domestic China that there are several serious challenges within the Middle Kingdom. These problems are not just mere speculation, but are, in fact, fundamental issues that could quite possibly derail Asia's present-day financial juggernaut. At present, these complex and multiple dilemmas are very threatening to the long-term leadership of the Chinese Communist Party in Beijing. However, within this particular section of the present chapter, I will only address a few of these primary concerns.

First, there is a growing cacophony of voices within China's panoply of small towns and in its rural regions as well. They are demanding that they be allowed to participate more directly in the decisions concerning local development. Second, the Chinese people want the eradication of the dispiriting and suffocating corruption that is strangling their local and national politics. Third, the Beijing government must confront the gross and ever-widening economic inequities in China—especially within the central and western provinces of China. There is strong evidence that the increasing amount of civil unrest in the interior regions of China is linked to peasants' demanding that more of China's resources be spent on their immediate needs—education, roads, sanitation, housing, clean water, more access to commercial goods, etc. They know the cities on the east coast are flourishing, and now they want their share of the nation's prosperity. Finally, there is an elevating recognition, within the national leadership, to drastically diminish the levels of pollution in the industrial areas and rural regions throughout China. This condition is beginning to hurt productivity and the quality of life in many parts of the country. This *particular* issue could very well be the ticking time bomb that could explode and exacerbate all the issues previously mention in this paragraph, and ignite a full blown social revolt inside the Middle Kingdom.

A plethora of issues—the economy, the environment, corruption, and the growing gap between the rich and the poor—represent the *root* causes for the dramatic rise in civil unrest throughout China. James Fallows, an *Atlantic Monthly* national correspondent, wrote in the December 2006 issue about what he learned during his visit to Shanghai, that "a nearly unbelievable 87,000 'public order disturbances' took place in China last year, according to China's own Public Security Ministry, up from an already alarming 58,000 in 2003."[67] With these problems bearing down on China, Fallows asks the question that many analysts are asking themselves with concern to China's future: "Can China continue to adapt?"[68]

In China, even within provinces that are experiencing robust economic prosperity, like Guangdong, the local citizenry is demanding a larger voice on all issues involving their respective villages and towns, especially issues concerning their economic development. Esther Pan, a staff writer on Asian issues at the Council on Foreign Relations (CFR), commented, "Local citizens feel they don't have enough of a say in how their area is changing, they see local officials and their relatives getting rich from bribes and stolen funds, and they are angry and frustrated, experts say."[69] Ms. Pan, who has written on Asian affairs at the CFR since 2003, notes that local groups often look to the national Communist Party to eliminate corruption but even their efforts fall short of expectations: "It (Chinese Communist Party) wants to root it (corruption) out, but it's so systemic at the local administration level there's little party leaders can do from Beijing . . . "[70] This growing frustration at the grassroots level, particularly in China's small towns and rural communities, is putting tremendous pressure upon the national government to accept and implement new legal reforms. There are also constant demands for an expanded role for the local courts, because the outcry for fairness and justice is threatening the social stability of China—which of course threatens its future economic growth.

Professor Jerome Cohen, at the NYU School of Law, states, "The Chinese government is plainly facing a domestic crisis of confidence caused by the failure of its institutions to deal adequately with a rising tide of public grievances relating to environmental pollution, real estate manipulation, unauthorized local financial demands, corruption, discrimination and other official abuses."[71] Professor Cohen, a renowned expert on the Chinese legal system, believes that the movement toward achieving legal reforms will not be deterred by corrupt elements, or officials, within Chinese society: " . . . We can expect robust law reform efforts to continue in China, even in the field of criminal justice. The PRC (People's Republic of China) is still considering whether or not to ratify the International Covenant on Civil and Political Rights (ICCPR), which it signed in 1998."[72] There is little doubt that these grassroots efforts demanding the eradication of local corruption will, as a consequence, strengthen the overall future development of China during the twenty-first century. The question of whether Beijing is willing to enforce its will—anticorruption laws—upon corrupt local officials throughout China remains unanswered.

The widening income gap, between individuals and families, and between those who live on the east coast and those who live in the cities, towns, and villages in the interior of the country, is growing and causing class-based stress throughout China. Though political free speech and access to multiple forms of information may be quite limited in the Middle Kingdom, nevertheless, the people know that their comrades on the east coast, particularly in the cities—Hong Kong, Shanghai, and Beijing—have it a lot better than they. Will Hutton provides startling statistics with an example that shows the huge disparities between Shanghai—per capita income exceeding $15,000—and the province of Guizhou in the rural west—per capita income of only $1,247.[73] It is this condition of massive income inequities existing in China which represents a real danger for the future stability of China.

An article in the *Wall Street Journal* chronicled the life of one Chinese laborer, Wei Zhongwen, who left rural China, and his family, to find work in Beijing. He succeeded in landing a construction job, like 2 million other labor migrants living in Beijing, which enabled him to send 80 percent of his monthly pay ($300) to his family. They live on a family farm in Yushu County, which lies within the northeastern part of Jilin Province. His family left behind, within the interior region of China, is classified as a "3861 army." This rather opaque governmental term indicates that women and children are receiving funding from an absent husband. Wei works fifteen-hour days—seven days per week—and is often exhausted from the endless demands from corrupt bosses who often don't pay the workers the money owed them. Plus, construction work in China is the second most dangerous occupation—right behind coal mining. In 2005, it was reported to the national government that 2,607 fatalities occurred on construction sites.[74]

Nevertheless, despite the loneliness and the multitude of occupational hazards within the construction industry, Wei's earnings have paid for a new five-room home for his extended family, a twenty-one-inch color television set, and his daughter's secondary education.[75] Wei's story represents just a glimpse of the daily ordeals, personal pain, and the undeniable economic gains experienced by millions of migrants who have drifted into China's large cities seeking higher earnings and a better way of life for their families.

Hence, Chinese laborers want, and are receiving, a larger portion of the prosperity that has resulted from the current economic expansion and enrichment within China. Conn Hallinan, a foreign policy analyst for *Foreign Policy in Focus* and a lecturer in journalism at the University of Santa Cruz, however, discovered a quote from a Chinese newspaper, *Xinhua News*, stating, "The income gap, which has exceeded reasonable limits, exhibits a further widening trend. If it continues this way for a long time, the phenomenon may give rise to various sorts of social instability."[76] Hallinan notes that this potential for "instability" is already occurring and is growing in frequency throughout China, particularly in inland communities who feel they have been forgotten by the Beijing government. In 2004, there were at least 74,000 "instabilities" involving almost 4 million people, and petitions to adjudicate grievances reached an all-time high in 2005. In April 2006, the issue of income disparity was the chief topic at the National People's Congress meeting.[77]

Australian scholar Jane Golley contributed a chapter to the book *China 2003: New Engine for Growth*, which explained how the southeastern part of China progressed in nineteenth century due to Western foreign trade, thus resulting in the central and western parts of China lagging behind in terms of economic development. However, this legacy lives on today despite promises by Mao Zedong, after the successful Communist Revolution in 1949, to rectify this financial imbalance. It never happened.[78]

Professor Golley, who teaches economics at Australian National University, warned against simplistic statements about the nature of wealth in China:

> It's important to recognize that there is more than one China. You can see the economic inequalities in Beijing. You can see it if you get on the train and travel for an hour, or travel for 50 hours. You'll see every range from wealth to poverty that you can imagine.[79]

Golley also points out that the standard of living has risen for everyone in the last twenty years. In 2008, the Summer Olympics will be held in Beijing and the world will see how much China has developed economically, but she believes that pollution represents the nation's next biggest hurdle.[80]

The last issue to be addressed in this section will indeed be the pollution crisis gripping China. In its rush to catch up to the major Western industrial powers, the Chinese, to put it simply, cut environmental corners to take the nation to the next level in terms of economic development. Of course, there are always consequences for overly ambitious behavior of any kind, and China's obsession for economic development is very similar to America's push toward urbanization and industrialization in the late nineteenth century. So far, there has been no Chinese *equivalent* of Theodore Roosevelt to appear on the political scene to recognize and take initial steps toward reforming development policies and preserving large sectors of China for posterity. Nevertheless, the pollution is beginning to take its toll on China and the people, and it might soon affect the phenomenal economic growth that the country has experienced for the last twenty-five years.

In July 2005, residents of Xinchang village, located about 180 miles south of Shanghai, attacked a local pharmaceutical plant because it was believed that the facility was an environmental hazard to the local community. As mentioned before in this chapter, the local citizens became enraged by what they perceived as indifference from the local governmental officials towards a serious grievance filed against this particular factory. The riot that ensued, involving perhaps as many as 15,000 people, took place in the Zhejiang Province—which is one of China's wealthier regions. The plant in question had been there for over ten years, but the local populace was convinced that its presence was detrimental to their health. The government stepped in to calm the local community by suspending the plant's activities. However, the local citizens demanded its permanent closure, because wheat production had dropped significantly. The local farmers were also convinced that the plant and its wastes were the root causes for the shortfall in their wheat production, and that the food grown there was no longer healthy for consumption.[81]

A few months later, in October 2005, the top Chinese environmental official, Zhang Lijun, startled his superiors, and China observers, by proclaiming that "pollution levels here could more than quadruple within 15 years if the country does not curb its rapid growth in energy consumption and automobile use."[82] Jim Yardley, a reporter for the *New York Times*, writes, "China, it seems, has reached a tipping point familiar to many developed countries, including the United States, that have raced headlong after economic development only to look up suddenly and see the environmental carnage."[83] Yardley goes on to say that China, unfortunately, due to its size and degree of pollution, represents a much greater danger to itself and the world.[84]

Robert Watson, a senior scientist with the Natural Resources Defense Council, believed that Mr. Zhang's prognosis concerning future levels of China's pollution was a bit on the high side. Yet Watson agreed with Zhang's basic assertion that the country's pollution levels are certainly going to spike upwards in the near future: "It could double or triple without too much trouble. And that's a scary thought, given how bad things are right now."[85]

The one environmental issue that has captured headlines throughout China and the world is the critical problem of water pollution. In December 2005, the provincial capital, Harbin, located in the territory formerly known as Manchuria, experienced a massive spillage of benzene into the Songhua River. This accident triggered a civic emergency and forced local officials to shut off all water supplies to approximately 3.8 million citizens. In the end, this crisis caught the attention of the international media despite efforts by the national government to hide this incident from outside scrutiny. The media coverage caused an unintended backlash throughout China. The people demanded to know how dangerous their environmental problems actually were within the country. And it became apparent to the Chinese citizenry, and outside observers, that these episodes of serious water violations were occurring more often than they had realized.[86] Elizabeth C. Economy, author of *The River Runs Black*, writes that "these things happen all the time, all over the place, probably on a weekly basis."[87]

A Chinese governmental report stated that 70 percent of the nation's lakes and waterways are polluted. A vice minister for water resources, within the Chinese national government, believes approximately 360 million rural citizens are without safe drinking water. And, now large findings of cancer are found in villages and towns along China's waterways.[88] In January 2006, this growing environmental crisis struck two more major Chinese cities. In the industrial city of Zhuzhou, in the Hunan Province, workers cleaning up a wastewater ditch mistakenly diverted the sewage water into the Xiangjiang River. The substance dumped in the river was cadmium, a metal used in manufacturing and linked to neurological disorders and cancer.

In December 2005, this same substance was spilt into the Beijiang River in Guangdong Province, which threatened the health of millions inside the region. In Hunan, Jiang Yimin, director of the provincial Environmental Protection Bureau, stated that the sixty-mile slick of cadmium has already passed the provincial capital, Changsha, without corrupting local water supplies.[89] The other major spill, in January 2006, occurred in the Henan Province due to diesel fuel being dumped in the Yellow River. This fuel slick reached neighboring Shandong Province and forced officials, even in the provincial capital, Jinan, to deactivate sixty-three pumping stations from extracting water from the river.[90] Though the Chinese national government talks about cleaning up the rivers, the eventual costs will be astronomical. Professor Economy points out that a 2004 Chinese governmental study discovered that half of the nation's sewage treatment facilities, built during China's last five-year economic plan, are not functioning due to high operational costs.[91]

Thus, tragically, in many cases, the facilities that are presently available in many areas to clean up the pollution in China's waterways are not being used, because the overarching priority is to keep the economy functioning and growing. Hence, China is stealing from Peter (China's environment) to pay Paul (economic growth). Obviously, this convoluted thinking will not prevail in the future. Though, to be fair, China is making some adjustments due to environmental realities. In 2006, a governmental report recommended that only four of the proposed thirteen dams should be constructed on the Nu River in southwestern China. Despite the belief that the original Nu River plan would produce more electricity than the controversial Three Gorges Dam, near completion, the environmental fallout and the massive human displacement were causing a storm of domestic and international protests. What the government report actually said remains a state secret.[92]

It is this lack of government transparency (due to corruption and secrecy) by the Chinese central government, in Beijing, that accentuates the overall mistrust and suspicions shared by millions of China's citizens, particularly rural dwellers, toward its central government. And, along with the significant corruption present at the local level, it is not hard to understand why there is a lack of faith in the nation's decision-making processes. This cynicism permeates all issues within Chinese society—employment, health care, education, income equity, standard-of-living issues, etc.

As in any capitalist society—even in Communist China—the questions concerning who gets what from the system, and who does the sacrificing to reach these arbitrary national goals, are becoming a growing concern for millions of Chinese. John Gittings, a British journalist, has witnessed China's evolvement since the Cultural Revolution in the late 1960s. He recognizes that past governments had a tendency to evade tough decisions and their responsibilities under the guise of nationalism or a perceived threat to party rule and sees the new generation of leaders in China in a much more positive light. He writes that they are now "more aware of the need to bridge social divisions, to tackle environmental blight, to tackle bureaucratic obscurantism and encourage more open communication."[93]

Gittings believes that the main responsibility of the present generation of leaders is to keep moving the country steadily forward. He sees the main threats to China's future to be the "deteriorating environment" and the "uncertainties of the world trade system on which the health of the Chinese economy increasingly depends."[94]

CHINA SHAKES THE ASIA-PACIFIC RIM

What is China to America? What is China to the Asia-Pacific Rim? In truth, the answers to these questions are clear and unclear, simultaneously. The range of opinions within the region represents a vast spectrum of interpretations. Though, as expected, the main arguments are being simplistically divided into two camps: first, those who see China's emergence in Asia as a *threat* to U.S. leadership, and secondly, those who interpret China's recent rise as *nonthreatening*—for now. The one thing they all agree upon is that China *is* changing the dynamics of the region, and the American response to this transition holds the key to the region's future.

An equally important question emerges: Will the Asia-Pacific region remain a shining model for those identified as the Third World and developing nations, in terms of future economic prosperity? Many of these nations are slowly but steadily integrating themselves within the global system, which consists of capital, commerce, education, information, labor, and technology. Even repressive governments, such as China, Vietnam, North Korea, and Burma, are realizing that their long-term economic futures and political viability are increasingly tied to this emerging regional and global economic model.

Thus, this section will focus on three thematic questions concerning Asia-Pacific and the twenty-first century: First, how will America respond to China's rise in Asia-Pacific? Some perceive the China challenge as the defining determinant for the U.S. position in the Pacific region during the twenty-first century. Secondly, how are America's key allies—Australia, Japan, and South Korea—adjusting to China's new economic prowess and military influence in the region? And, finally, can America maintain the fundamental framework that has created and ensured unity and understanding, in terms of collective security, between itself and its key regional allies since 1950?

To answer the first thematic question, I believe America will respond to China's rise with policies and a strategy consisting of passive/aggressive characteristics. This is a typical response by a hegemonic power (America, in this case) that is internally threatened but does not want a specific individual, or nation (China, case in point), to think they are vulnerable due to their emergence as a global power. In short, the U.S. is still figuring out what to do about this evolving economic and military powerhouse in East Asia.

The Chinese, of course, are deciding (with great caution) how they can coexist with an established hegemonic power who observes their emergence with a noticeable degree of anxiety, and, perhaps, even fear. Without question, the future of China-U.S. relations remains speculative, and it also represents the *unknown* variable concerning Asia-Pacific's future status. Nevertheless, to say that war is *eminent* between these two powerful nations is extremely premature. Yet it is equally foolish to ignore the tensions existing between them. Why? Because, their respective agendas and vital interests within the region are very similar and yet increasingly conflicting within a relatively small geographical arena.

In the last five years, America and China have taken turns assisting and criticizing each other on a number of issues confronting Asia-Pacific. For instance, the North Korean situation is a perfect example where both sides have had to compromise to find a workable solution. Since 2001, the U.S. has been distracted by the war on terror in Afghanistan and Iraq. Both wars have absorbed enormous amounts of American financial and human resources. Not unexpectedly, when the North Korean leader, Kim Jong-il, announced, in 2005, that his country was reinstituting its nuclear weapons program, the Bush administration reluctantly looked to China for diplomatic assistance with this dangerous regime. In truth, the U.S. is stretched dangerously thin, diplomatically and militarily, particularly since its ill-founded invasion of Iraq. And the Bush administration has acknowledged that China has maintained a strong relationship with North Korea since the end of WWII.

Of course, the neoconservatives within the Bush White House intensely dislike this admission of diplomatic inadequacy which exposes the inherent weaknesses within their overall plan toward achieving global dominance. Nevertheless, the U.S. government urgently asked and received assistance from President Hu Jintao, and the Chinese Communist government, when North Korea stunned Asia and America with its first ever nuclear test in October 2006. As a result, after direct Chinese intervention, the North Korean leader, Kim Jong-il, agreed to return to the six-party talks involving China, North and South Korea, Japan, the U.S., and Russia.[95] It is important to understand that China's assertive diplomatic actions towards North Korea are not due to an ideological kinship. In reality, China confronts an irrefutable truth that they have huge financial interests at stake. If Northeast Asia is engulfed by a regional war, those 9–10 percent annual economic growth figures enjoyed by China for the last twenty-five years will become a sweet memory for President Hu's government. And such a war's collateral damage may include the termination of the Chinese Communist Party's leadership in China as well.

Nevertheless, China is not permitting American hegemonic unilateralism to be the only game, in terms of future economic and energy policies, in the region. China, as mentioned earlier in the book, created the Shanghai Cooperation Organization (SCO), and was a strong supporter of the East Asian Summit (EAS) that was convened for the first time in December 2005. In both cases, it is correct to perceive these two developments as future harbingers toward challenging American economic dominance in Asia-Pacific. China is letting the U.S. know, on no uncertain terms, that the economic future of the region will not be predominately designed and directed toward fulfilling U.S. interests.

Though, as I have mentioned, again, earlier in the book, no one wants to see America roll back its presence in the region to the Hawaiian Islands. However, many nations (and allies) want a larger voice in determining the region's economic and geopolitical future. In terms of soft power, China is not an attractive alternative for many countries in the region, in terms of political freedoms, electoral democracy, and the ability to dissent against unpopular policies. However, their form of parochial nationalism is quite infectious and it represents a real threat to America's overall support in the region—if the U.S. ignores calls for greater participation in regional matters.

Finally, the Americans and Chinese need each other much more than their respective publics realize or understand. Simply stated, America depends on China buying U.S. Treasury notes every day to pay for our overindulgent capitalistic lifestyle. Laura Tyson, a former economic advisor on President Bill Clinton's Council of Economic Advisors, once commented rather poignantly, "America spends, Asia lends."[96] America's elected officials don't have the political nerve, or the intellectual integrity, to inform their constituents that the nation's national debt is now approaching $9 trillion.

In short, the national economy is not producing enough wealth to pay for all the things that Americans believe they are entitled to in life. As a consequence, the Chinese government, in recent years, has been strongly persuaded by the American government to purchase billions of dollars of U.S. Treasury notes to finance America's increasingly obese society, its grotesque debt from mindless consumerism, and the out-of-control spending by the U.S. government itself.

Conversely, China can not force the U.S. to change its domestic spending habits because much of the debt is due to buying cheap Chinese goods at stores, such as Wal-Mart, K-Mart, Meijers, etc. China's mind-boggling economic progression over the last twenty years, and relative social stability, would evaporate overnight if the U.S. market plunged into financial chaos. Both nations would wake up to high unemployment and social upheaval. In an almost Shakespearean sense, America and China, like two scorpions trapped within a bottle, each possesses the capacity to destroy the other—financially. Thus, it is in the interest of both countries to maintain this financial charade.

War, whether by financial fiat, or by military confrontation, is to be avoided at all costs. There are several critical issues, such as Taiwan's future sovereignty, North Korea's nuclear missile program, oil and gas ownership within the Spratly Islands in the South China Sea, and Japan's future military role in East Asia, which are extremely sensitive for America and China. They occasionally flare up in the course of doing regional business, but, so far, have been resolved quietly and efficiently. A U.S.-China war of any kind will accomplish absolutely nothing in terms of achieving common economic and geopolitical objectives within the region—for both countries.

To put a finer point on this volatile situation, the U.S. and China are increasingly seen by most citizens in the region as the dual caretakers of it for the twenty-first century. This acknowledged reality is also why many will be on edge during the coming years and decades. Can this *partnership* produce the type of peace and prosperity desired by the people and nations within the Asia-Pacific region? America, being the only superpower at this time, carries the brunt of the responsibility for creating a constructive and productive relationship with China. Rest assured, the people in this region are watching intensely the actions of both very carefully.

The second thematic question concerning how America's key allies will react to the growing economic and military presence of China in Asia-Pacific is already taking shape. I visited South Korea (2005), Australia (2006), China, South Korea (again), and Japan (2007) within the last three years. Therefore, I will answer this particular question by providing an overview of each nation relating to their current, and probable, relations with America and China. As expected, I cautiously proceed upon the unpredictable terra firma known as the Asia-Pacific Rim—without fear or favor—and I present a few of my own impressions and thoughts about America's key allies: Australia, South Korea, and Japan (and China).

First, I will examine Australia. My last visit to this island continent was in May–June 2006. I have already presented in a previous chapter the numerous interviews, opinions, and writings acquired during my travels within this beautiful country. Nevertheless, here are some additional distilled impressions and thoughts about the future challenges confronting this remarkable nation, and a people who are experiencing enormous change due to its relations with Asia-Pacific.

I can't get the impression out of my mind of Australia being so small and vulnerable. It is true that their overall territorial sovereignty is huge—essentially equal to the U.S., but its miniscule population (20 million—$\frac{1}{15}$ of the U.S.) is dangerously small, in terms of national defense. Even if Australia acquired top-shelf technological military weaponry, their tiny military forces (52,000 in total) are basically equal to the size of the New York City Police Department. In truth, it would be no match for a massive invasion force from one of its Asian neighbors.

Australia, in truth, lives precariously on the southern cusp of the East Asian hemisphere. Its national defense is tied to a nation (America) that is dangerously in debt ($9 trillion) and overextended militarily (Afghanistan and Iraq). And its current and future economic prosperity is tied to a Communist nation—China. Yet I kept hearing from academics, politicians, writers, and regional observers that everything is fine and that the future will continue to be bright and prosperous.

Yet the tone, or lilt, in all their voices had a shred of shrillness, in their modulation, reflecting a degree of doubt within their statements of hopefulness. In short, they appeared to be determined to convince themselves, more than me, about the future of Australia. It is this interpretational image that I took away from my last trip to Australia. Yes, they are a wealthier society. Yes, the people have reelected Prime Minister John Howard three times, because he promises to keep the economic good times rolling along. Yes, Australia has signed numerous trade (primarily natural resources) deals that will continue to bring billions into the national treasury. Yes, Australia is playing a larger and more influential role in the South Pacific region, and internationally.

But something wasn't quite right. I think, despite their increased wealth and influence regionally and globally, there was a sense that this situation was fraught with danger. China's influence in Australian domestic and foreign affairs was acknowledged by all, but everyone also reiterated that Australia could maintain its *balanced diplomacy* between America and China. Like America, Australia's economic future is increasingly tied to China's own expansion. A catch-22 situation is evolving for Australia with the two major powers, America and China, pulling on the opposite ends of the rope—with Australia in the middle.

For Australians to say that this realpolitik dilemma does not exist, or that they will not have to make a choice between the U.S. and China, somewhere down the road, is simply wishful thinking. There is no doubt in *my* mind, the moment of truth will arrive for Australia, and their *decision* could very well determine the country's destiny for the rest of the twenty-first century. The unsettling truth for Australia, though they consider themselves a middle power, is that they are simply too small to survive as a neutral entity. The wake that would result from a U.S.-China confrontation would sweep over Australia, and Asia-Pacific, causing serious collateral damage throughout the entire region. Many analysts that I spoke to made it quite clear—Australia wants peace and stability. It is a relatively healthy country, but, without a doubt, a war between major powers in the region would certainly shake the country to its very foundation.

South Korea is, of course, in a very different situation. Though, like Australia, it greatly depends upon America and China for its national security and economic prosperity, respectively. However, it is these same two countries who are delaying the eventual unification of the Korean peninsula. At least this was the perception communicated at the fifth anniversary of the North-South Summit that took place, in June 2005, at the Shilla Hotel in Seoul, South Korea. In June 2000, South Korean President Kim Dae-jung and North Korean leader Kim Jong-il met at Pyongyang International Airport, shook hands, smiled before the world media, and, more importantly, for the first time since the end of the Korean War (1953) brought hope to this troubled peninsula.

As I mentioned in an earlier chapter, I thought South Korea, in 2005, had a noticeably different nationalistic feel to it. The people and their society appeared confident and much more willing to assert themselves in their own lives, and in their relations with other countries. This was quite evident to me at the internationally attended conference commemorating the historic meeting between the North and the South. Again, there is no doubt in my mind that the Korean peninsula will unify—I think within the next ten years.

However, I strongly believe that the countries surrounding the Korean peninsula are less than enthusiastic about the eventuality of such a recon- ciliation taking place between these two Cold War adversaries. And I also believe that most Koreans *understand* that their primary neighbors, China and Japan, feel this way. Therefore, future progress toward national consol- idation will probably be a slow and sluggish process. Why?

First, Japan is fearful of having a strong and unified Korea as its neighbor because *their* recent collective history is one of Japanese occupation, repres- sion, and violence toward the Koreans since the late nineteenth century. Un- like America, history is not considered unimportant and inconsequential to Koreans. They are proud of their recent accomplishments as a society— meaning their newfound economic and military strength. And Koreans see not China, but Japan as their greatest threat—geopolitically. All you have to do is watch a sporting event between these two nations, even on television, and the hair on your arms will stiffen from the intense kinetic energy pro- duced by the fans of these two nations.

Unfortunately, Korean-Japanese relations are a long way from achieving a high level of confidence and trust on both sides. Plus, it is important to understand that Japan has never looked across the Tsushima Strait (120 miles) and witnessed a strong Korea. This fact, alone, has had a sobering ef- fect upon the Japanese leadership. Finally, from a geopolitical standpoint, Japan is currently confronted with the dual reality of a strong (South) Ko- rea and China, simultaneously. This situation has never happened in the re- gion's prior history. Nevertheless, these historical phenomena must be rec- ognized and respected by the Japanese, or regional relations could quickly deteriorate into a Cold War–type of existence in Northeast Asia.

Second, China is concerned about a unified Korea for other reasons. First, the Chinese Communists are worried about the potential of having a strong and unified Korea with Western values, a modern military, and an estab- lished democracy on its northern border. This does not bode well for the Bei- jing leadership, which is trying desperately to keep the Communist system of government in power, despite an annually growing number of public dis- turbances throughout the country. The Middle Kingdom, historically, has looked upon the "Hermit Kingdom" as an inferior and subservient entity.

However, in 2006, South Korea is much wealthier and more advanced technologically than China. And, if you combined both militaries on the Korean peninsula, there would be approximately 1.6 million in uniform. This is essentially equal to China's ground forces. If you add in the ad- vanced weaponry that the North and South both possess, then you can see why China is a bit nervous about allowing, or promoting, Korean unity. Though North Korea is recognized internationally as being underdeveloped economically, South Korea's economy is ranked eleventh in the world. And South Korea, considered one of Asia's economic tigers—along with Singapore and Taiwan—and North Korea have both stated publicly that they would be willing to accept the presence of U.S. military bases upon the peninsula even after unification. Why?

Well, simply put, both Korean nations are wary about China's future intentions in Northeast Asia. With the presence of U.S. troops on the peninsula, this would mitigate, to some degree, China's desire to dominate the Korean peninsula as it did in prior centuries. Presently, despite serious misgivings by many Koreans concerning America's presence on the peninsula, it is still perceived as being much more benign, militarily and politically, than the potential of having a concerted Chinese, or Japanese, influence exerted upon them. You can make a credible argument by stating the balance-of-power theory remains a real part of the Korean reality. Yet, in the coming years, perhaps within a decade, I remain certain that the Cold War era will end on the Korean peninsula.

However, I am equally certain that a new power equation will emerge in Northeast Asia. In the future, the Korean nation will find itself constantly seeking the middle ground within a geopolitical struggle between its two powerful benefactors—China and America. Though, there is considerable opinion that a Sino-Japanese confrontation is never far from the realm of possibility, and such an event would very easily replace the issue of China-U.S. regional competition within the Korean foreign ministry. But, for the time being, the brewing hegemonic competition for leadership of the Asia-Pacific Rim between the Americans and Chinese will certainly tax and fully test the dexterity of Korea's diplomatic skills during the twenty-first century. Koreans know firsthand what happens when politics fails (Korean War, 1950–1953), because it took over fifty years for them to get to this point of actually discussing the possibility of unification and, eventually, achieving a significant degree of self-autonomy. Observers of the region are quite cognizant of the fact that there is a lot on the line for both North Korea and South Korea.

In concluding this chapter, I want to express a few thoughts on the *inevitability* of war occurring in Northeast Asia, due to the accepted premise that a titanic struggle between China and America will develop because both are determined and obsessed about exercising hegemonic dominance over Asia-Pacific during the twenty-first century. Those who perpetuate and support this thesis can, indeed, make a credible and historically based argument that can clearly lead one to agree that such a fate is inevitable.

Yet I remember what my old friend and historian Howard Zinn, professor emeritus at Boston University, has told me on numerous occasions during conversations, and from listening to him deliver lectures at colleges and universities in the Midwest, that the only thing predictable about history is its unpredictability. The twentieth century is clearly evidence of that truism. In truth, there are no absolutes about the future, based on what has happened in the past. However, you can learn certain lessons, and truths, from history and apply them to the present and future, but it's never a perfect fit.[97]

I believe his basic assumption and judgment concerning the potential use and understanding of history to be sound and wise. Everyone has a different take on the importance of history, and America's corporate media has often distorted it to fit their arbitrary and self-interested agendas. Unfortunately, much of today's news, throughout the world, is owned and shaped by corporate interests or government censors. The end product is often diluted of its informational importance or relevance. It lacks the journalistic substance needed to educate an uninformed citizenry, who desperately depends upon news outlets for its basic understanding of the world's challenges and complexities.

In short, the more we know about cultures and people, different from ourselves, the better off we are in understanding what makes them tick as individuals and societies. Without this crucial knowledge, we are simply wandering in the dark. This uninformed and vulnerable condition puts us at the mercy of reactionary demagogues and warmongers whose collective paranoia interprets all alien cultures and people as enemies of the state. The recent debacles in Afghanistan and Iraq are sad examples of this irrefutable truth.

Therefore, the *key* and *vital* question remains unaltered and unanswered: Can America and China avoid a military conflagration during the twenty-first century, due to their *perceived* individual hegemonic interests within Asia-Pacific? The real answer is that no one truthfully knows. Yet history does provide a sterling example for both countries to consider—the Shanghai Communiqué—created in February 1972. It was this publicly announced joint statement, agreed to by U.S. President Richard Nixon and China's Chairman Mao Zedong at the end of their historic meeting, which ushered in a new era of relations between the two major Asia-Pacific powers. It helped to end the U.S. involvement in the Vietnam War, and it also marked the end of the noncommunicative Cold War diplomacy that existed between the most powerful democracy in the world and the most populated (and Communist) nation on earth. This diplomatic breakthrough, though viewed with skepticism by conservative reactionaries in America, was later judged by almost all foreign policy analysts and historians to be a tremendous diplomatic achievement.

Zhang Yuping, who is vice dean in the College of Humanities and Law at North China University of Technology, was a visiting scholar at Central

Michigan University during the academic year 2005–2006. Professor Zhang stated in an interview that "Mao greatly influenced my generation. He did everything for the people. The Cultural Revolution was right at the beginning, but later on things went badly."[98] Though, in the West, a number of present-day scholars—concerning Chinese history since 1949—have described Mao as a rigid doctrinal tyrant, or as an egomaniacal dictator without a conscience. Despite these recent works of scholarship describing Mao in rather brutal and unflattering terms, Professor Zhang continues to see Mao in a favorable light, "Mao was probably 80 percent good and 20 percent bad in my opinion. He gave China and the Chinese people strong leadership during his life, but, it is true, he did have some weaknesses."[99]

Perhaps, Professor Zinn's analysis is essentially correct. Perhaps, our current situation with China touches upon different issues, in a different time. All of which represents an unquestioned degree of unpredictability. Yet can we not learn something from the courageous and visionary events that occurred, in 1972, within the pages of American diplomatic history? I believe so. President Nixon, Chairman Mao, National Security Advisor Henry Kissinger, and Chinese Premier Zhou Enlai went beyond the realm of commonly held wisdom, and geopolitical dogma, and changed the course of history between the U.S. and China. Can it be done again?

Former National Security Advisor Zbigniew Brzezinski, during the Carter presidency (1977–1981), believes China has shown great wisdom in running its affairs since the fall of the Berlin Wall in 1989, and that they have not made the same mistakes committed by Soviet leader Mikhail Gorbachev during the shocking collapse of the Soviet state in 1991.[100] Brzezinski, author of *The Grand Failure: The Birth and Death of Communism in the Twentieth Century*, presciently predicted the rapid downfall of the Soviet Union due to its serious internal and philosophical contradictions that simply undermined the structural integrity of the most powerful Communist state in the world.

Since 1978, Chinese leaders such as Deng Xiaoping and Jiang Zemin, and current president Hu Jintao, have avoided the dangerous pitfalls that brought down the Communist Party apparatus in the Soviet Union in December 1991. However, in 2007, China is sailing in uncharted political waters. Professor Brzezinski believes, "The Chinese are moving fairly fast from their revolutionary roots."[101] He also believes their current economic policies irrefutably show that "China is simply not following Communist doctrine."[102] If this is so, and it certainly appears it is, then perhaps this moment represents another opportunity in history for bold thinkers and visionaries, in America and China, to construct and design a new geopolitical paradigm in which both countries can coexist and thrive simultaneously.

In 1972, the U.S. and China found acceptable common ground from which both nations could mutually benefit. Two countries with brave and visionary leaders broke down the ideological barriers separating them from their desired geopolitical agendas. Smart and wise people, in both countries, began the deescalation of Cold War tensions between themselves and those who depended on them for power and influence within their respective governments. In effect, Nixon and Mao began the incremental process of dismantling the intense and rigid ideological artifice that was mutually constructed to separate America and China since 1949.

In 2007, is it beyond the pale, that perhaps our current political leaders, or future leaders, representing the American government, can create a new version of the Nixon-Kissinger stratagem which will result in a new communiqué concerning America, China, and Asia-Pacific in the twenty-first century? Put directly, can America once again boldly seek and achieve another groundbreaking act of diplomacy with China? I believe the ball is in *America's* court. History has shown, irrefutably, that we did it once. Can we accomplish it again? Do we have the vision and the will to achieve it again?

According to MIT Professor Noam Chomsky, the brilliant and often controversial linguist and U.S. foreign policy critic, the U.S. may have no other alternative but to build a new and constructive relationship with China during the twenty-first century. Chomsky, a globally renowned analyst of American foreign policy, believes the current cacophony of voices attempting to define U.S.-China future relations are "purely speculative and there is no way, that I can see, to guess which is more plausible."[103]

However, Professor Chomsky does see China becoming increasingly proactive in its foreign relations with other parts of the world. He believes that President Bush and his neoconservative allies are confronted with a situation they can do little about in the short-term:

Unlike Europe, it (China) can't be intimidated . . . Another factor is America's huge financial resources (investments) in Northeast Asia . . . Its (China) trade and diplomatic inroads into regions that the U.S. has assumed it controlled, like Latin America and even Saudi Arabia . . . On the other hand, the Chinese export economy is an enormous gift to U.S. corporations. American manufacturers can produce with extremely cheap and brutally exploited labor, with few regulatory conditions or environmental concerns, and it can export cheap goods at huge profits, undermining their major domestic enemies—unions and American working-class wages. And importers, like Wal-Mart, benefit from these conditions in China. (American) financial institutions are itching to get into the act. So, it's a growing and disturbing dilemma for both the American political establishment and U.S. workers as well.[104]

I, myself, refuse to succumb to the dark impulses and bombastic rhetoric that is often associated with present-day public debates concerning the future challenges confronting U.S.-China relations. However, with history as my road map for the twenty-first century, I believe there *are* individuals with the necessary courage, knowledge, and wisdom, in both America and China, to help their respective countries find new common ground, and to recognize their mutual interests—regionally and globally. This pragmatic, rational, and time-proven methodology has the potential to transform a possible adversarial relationship into a new partnership that could fundamentally transform the Asia-Pacific Rim during the twenty-first century.

In essence, America and China have the potential to create a new and powerful dynamism throughout Asia-Pacific. It would be based upon constructive, hard-nosed, and transparent negotiations, with coefforts to maintain the region's prosperity, and a mutual acknowledgement and understanding of their shared responsibilities. Such a partnership could propel the region—economically, politically, and socially—beyond expectations. Thus, a new era, the *Pacific Century*, with unprecedented influence and power in the twenty-first century, could fundamentally reconfigure the world as we know it.

The frightening aspect to this type of speculative thinking is that the potential for such a reality exists—if visionary leaders in both countries emerged to make it happen. The historic significance of such a partnership is simply mind-boggling. Could the audacity and courage displayed by Mao and Nixon, in 1972, be reconstructed in the new millennium? To be precise, can history itself be repeated?

NOTES

Zhongguo, according to en.wikipedia.org/wiki/Zhongguo, is actually a Chinese Mandarin word originally used to identify China. It consisted of two parts: *Zhong*, which means "middle" or "central," and *guo*, which means "country" or "kingdom."

1. Henry Kissinger, "China Shifts Centre of Gravity," *The Australian*, 13 June 2005. This article was published in Australia's only nationally published newspaper.

2. Jonathan D. Spence, "The Once and Future China," *Foreign Policy*, January/February 2005.

3. David Shambaugh lecture, "The Changing Nature of the Regional Systems in Asia-Pacific," Chicago Council of Foreign Affairs, 26 January 2006.

4. Ibid.

5. Ibid.

6. Natalia Rigol, "A Game of Giants: The Future of Sino-U.S. Relations," *Harvard International Review*, Spring 2005.

7. Ibid.

8. Merle Goldman lecture at Alma College (Michigan), 16 October 2006; Professor Goldman focused upon China's future and its economic reforms.

9. John Perkins, *Confessions of an Economic Hit Man* (New York: Plume Book, 2006). John Perkins wrote a fascinating memoir on his business dealings in Central

and South America on the behalf of powerful U.S. corporations. This "insider" book stunned even the most jaded U.S. foreign policy critics.

10. Rigol, "A Game of Giants," 2005.

11. Eric Heginbotham and Christopher P. Twomey, "America's Bismarckian Asia Policy," *Current History*, September 2005, pp. 243–50.

12. Ibid.

13. Joseph S. Nye, Jr., *Soft Power: The Means to Succeed in World Politics* (New York: Public Affairs, 2004).

14. Heginbotham and Twomey, "America's Bismarckian Asian Policy," pp. 243–50.

15. Kerry Dumbaugh, "China-U.S. Relations: Current Issues and Implications for U.S. Policy," *CRS Report for Congress*, Congressional Research Service, The Library of Congress, 20 January 2006.

16. Ibid.

17. Ibid.

18. Interview with Professor Patrick Shan, 20 October 2006, Grand Valley State University.

19. Ibid.

20. Lionel Beehner, "The Rise of the Shanghai Cooperation Organization," *Council on Foreign Relations*, 12 June 2006.

21. John Mearsheimer, "The Rise of China Will Not Be Peaceful at All," *The Australian*, 18 November 2005.

22. Ibid.

23. Michael T. Klare, "Revving Up the China Threat," *The Nation*, 24 October 2005.

24. Ibid.

25. Ibid.

26. Gregory Clark, "No Rest for 'China Threat' Lobby," *Japan Times*, 7 January 2006.

27. Ross Terrill, *The New Chinese Empire: And What It Means for the United States* (Cambridge, MA: Perseus Books Group, 2003), p. 28.

28. Clark, "No Rest for 'China Threat' Lobby."

29. Ibid.

30. Terrill, *The New Chinese Empire*, p. 26.

31. Ibid.

32. Ibid.

33. Office of the Secretary of Defense, "The Military Power of the People's Republic of China," *Annual Report to Congress*, 2005.

34. Ibid.

35. Mure Dickie, Kathrin Hille, and Demetri Sevastopulo, "Report Strikes Beijing Nerve at Politically Sensitive Time," *Financial Times*, 21 July 2005.

36. Ibid.

37. Alfred Thayer Mahan, *The Influence of Sea Power upon History* (originally published in 1890). It represents one of the most influential military essays ever written concerning the use of naval power on the global stage. In short, a nation uses its naval power to protect its vital interests throughout the world.

38. Robert D. Kaplan, "How We Would Fight China," *The Atlantic Monthly*, June 2005, p. 49.

39. Ibid., p. 64.

40. Richard N. Haass, "What to Do about China," *U.S. News and World Report*, 20 June 2005, p. 52.

41. Ibid.

42. Ibid.

43. David Rothkopf, *Running the World: The Inside Story of the National Security Council and the Architects of American Power* (New York: Public Affairs, 2005), pp. 452–53.

44. Bruce Cumings, "The World Shakes China," *The National Interest*, Spring 1996. Cumings uses this famous Napoleon quote in his article, but he also mentions that he is not sure if the quote is 100 percent accurate. Nevertheless, I have used it in this chapter on China.

45. Gilbert Achcar, "Assessing China," www.zmag.org, 25 June 2005.

46. Joe Guy Collier, "Growth in China Gives GM a Boost," *Detroit Free Press*, 6 January 2006.

47. *News Brief*, "GM, Ford See Sales in China Jump," *The Detroit News*, 9 January 2007, p. 2C. This was just a small news article tucked away on page 2 of the newspaper's business section. You got the impression that they didn't want too many of their readers finding it.

48. Ibid.

49. Keith Bradsher, "China Seeking Auto Industry, Piece by Piece," *The New York Times*, 17 February 2006.

50. Interview with Christine Milne, 5 June 2006, Hobart, Tasmania

51. Robert Wilson, "China Exports Take Aim at Australia," *The Australian*, 29 March 2006.

52. I found an article by Ameet Sachdev—"Trade, China and Steel"—published in the *Chicago Tribune* in August 2005 on the website of Daniel W. Drezner, (www.danieldrezner.com). The article focused upon Nucor CEO Daniel R. DiMicco and the problems confronting the U.S. steel industry in the global marketplace.

53. Ibid.

54. Oded Shenkar, *The Chinese Century: The Rising Chinese Economy and Its Impact on the Global Economy, the Balance of Power, and Your Job* (Upper Saddle River, NJ: Wharton School Publishing, 2006), p. 2.

55. Ibid., p. 3.

56. Ibid.

57. Ibid., p. 136.

58. Ibid.

59. Ibid., p. 138.

60. Editorial, "China, the World's 4th Largest Economy?" *Asia Times*, 14 December 2005.

61. Lester R. Brown, "China Is Replacing U.S. as World's Leading Consumer," *New Perspectives Quarterly*, Spring 2005.

62. Ibid.

63. Lester R. Brown, *Plan B 2.0: Rescuing a Planet under Stress and a Civilization in Trouble* (New York: W.W. Norton & Company, 2006), pp. 10–11.

64. Will Hutton, *The Writing on the Wall: Why We Must Embrace China as a Partner or Face It as an Enemy* (New York: Free Press, 2006), pp. 303–4. I believe it is

appropriate to list Suzanne Berger's book since it was the basis of Hutton's argument concerning the myth of the outsourcing of low-wage jobs.

Suzanne Berger, *How We Compete: What Companies around the World Are Doing to Make It in Today's Global Economy* (New York: Currency, a division of Random House, 2005).

65. Ibid., p. 304.

66. Ibid.

67. James Fallows, "Postcards from Tomorrow Square," *The Atlantic Monthly*, December 2006, p. 110.

68. Ibid.

69. Esther Pan, "China's Angry Peasants," *Council on Foreign Relations*, 15 December 2005. Ms. Pan answered a number of questions concerning the issues angering Chinese peasants.

70. Ibid.

71. Jerome A. Cohen, "Law in Political Transitions: Lessons from East Asia and the Road Ahead for China," *Council on Foreign Relations*, 26 July 2005.

72. Ibid.

73. Hutton, *The Writing on the Wall*, p. 30.

74. Mei Fong, "So Much Work, So Little Time," *The Wall Street Journal* (Weekend Edition), 23–24 December 2006, p. A1 and p. A.

75. Ibid.

76. Conn Hallinan, "China: A Troubled Dragon," *Foreign Policy in Focus*, 11 May 2006.

77. Ibid.

78. Jane Golley, "Contemplating China," *ANU Reporter*, Autumn 2006, pp. 7–8.

79. Ibid.

80. Ibid.

81. Howard W. French, "Anger in China Rises over Threat to Environment," *The New York Times*, 19 July 2005.

82. Jim Yardley, "China's Next Big Boom Could Be the Foul Air," *The New York Times*, 30 October 2005.

83. Ibid.

84. Ibid.

85. Ibid.

86. Jim Yardley, "China Chemical Spills Spur Plan to Guard Water Supply," *The New York Times*, 12 January 2006.

87. Ibid.

88. Ibid.

89. Ibid.

90. Ibid.

91. Ibid.

92. Ibid.

93. John Gittings, *The Changing Face of China: From Mao to Market* (New York: Oxford University Press, 2005), p. 327.

94. Ibid., p. 328.

95. Journalist Andrea Mitchell did a story for NBC news, and an article on the *MSNBC* website reflected that story, titled, "Report: Kim 'Sorry' about North Korea

Nuclear Test," 20 October 2006. The story on the MSNBC website was a collective effort with information provided by Reuters, NBC, MSNBC, and the Associated Press.

96. I retrieved this attributed quote to Professor Laura Tyson from a blog concerning Professor Noam Chomsky's views on subjects dealing with the American empire from the 1940s to today. This quote showed up in Chomsky's brief overview concerning the current situation between the United States and Asia.

97. Based upon numerous conversations and lectures involving Professor Howard Zinn from 1994 to 2007.

98. Interview with Zhang Yuping, 25 April 2006. Afterwards, Professor Zhang invited me to speak to the students at North China University of Technology in the spring of 2007. I accepted.

99. Ibid.

100. Interview with Professor Zbigniew Brzezinski, 8 January 2007.

101. Ibid.

102. Ibid.

103. Noam Chomsky, email correspondence, 2 January 2006.

104. Ibid.

5

America: The Eagle in Transition

What are we to make out of China's irrefutable economic and military development over the last twenty-five years? It is my belief that America's footprint, or hegemonic capabilities, will diminish, to some degree, for a number of reasons during the twenty-first century. Part of my analysis is based upon the current economic developments and trends emerging in the Pacific Rim region, and in America. Another factor in my evaluation is founded upon the *shifting* of power or the *perception* by our regional allies that U.S. *hegemonic* power is slowly evolving toward a new hegemonic entity, and away from America. A growing consensus within the U.S. foreign policy establishment believes that the *source* of America's incremental descent, within the Pacific Rim, is China. It is a nation that does not hide the fact that it has a regional and global agenda. Yet there exists institutional confusion, within America and China, on what China actually wants to accomplish in the near and distant future. Tim Shorrock reported in *Asia Times*, in 2002, "The country's (China) government and intellectual elite are deeply split about how to deal with the world's only superpower and (how to) handle relations with the global community."[1] Thus, the *real* question remains unanswered for many Asians and Americans, on whether China's rise will be peaceful, or will it represent the beginning of a period of contention and conflict. It is my belief that the Asia-Pacific region will become the world's primary geopolitical focus during the twenty-first century.

THE CHINA CHALLENGE

As mentioned in the introduction, both America and China are wrestling with the question of future responses to each other over known and unknown questions that will arise during the course of the twenty-first century in the Pacific Rim. Henry Kissinger, former U.S. secretary of state and director of the National Security Council during the presidential administrations of Richard Nixon and Gerald Ford, addressed this future dilemma in his book, *Does America Need a Foreign Policy?*, by emphasizing that America and China need to find common ground and work together to keep Asia-Pacific stable and prosperous. Dr. Kissinger does acknowledge that there are those, in both countries, who see inevitable conflict between these two major powers. Yet he reiterates that this conflict scenario will not produce the type of long-term results, concerning peace and stability in East Asia, sought after by these hawkish proponents.[2]

Kissinger, the former Harvard government professor, has been directly involved with the Chinese government since his secret mission to China, in 1971, on the behalf of President Nixon, to reestablish diplomatic relations between the two nations. Therefore, based upon thirty-five years of experience negotiating with various Chinese leaders, Dr. Kissinger sees a different course of action as being the most constructive and productive for future relations between America and China:

> China policy should be liberated from familiar slogans. The issue is not how to label the relationship but what content it can be given. Cooperative relations are not a favor either country bestows on the other. They are in the common interests of both countries. There are enough issues to test the seriousness of both sides. . . . A permanent dialogue is needed as the best means to create a more stable world or, at a minimum, to demonstrate to the American people and America's allies why it is not possible.[3]

It should be noted that Dr. Kissinger has significant financial interests in China, and has maintained strong political ties to the Chinese government since his departure from the U.S. State Department in 1977. To be specific, he receives large consultancy fees from China's government and business hierarchies for his analysis concerning global affairs, while representing Kissinger Associates. Nevertheless, it is also true that every president since Nixon has requested his advice on China and its future intentions for the Pacific Rim. In short, Kissinger sees a grudging, but respectful, relationship between these two powers. He sees a tense but constructive geopolitical equilibrium developing in East Asia, because he is absolutely convinced that there is simply too much at stake for both countries to be dragged into a devastating conflagration that would bring down the whole region.[4]

However, there are analysts and scholars who say that mankind has no choice on this matter, because history presents an irrefutable counter-argument on this balance-of-power subject. In short, it is strongly believed by these students of world history that conflict between an established hegemonic power and one that is rising to hegemonic status, especially in the same region, will occur with a large degree of certainty. Why? Their argument is based upon the historical fact that aspiring hegemonic powers almost always collide due to having the same agenda—to dominate world affairs. And, as in politics and sports, you can only have one champion, or winner, after the competition is over. History has shown that there is an unwritten law concerning human affairs—there is a never-ending process of one individual, or nation, seeking to stand above the rest. There is a certain stability and understanding amongst competitors—of all stripes—that respect this cosmic truth concerning universal competition.

In the first decade of the twenty-first century, many American foreign policy analysts, concerning the Pacific Rim, perceive China as the new enemy to confront (and contain) because the Chinese have not denied their desire to become a hegemonic force in East Asia. These same "experts" will often say that America represents the *indispensable nation* throughout the region, and the world, in terms of establishing and maintaining peace and stability. In truth, though, these true believers of America's global mission actually interpret the U.S. being much more than a *balancing force* or an exemplary *shining city on the hill* for East Asians to respect or emulate. They, in fact, really desire America to remain *the* unquestioned power in the region, and the world.

In short, these individuals interpret the rise of China as a *very* negative development. Many Asian analysts and regional observers of power politics in East Asia are convinced that the potential for conflict between the U.S. and China is heightened because history has repeatedly shown that an emerging hegemonic power—regionally or globally—is often perceived immediately as a direct threat to the *existing* force structure developed by the recognized hegemonic power.

John Mearsheimer, the R. Wendell Harrison distinguished service professor of political science at the University of Chicago, states quite confidently in his book, *The Tragedy of Great Power Politics*, that history has shown that two competitive hegemonic powers, regionally or globally, will experience conflict because that is the nature of global powers exercising their economic and military influence upon the world stage.[5]

The counter-argument is that we (America) can not jump to immediate conclusions, even if history indicates that hegemonic powers have a strong tendency to collide due to their regional, or global expansionist (economic or military, or both) agendas. However, students of history also know that there are few absolutes in human history, except for the unpredictability of human endeavors. Thus, critics of Mearsheimer's thesis, concerning the almost certainty of great-power conflict, remain unconvinced that the U.S. and China are cosmically destined to go to war.

Zbigniew Brzezinski, the former national security advisor to President Jimmy Carter, and currently a counselor at the Center for Strategic and International Studies, believes that China's future aggression against America is exaggerated and overdone by great-power advocates. Brzezinski, who is also a professor of foreign policy at Johns Hopkins University, strongly believes that China's major priority is to develop its economy. Their military buildup does not alarm him because he does not see any unusual trends emerging that would indicate that China is becoming a significant threat to U.S. interests, regionally or globally, in the relatively near future. And any analysis concerning long-term threats is purely speculative.[6]

Yet the basis of this intense argument of whether China is a short-term or long-term threat might be moot, due to a looming and potential financial crisis emerging in America. Though a total meltdown (i.e., circa 1929) is highly doubtful, nevertheless, the fiscal integrity of the national budget appears to be in danger. Specifically, the national debt—almost $9 trillion—continues to grow at an alarming rate, and the country's (global) trade deficit continues to reach new heights of disequilibrium. To be precise, President Bush's economic policies are putting America's financial house in a precarious situation. This frightening prospect of possessing massive debt—domestically and internationally—represents a direct threat to America's future capacity to project economic and military power throughout the world.

If a financial crisis does occur, as many speculate, it will be due to numerous reasons:

1. Large expenditures on overseas wars—Iraq, Afghanistan, and other antiterrorist activities
2. Weather-related catastrophes at home (i.e., Hurricane Katrina)
3. Dysfunctional and costly homeland security projects
4. Crumbling public infrastructure—schools, roads, health care system—that are threatening our future economic vitality
5. Baby boomer retirees threatening the financial solvency of the Social Security system and various health care programs for the aged
6. Income disparities growing steadily within U.S. society (They represent the largest income gap in the industrialized world.)
7. Continued massive trade deficits, especially with China; growing national debt continuing unabated

Essentially, America's capacity to project global power—even protecting the nation's vital interests—could be compromised if the U.S. financial infrastructure collapses due to the national debts incurred, as mentioned earlier. Presently, however, there is irrefutable evidence that America's global financial standing is slowly deteriorating. In essence, these potential fiscal dilemmas—domestically and internationally—are slowly crippling our capacity to influence global events. To be specific, these economic developments are quite real, and they are now starting to have a direct effect upon our global status. Investigative financial reporter for the International Press Service Emad Mekay wrote that the Geneva-based World Economic Forum (WEF) issued its 2006–2007 Global Competitiveness Index (GCI). The U.S. has dropped from the number one ranking in the world, to now being ranked sixth.[7] Mekay, who has written major exposes on the World Bank, the Asian Development Bank, and the International Monetary Fund, states that America's sudden decline is due, according to this highly respected international economic institution, to its high spending on the war on terrorism and homeland security and the lowering of taxes. All of these factors represent a serious potential for triggering a fiscal crisis in the U.S.[8]

Paul Kennedy, a prominent history professor at Yale University, provided in his epic work, in 1987, *The Rise and Fall of the Great Powers*, a vivid description of how the great powers of the past fell apart, and quickly, primarily due to financial reasons and a military overstretched by global obligations. Quite often the great powers of the past fought one too many wars that eventually compromised the financial capabilities of these hegemonic states. Once a great power's financial/industrial base is fundamentally compromised, their sphere of influence contracts, regionally and internationally.[9]

Many readers, in the late 1980s, interpreted Kennedy's work as a prophetic warning to America's government and society. Twenty years later, the U.S. is facing a massive and growing national debt, alarming domestic budget deficits, and exploding international trade imbalances, especially with China. When the economic good times returned in the mid-1990s with the dot.com explosion, many critics, such as foreign policy scholars Joseph Nye and Niall Ferguson, chastised Kennedy for his negative predictions concerning America's future.[10]

However, in 2007, Professor Kennedy's economic/power thesis, published in 1987, toward the end of the Reagan administration (1981–1989), is making an unexpected comeback in American thinking. Kennedy's critics are now lying low. Why? Well, it doesn't take an MIT economist to tell Americans that the U.S. financial situation is increasingly shaky. The U.S. dollar has lost approximately 25 percent of its value—based on my trips to South Korea and Australia in 2005 and 2006, respectively. And the U.S. continues to pay for two expensive wars in Afghanistan and Iraq. Oil prices, in 2006–2007, have on occasion spiked to record highs, and a gallon of gas has risen to approximately $2.50. As expected, American consumers are now feeling the budgetary pinch as their cost-of-living expenses continue to rise, though most U.S. workers are also currently experiencing a decline in their purchasing power; and future employment prospects are becoming increasingly complex, grim, and unpredictable for millions of Americans.

According to Forrester Research, in 2003, U.S. companies were expected to transfer 3.3 million jobs in the next twelve years (2003–2015) overseas.[11] Since 2000, the manufacturing industries hardest hit, in states such as Michigan—my adopted home state—were auto, furniture, toys, textiles, and household goods. Most of these solid-paying blue-collar jobs are now being relocated to Asia. After several decades of U.S. industrial dominance, and relatively little concern for foreign competition, it appears the chickens have truly come home to roost for blue-collar America. In late December 2006, the U.S. public received another jolt of reality just before Christmas Eve. The *New York Times* printed a story on page 1, in their business section, stating that "after seventy-five years, the world's automobile industry is about to get a new No. 1."[12]

Toyota's surging sales had finally put it in a position to end the seventy-five-year reign of General Motors (GM) as the world's automotive king. The news, however, was not totally unexpected because Toyota stated, in 2003, that one of their primary goals was to replace GM as the world's leading automaker by 2010.[13] Nevertheless, the news still hit U.S. autoworkers hard. Ricardo Yrias, a fifty-two-year-old assembly line worker at GM's truck factory in Flint, Michigan, stated a common sentiment amongst the workers: "As far as pride, it hurts."[14]

Micheline Maynard and Martin Fackler, the authors of this painful story concerning the U.S. auto industry, wrote that the Toyota Motor Company had issued its 2007 sales forecast (9.34 million cars) in late December 2006. These prospective sales projections, based upon global research, would propel Toyota past GM (9.2 million cars) as the largest seller of automobiles in the world by the end of next year. GM, an American icon within the global business community, had *dominated* the car industry for decades. In fact, it has been the number one seller of autos since 1931.[15]

In another article, in the same business section as the GM-Toyota story mentioned above, an Associated Press wire story told how the Ford Motor Company was fighting for its automotive life. The article stated that Ford is going to invest $1 billion into six of their southeastern Michigan auto plants over the next five to seven years. In return, the state of Michigan will provide Ford with $151 million in tax incentives over the next twenty years. This legendary and longtime automotive giant believed that this investment would help retain 13,740 Ford jobs in Michigan.[16]

It should be noted, however, that to say that globalization represents the *primary* reason for the destruction of the U.S. auto industry is not entirely accurate. It is true that GM and Ford, and their respective shareholders, are making *huge* profits from their overseas production facilities in China. It is also true that China's low labor costs (nonunion), and the government providing a national health care program to its citizens, are tremendous inducements for these struggling auto giants to move their facilities to the Middle Kingdom.

In short, a GM car, or a Ford car, made in China simply costs less to produce because the overall production costs are dramatically lower in China. Finally, to be entirely truthful, the *quality* of their respective cars has not diminished either during this global transition. This is not the first time a major U.S. industry has suffered due to intense international competition, primarily from East Asia. An earlier generation witnessed the U.S. steel industry painfully and permanently lay off approximately 70 percent of its workforce from 1980 (398,000 workers) to 1997 (112,000 workers), due to the modern and highly efficient steel mills in Japan and South Korea.[17] Not unexpectedly, the steel plants in Ohio, Pennsylvania, Michigan, and Illinois that were fortunate enough to survive the economic hurricane that devastated the industry, during the 1980s, were equipped with cutting-edge technology. Conversely, quite expectedly, the quality of steel produced improved markedly, and overall steel production rose dramatically by more than 35 percent.[18]

In essence, here is the new global economic equation that all nations must respect: less workers + more productivity + technology = efficiency + higher profits for shareholders + compressed workers' wages. This economic scenario is being played out in every manufacturing industry throughout the world.

As mentioned earlier in this chapter, the post-WWII baby boomers are on the verge of retirement en masse. Thus, they represent a terrifying financial tsunami in terms of potential costs for the U.S. government. The astronomical budgetary numbers associated with this generational eventuality are sobering and very threatening. Of course, very few American politicians have the courage to tell their constituents the truth about the oncoming fiscal train wreck that awaits them as the moment of truth draws closer. Harvard University historian Niall Ferguson, author of *Colossus: The Price of America's Empire*, believes the U.S. is heading for a day of reckoning in terms of the financial costs related to the post-WWII retirees. In 2008, when the baby boomers' deluge begins, some economists believe that income taxes, or payroll taxes, will have to be increased 69 percent and 95 percent, respectively, to meet the government's obligations.[19]

Therefore, no matter how you spin these economic issues, the employment and retirement challenges, and obligations, confronting America and its governmental institutions are going to be incredibly daunting as the twenty-first century matures.

Finally, there are those observers who believe that America is in the process of containing China. These individuals do not believe America wants war immediately, but they also do not think that the U.S. will *share* its hegemonic status with the Middle Kingdom. Hence, they believe that America has chosen a *third* path in dealing with China. In short, these analysts, scholars, and "experts" (consumers beware) see the U.S. utilizing various means to *manage* China's development, subtly and strategically.

Henceforth, America is actively creating a new web of acknowledgements, alliances, agreements, and understandings with countries throughout the Pacific Rim and Central Asia. This process can be accurately described as "soft containment" with a hard objective—keep China's influence minimized if possible. *I* am one of those who believe this is the *real* policy toward China today.

In the next section, I will briefly examine the new developments in the Asia-Pacific Rim region. Though, collectively, these new developments are not totally understood by the American public, due to the paltry amount of foreign news presented on the major television networks in the U.S. Yet it is becoming increasingly apparent to many observers, in America and Asia, that U.S. diplomatic and military activities in this strategic arena of the world represent nothing more than the concentrated exercise of balance-of-power strategies directed toward a rising regional power, in this specific case, China.

OLD WINE, NEW BOTTLE

The United States instituted a Cold War strategy called *containment* in the late 1940s against the Soviet Union. One of my foreign policy heroes, George F. Kennan, created a detailed summation of post-WWII Soviet intentions in his famous 8,000-word "Long Telegram" sent to the U.S. State Department in 1946. In short, the Soviet Union was seen as a challenger to the U.S. hegemonic position after World War II. The U.S. government needed a coherent and comprehensive plan to deal with future Soviet aggressions in the world, but especially for western Europe. Kennan became a foreign policy star after the implementation of this post-WWII stratagem, but he later regretted it being invoked and directed toward every geopolitical situation throughout the world, especially in Asia—Korea and Vietnam. Despite what Kennan considered its misapplication, this visionary blueprint to prevent Russian dominance in western Europe was the *philosophical* backbone of U.S. deterrence throughout the world until the collapse of the Soviet Union in December 1991. Ironically, Kennan outlived the Cold War and all his contemporaries and critics, dying at the age of 101 in 2004.

Like Professor Kennedy's *Rise and Fall* thesis, it appears that Kennan's sixty-year-old containment blueprint is making a comeback and being reimplemented in 2007, but this time it's directed toward East and Central

Asia with China in mind. If we go clockwise from the top of Northeast Asia to the Central Asian republics, formerly of the Soviet Union, you will find a common thread connecting this vastly different group of countries—strong ties to the U.S. due to China's rise in the Asian region. I will simply go down the list of nations and provide a very brief overview of them and their relations with America.

Russia

President Vladimir Putin, despite the occasional dalliance with China, remains on relatively good terms with America and U.S. President George W. Bush. Despite President Putin's lackluster record concerning democracy, and his increasing use of authoritarian rule within Russia, his help on the war on terror is greatly desired by the American government. Also, Russia can play a key role in hopefully preventing Iran and North Korea from becoming permanent nuclear powers. In the meantime, though, the Russians continue to tolerate NATO's continued encroachment upon the motherland, and they have not yet openly resisted the growing U.S. presence in Central Asia. In short, it is imperative that the U.S. receive Russian assistance with Iran, Afghanistan, and China—all of which are key targets within America's grand strategy for the Eurasian region. One of the better books written concerning the deteriorating political and social situations within Russia is titled, *Kremlin Rising*, by Peter Baker and Susan Glasser.[20] They present a grim analysis of modern-day Russia, which few Americans know about or understand.

Japan

Their bilateral defense agreement with the U.S. grows in importance, due to China's surging economic and military presence in Northeast Asia. Plus, North Korea's testing of a nuclear weapon, in 2006, raises the security stakes tremendously for the Japanese government. Article 9 (the antiwar amendment) within the Japanese constitution is being revisited by conservatives and those who seek a functioning and "normal" foreign policy for Japan. Specifically, these proponents are seeking to change the understanding of Article 9. They want more autonomy for Japan to decide for themselves what is in the nation's interests in East Asia, and not be seen as just an appendage of U.S. policies in the region. An excellent book concerning whether the Japanese should seek a new path in its national affairs is titled, *Japan: A Reinterpretation*, written by Patrick Smith in 1997.[21] I lived in Okinawa, Japan, at the time of its publication. Many thought his award-winning book caught the growing angst that exists within the Japanese government and society about their future as a nation in East Asia.

South Korea

It is an increasingly difficult relationship for America. South Koreans are exercising more autonomy in their foreign policy decision making than desired by Washington, DC. However, despite growing tensions within their relationship, the U.S. has promised to maintain 25,000 troops in-country after 2008. And the existing troops located in Seoul will be relocated down the peninsula about forty miles south of Seoul, the nation's capital. South Korea's last two presidents, Kim Dae-jung and Roh Moo-hyun, have exercised greater policy independence than previous leaders, particularly with regard to Kim Jong-il's North Korea. Yet South Korea needs the U.S. military presence to remain in-country because of China's growing influence in Northeast Asia. China has become South Korea's number one trading partner. However, the South Koreans do not want to become engulfed by China's hegemonic shadow. Thus, U.S. troops will remain upon the Korean peninsula into the foreseeable future. The best of the recent books describing the changing political environment on the Korean peninsula are entitled, *The Two Koreas* and *The Koreans*, authored by Don Oberdorfer and Michael Breen, respectively. Though, the *best* historian on Korean history, in my opinion, is Professor Bruce Cumings at the University of Chicago.

Vietnam

They are quietly reforming (i.e., capitalism) their economy, and they are seeking foreign investment, particularly from the U.S. They offered America the reuse of the Cam Ranh Bay military facility. The U.S. initially said no, but if China continues to develop, especially militarily, the U.S. may re-think its position. Thus, expect more entreaties from the Vietnamese for the U.S. to reestablish its military in-country—creating a South Korea–like presence. I think the U.S. would have accepted the original offer but the Vietnam War is still a little too close to the American psyche. And China would have definitely been very displeased to find U.S. military forces near its northern and southern borders. Also, cries of containment would be heard from the Chinese leadership in Beijing, and, to be truthful, they would possess a certain degree of credibility. Nevertheless, as China grows in stature in Southeast Asia, expect other small nations in the region to request closer ties to America.

Philippines

They expelled U.S. military forces, in 1991, closing down Subic Bay Naval Base and Clark Air Force Base. In recent years, they have quietly conducted a number of military exercises with the U.S., despite a strong anti-U.S. faction within the Philippine National Parliament. Nevertheless, the Philippines need America's help because of a strong Islamic presence in their country (outer islands) also because of China's aggressive activities surrounding the Spratly Islands—where the Philippines have laid claim to a portion of the oil and gas beneath them. Hence, a strong U.S. military presence in the region remains vital to the security of the Philippines, and to hopefully persuade China to be more gracious with its neighbors on the issue concerning the Spratly Islands' resources.

India

In 2006, President George W. Bush cut a new deal with India to supply them with updated nuclear technology, despite their refusal to recognize or sign the Non-Proliferation Treaty (NPT) concerning nuclear weapons. Many analysts interpreted this agreement with India as a classic example of diplomatic hypocrisy. America rewards India for its defiance, and punishes North Korea for ignoring the very same international standards. In short, Bush had inadvertently undermined America's own moral arguments, amongst its regional allies, concerning North Korea's nuclear weapons program. However, I believe the *real* agenda for the U.S. was to seek India's assistance toward creating triangular diplomacy in Asia, as a counter-balance to China's growing power within the region. Historically, this is not the first time this geopolitical strategy has been implemented by the U.S. in East Asia. In 1972, during the Cold War, the United States (i.e., President Richard Nixon and National Security Advisor Henry Kissinger) visited and negotiated with Communist China (i.e., Chairman Mao Zedong and Premier Zhou Enlai), to create triangular diplomacy as a counter-weight against potential expansionism by the Soviet Union, because the U.S. was on the verge of losing the Vietnam War. In 2007, President Bush is reconfiguring triangular diplomacy by recruiting India to assist America in counter-balancing the emergence of a powerful China in East Asia. Why? It appears that the U.S. is, once again, on the verge of losing another ill-advised military adventure, this time in Iraq. Therefore, as expected, U.S. foreign policy *realists* believe that a U.S. defeat in Iraq (and possibly in Afghanistan) will result in a loss of prestige around the world. Henceforth, this potential outcome may embolden the Chinese to act more aggressively in international affairs.

Central Asia

The U.S. is in the process of developing stronger relations with these former Soviet states: Kyrgyzstan, Tajikistan, Turkmenistan, and Uzbekistan. Strategically, Central Asia lies at the heart of the historic *grand chessboard*, Eurasia. Thus, it's geographically situated between the Middle East and China. Several of these newly established states, created after the Cold War, have U.S. military bases situated inside them to resist a *potentially* resurgent Russia, or to contain a powerful China in the region. Of course, the oil and gas deposits within the Caspian Sea area are of great strategic importance, especially to an increasingly oil-hungry China. Also, the control of the Eurasian landmass is seen by some analysts, historically, as being absolutely vital to a nation's global influence (Halford Mackinder's Eurasian theory).

CONTAINMENT: WILL IT WORK AGAINST CHINA?

There is an emerging consensus that the U.S. is implementing an updated and revised version of Cold War containment upon the People's Republic of China. I believe this to be true. An honest appraisal of U.S. interests in Asia (as noted above) indicates that China's emergence has not only caught the attention of the American government, but has initiated a series of political and military activities to subtly encircle the Middle Kingdom and attempt to limit its future influence in East Asia. *Containment*, as a geopolitical philosophy, has been a very effective stratagem throughout American history.

Upon historical hindsight, it can be stated, to a degree of truth, that containment represents a fundamental strategic philosophy that has been implemented since the early nineteenth century. George F. Kennan, though a renowned U.S. foreign policy analyst in the latter half of the twentieth century, was also a great admirer of John Quincy Adams' diplomatic accomplishments and philosophy in the early nineteenth century. In point of fact, it can be strongly argued that it was Adams who created the first version of containment with the penning of the Monroe Doctrine in 1823. And, perhaps, elements of Adams' work can be seen in parts of the philosophical foundation, and strategic vision, that Kennan later created in the mid-twentieth century toward curbing the global influence of the Soviet Union.

Adams, then secretary of state under President James Monroe, defined the U.S. position in the Western Hemisphere, in the early 1820s, concerning those European nations seeking an opportunity to recolonize several Latin American states after Spain's demise. In fact, what Secretary Adams, whom many historians consider America's greatest secretary of state, was actually doing was containing European territorial ambitions within the Western Hemisphere. Upon hindsight, the U.S. was successful in its bold diplomatic efforts to keep Europe out of the region, due to a strong British naval presence in the Atlantic and Caribbean. However, I believe, it can also be effectively argued that the Monroe Doctrine was the first usage of this strategic containment philosophy designed to confront great-power expansionism without the immediate threat of war.

It is also believed by a growing list of prominent U.S. scholars that a new doctrine of antiexpansionism is now being reapplied toward China in the opening decade of the twenty-first century. Its successful implementation against European powers in the nineteenth century, with concern to the Western Hemisphere, and the Soviet Union in the latter half of the twentieth century in western Europe, is clear evidence of its effectiveness. Yet its successful implementation against China, at the beginning of the twenty-first century, remains questionable.

Historically, China has not looked fondly upon intrusive and threatening outsiders. In fact, China has looked upon the outside world with a considerable amount of skepticism and scorn. First, the Chinese are very proud of their ancient culture and numerous historical achievements in the fields of education, philosophy, literature, and science. Secondly, the dark chapter of Chinese history represented by Europe's (including Japan and America as well) successful attempts to implement exploitive colonialism and imperialism within China, beginning in the mid-nineteenth century until WWII, has left the Chinese hypersensitive to any pressure or threats from external sources. Therefore, it would not surprise this author to see China take calculated steps in limiting U.S. efforts toward achieving this new containment objective in East Asia. The American Eagle encirclement of the Middle Kingdom could very well bring out the worst in the Chinese Dragon.

Michael T. Klare, director of peace and world security studies at Hampshire College, sees a dangerous future for America and its recent efforts to contain China since 2001. Professor Klare, author of *Blood and Oil: The Dangers and Consequences of America's Growing Dependency on Imported Petroleum*, believes that the events of 9/11 only delayed further planning by the first Bush administration (2001–2004) to continue its long-term efforts toward neutralizing China's influence in East Asia. However, Klare writes that the second Bush administration is now, once again, focusing its attentions upon China. He writes, "By the time the second Bush administration came into office, however, the pool of potential rivals had been narrowed in elite thinking to just one: the People's Republic of China. Only China, it was claimed, possessed the economic and military capacity to challenge the United States as an aspiring superpower; and so perpetuating U.S. global predominance meant containing Chinese power."[22]

Professor Klare declares the efforts to bring democracy to the Middle East may be the primary focus of current concerns within the White House, but "they do not govern key decisions regarding the allocation of long-term military resources. The truly commanding objective—the underlying basis for budgets and troop developments—is the containment of China . . . its paramount focus on China is risking a new Asian arms race with potentially catastrophic consequences."[23]

In contrast, it is interesting to analyze China's response to America's activities toward containing them. According to Klare, China is reaching out and providing extraordinary economic benefits to America's key allies: Australia, Japan, South Korea, and India. This savvy and farsighted strategy has loosened up, to some degree, the rigidity of their support for U.S. objectives in Asia-Pacific. Ironically, it is also China's neighbors, several of whom support U.S. interests, who are inadvertently helping the Chinese to grow— economically and militarily.

In 2006, China's President Hu Jintao shocked accepted protocol during his visit to the U.S. by visiting the headquarters of American corporate icons Boeing and Microsoft before visiting the White House. It was an effective stratagem to remind the American business community (and the U.S. Congress) that a lot of money is to be made by *doing* business with China.[24] In retrospect, this clever and nuanced twist of China's foreign policy quite effectively promoted good 'ole fashion corporate greed in the U.S. Thus, the move diminished potential neoconservative plans toward containing and threatening China's future as an Asian power, and its recognized territorial sovereignty.

Chalmers Johnson, professor emeritus at the University of California, San Diego, and former CIA analyst, wrote an interesting paper, "No Longer the 'Lone' Superpower: Coming to Terms with China," on the new reality facing America with the rise of China. Johnson, who is presently the director of the Japan Policy Research Institute, believes if we base our analysis concerning the future of East Asia, during the twenty-first century, on what occurred in the twentieth century, we might be in for a very troubling time.[25] According to Professor Johnson, "the major question for the twenty-first century is whether this fateful inability to adjust to changes in the global power-structure can be overcome."[26] Johnson also indicates that the U.S. and Great Britain were not very conciliatory toward the rise of new powers during the twentieth century—Germany, Japan, and Russia—which he believes led to two world wars, a forty-five-year Cold War, the Vietnam debacle, and numerous clandestine involvements with wars of national liberation. The former CIA analyst points to arrogance and racism as being the primary foundational factors of American, European, and Japanese colonialism and imperialism.[27]

Perhaps, a new multipolar global landscape will provide a different version of containment for America and China. Johnson quotes *Time* magazine writer Tony Karon: "All over the world, new bonds of trade and strategic cooperation are being forged around the U.S. China has not only begun to displace the U.S. as the dominant player in the Asia Pacific Economic Cooperation (APEC) . . . it is emerging as the major trading partner to some of Latin America's largest economies."[28] China is a part of an emerging independent marketplace in East Asia. In 2002, Yoichi Funabashi, a senior

Japanese political commentator, stated, "The ratio of intra-regional trade (in East Asia) to worldwide trade was 52 percent in 2002."[29]

After reading Professor Johnson's work on America's coming to terms with China, I came away thinking that two former methodologies of dealing with a rising hegemonic power will not work with present-day China. First, military confrontation with the Chinese would end globalization as we know it, because China is the economic locomotive for East Asia—where the fastest-growing economies exist in the world. Also, during the past decade, China has purchased billions of dollars worth of U.S. Treasury bills financing our overconsumption as a society, and American corporations have invested billions into the Chinese economy. *All* would be lost if a war occurred between these two major powers. Secondly, the implementation of some kind of containment policy will not work either. This places America's allies in an untenable position—pick America or China. America, for many Asia-Pacific nations, represents their security blanket against a rising China, or a resurgent Japan. Though all nations in Asia-Pacific trade with the U.S., there is no doubt, in anyone's mind, that it is the Chinese economy that is pulling the economic wagon in the region.

Finally, I want to present a final perspective on U.S. activities and policies in Asia. Lee Sustar, editor of the *Socialist Worker* newspaper, believes that the U.S. has been moving with undue haste during the past few years to consolidate its vulnerable positions in Central Asia and the Pacific. Sustar interprets Washington's overly energetic behavior in Central Asia and the Pacific as a result of its failing wars in Iraq and Afghanstan. The by-product of America's recent efforts in these two key regions is identified by Sustar as "Little NATO"—membership includes the U.S., Australia, Japan, the Philippines, and Thailand. Of course, the U.S. government and military told questioners that their real reason for enhancing relations with the Little NATO countries was the war on terror.[30]

In reality, these efforts were in concert with other efforts, according to Sustar, to "conceal the real aim of the operation: to encircle China by hard-wiring the military's regions to the Pentagon and positioning Special Forces and 'counter-terrorism' units."[31] Later on in the article, the editor of the *Socialist Worker* points out that the Pentagon's 2006 *Quadrennial Defense Review* identified China as the greatest threat to America's military supremacy throughout the world: "Of the major and emerging powers, China has the greatest potential to compete militarily with the United States and field disruptive military technologies that could over time offset traditional U.S. military advantages absent U.S. counter-strategies."[32]

The strain upon the U.S. military due to an unexpected high level of resistance in Iraq and Afghanistan have indeed taken its toll, but, according to Sustar, it has not deterred the U.S. government from its primary objective to pursue an encirclement strategy concerning the Middle Kingdom:

"Containing China is U.S. imperialism's overarching—and highly dangerous—goal."[33] Interestingly, even though Sustar is the editor of a leftist newspaper and his reflections echo the sentiments of fellow travelers throughout the world, his perspectives are very similar to foreign policy titan and conservative Republican Henry Kissinger. Both men are from distinctly different walks of life, politically, but both are equally dubious about the chances of success if the U.S. implements containment as a strategy against China in the twenty-first century.

I want to present some final observations on America, and its difficulties in Asia-Pacific during this period of historical transition in the early stages of the twenty-first century. Americans could find themselves very lonely if they mishandled the "China factor." I have learned from living, researching, studying, and working in this region for approximately a decade, America is greatly respected and remains a symbol of success to most Asians.

However, as always, "times are a changin'" as the old Bob Dylan song goes, and America is experiencing a fundamental and seismic shift in its influence throughout Asia-Pacific—economically and militarily. In this chapter, you have been exposed to different perspectives about what America should do, or not do, concerning its future relations with China. War, or the implementation of soft containment, is not the right remedy for the present geostrategic challenges confronting America with concern to China's rise in Asia-Pacific.

Either path will lead the United States toward disastrous results: The first path (war) will lead to the potential destruction of regional financial institutions, and regional trade and security agreements established after WWII. The post-WWI era is a prime example of how difficult it is to put the world back together after a global conflagration. The second path (containment) will potentially produce the political isolation of China—which may very well lead to the destruction of the established regional defense agreements amongst America's most ardent allies since the early 1950s. Put bluntly, several U.S. allies (Australia, South Korea, and Japan) are increasingly dependent upon business contracts with China's government to keep their national unemployment levels low, and their national economies productive and prosperous.

If our key allies in the region perceive America's having *provoked* a military confrontation with China over a rather *dubious* issue (i.e., trade tariffs, copyright laws, or currency manipulation), or a matter of *vital* interest to the Chinese (i.e., Taiwan, access to energy, or a preventive attack upon North Korea), America may very well find itself all alone in the biggest geographical backyard in the world—Asia-Pacific. I believe the next ten to fifteen years will be extraordinarily important for the future prosperity and stability of the most important region in the world—some have already termed it "The Pacific Century."

In the end, the U.S. and China must ask themselves this critical question: Is there the knowledge and wisdom, based upon *known* history in both countries, to prevent a deadly struggle amongst the great powers in the twenty-first century? If not, we already know the bloody, dispiriting, and haunting answer to this question: it will, once again, only produce a short-term euphoria for the winners, humiliation for the losers, and, tragically, another stark and dark chapter that rebukes the assumed advances associated with modern civilization and mankind.

NOTES

1. Tim Shorrock, "China's Elite Clearly Split over Foreign Policy," *Asia Times,* 15 February 2002.

2. Henry Kissinger, *Does America Need a Foreign Policy? Toward a Diplomacy for the Twenty-first Century* (New York: Simon & Schuster, 2001), pp. 145–49.

3. Ibid., p. 149.

4. Ibid., pp. 145–49.

5. John Mearsheimer, *The Tragedy of Great Power Politics* (New York: W.W. Norton & Company, 2001).

6. Zbigniew Brzezinski, *The Choice: Global Domination or Global Leadership* (New York: Basic Books, 2004), pp. 118–20.

7. Emad Mekay, "U.S. Warned on War Spending and Deficits," www.zmag.org, 1 October 2006.

8. Ibid.

9. Paul Kennedy, *The Rise and Fall of the Great Powers: Economic Change and Military Conflict from 1500 to 2000* (New York: Random House, 1987).

10. Joseph Nye, *Bound to Lead: The Changing Nature of American Power* (New York: Perseus Publishing, 1991). Niall Ferguson, *The Cash Nexus: Money and Power in the Modern World, 1700–2000* (New York: Basic Books, 2001).

11. Jyoti Thottam, "Where the Good Jobs Are Going," *Time,* 28 July 2003. I pulled this article off the website: www.time.com.

12. Micheline Maynard and Martin Fackler, "Toyota Is Poised to Supplant G.M. as World's Largest Carmaker," *The New York Times,* 23 December 2006, p. B1.

13. Ibid.

14. Ibid.

15. Ibid.

16. Associated Press, "Ford to Invest in Plants and Get Tax Breaks," *The New York Times,* 23 December 2006, p. B8.

17. Editors, "Grappling with the Globe," *American Heritage Magazine,* June 2001, Vol. 52, No. 4.

18. Ibid. Note: U.S. steel production rose from 95.2 million tons (1980) to 131 million tons (1997).

19. Niall Ferguson, *Colossus: The Price of America's Empire* (New York: Penguin Group, 2004).

20. Peter Baker and Susan Glasser, *Kremlin Rising: Vladimir Putin's Russia and the End of Revolution* (New York: Scribner's, a Lisa Drew Book, 2005). At an event at the bookstore called Politics and Prose, in Washington, DC, these two writers made it quite clear that Russian democracy is increasingly a sham.

21. Patrick Smith, *Japan: A Reinterpretation* (New York: Pantheon Books, 1997). This book was later selected as the winner of the Overseas Press Club Award for the best book on foreign affairs, and it was also chosen as one of the *New York Times* Notable Books of the Year.

22. Michael T. Klare, "Containing China," www.zmag.org, 18 April 2006.

23. Ibid.

24. Ibid.

25. Chalmers Johnson, "No Longer the 'Lone' Superpower: Coming to Terms with China," Japan Policy Research Institute, March 2005, JPRI Working Paper No. 105.

26. Ibid.

27. Ibid.

28. Ibid.

29. Ibid.

30. Lee Sustar, "Containing China: The United States on the Asian Chessboard," *International Socialist Review*, July–August 2006.

31. Ibid.

32. Ibid.

33. Ibid.

6

Australia: Serving Two Masters in Asia-Pacific

Extraordinary times are occurring in Asia-Pacific as the twenty-first century unfolds. And Australia, once considered a colonial outpost representing British interests in Southeast Asia, is now one of the most prosperous nations in the region. Yet I believe it has some difficult days ahead. It is currently enjoying a fifteen-year run of economic expansion due to primarily multibillion-dollar natural resource deals with Asia, particularly with China. This financial windfall is continuing under a security umbrella provided by the United States. Australia is a highly valued American ally in the South Pacific region. However, Australia finds itself increasingly in an uncomfortable situation that positions its vital interests in conflict with each other. The real possibility of a regional scenario (i.e., a military confrontation) involving America and China is not considered to be some think tank war game, or an unread government-produced white paper on Asia-Pacific, but a disturbingly potential reality that could derail Australia's "blue skies are forever" perception of their future. This chapter will address the current foreign policy and military initiatives of Australia in Asia-Pacific, particularly in Southeast Asia. It will provide a closer scrutiny of Australia's current economic development and the increasing degree of leverage that Asia has over the Australian economy. Finally, I will provide some perspectives from within Australian society concerning the major topics addressed in this chapter. These opinions and my own judgment will be presented to answer the question, "Can Australia serve two masters in Asia-Pacific in the twenty-first century?"

AMERICA'S DEPUTY SHERIFF IN EAST ASIA

When President George W. Bush visited Australia, in 2003, he referred to Australia as "America's Sheriff" in the (Southeast Asia) region.[1] This comment certainly caught the attention of Australians and their Asian neighbors. To say the least, it made a great many feel uncomfortable. Journalist Stephen Blank provided details concerning a study conducted, in 2003, by the Royal Australian Navy in conjunction with its naval theater missile defense system. The study identifies the current possibility of weapons of mass destruction (WMD) being used against Australia as the greatest threat to its security, rather than a military invasion, or the use of some kind of military intimidation.[2] These findings broaden the concept of the Australian Approach to Warfare (AWA). It is understood that Australia's Defense Forces (ADF) will, of course, deter and defeat an armed attack upon Australia, but these "forces" will also have the capability to assimilate themselves into the strategies and defense force units of other nations—particularly the United States.[3]

This new strategic perspective and Bush's startling description of Australia's new role in Asia-Pacific were certainly provocative, and they did initially receive some negative feedback from within the region. Former Malaysian Prime Minister Mahathir Mohamad was very critical of this brazen attitude and posturing. Mahathir has been a vociferous critic of Australian policies in Asia-Pacific for many years. He regards Australians in Asia as "some sort of a transplant from another region."[4] However, during the same week Australian Prime Minister John Howard announced the completion of a free trade agreement (FTA) with Thailand. Australia had also agreed to a FTA with Singapore earlier in the year. Thus, Australia became the first country to have achieved two FTA agreements with countries who are members of the Association of Southeast Asian Nations (ASEAN).[5]

If that wasn't enough to diminish Mahathir's biting criticism of Australia's proper place in Asia, then the visit by the president of China, Hu Jintao, in October 2003, certainly destroyed the basis of Mahathir's argument concerning Australia's legitimacy in the region. By the time President Hu's visit to Canberra ended, a commitment to study the viability of a future FTA involving both countries was announced, and China's largest offshore oil and gas producer, CNOOC Ltd, signed a $36 billion deal to purchase 12.5 percent equity stake in the Gorgon gas field off the northwestern coast of Australia.[6] These business deals represented clear evidence of Australia's increasing assimilation into the economic structural framework of Asia-Pacific. In retrospect, Mahathir's ill-tempered "transplant" remark appears to lack credibility and understanding of the new paradigm in East Asia. Instead, his comment appears to be a rash and prejudicial judgment based upon past events and relations, and is not reflective of Australia's new initiatives and role in the region.

Yet there remain critics, such as John Pilger, an award-winning investigative reporter and native Australian, who has often been very critical of the Australian government's actions in the region since the 1970s—especially concerning Indonesia and East Timor. Both of these countries remain a very sensitive topic to many Australians. He filmed a documentary called, *Death of a Nation*, which exposed the brutality of the Suharto dictatorship in Indonesia, and its mass murder of, perhaps, 200,000 citizens of East Timor in 1975. It was Indonesia's bloody absorption of East Timor (with Australian and U.S. support) after Portugal relinquished the territory, in 1975, as a colony that continues to upset many Australians. Also, five Australian journalists were shot to death by the Indonesian security forces during their intervention upon the island. In short, during the past thirty years, the relations between Australia and Indonesia have always been a bit strained.[7]

And, now Prime Minister Howard's embracement of his new role as "America's Sheriff" has particularly annoyed Pilger. Why? Howard now takes credit for East Timor's fledging but troubled democracy, even though, according to Pilger, Australia's prime minister was literally forced to send troops onto the island nation, in 1999, because of a surge of popular opinion to protect the East Timorese from another assault by members of the Kopassus, the infamous and notorious special forces unit that is well known for its brutal tactics throughout the Indonesian archipelago.[8]

However, Pilger believes that Australia's successful intervention of East Timor has rigidified into government policy for *all* destabilizing incidents or situations involving the island states just off the northern shores of Australia. Aussie troops have been sent to the Solomon Islands, a governmental team is currently situated in Papua New Guinea negotiating a quasi-FTA agreement, and growing instability in West Papua has also garnered the attention of the Howard government. Thus, Pilger interprets Australia's muscular foreign policy as just a means to exploit these islanders for their wealth. He states, "Since 1999, Australia has received more than a billion dollars in taxes on oil extracted from a field fully situated in East Timorese territory. Yet, East Timor has received nothing from the same field."[9] Quite clearly, Pilger has exposed the superficial morality of the West. In his estimation, the democratization of East Timor has produced very little except for the shameless plundering of this small island nation's resources in the South Pacific.[10]

However, a more disturbing and ominous role may be developing for "America's Sheriff" in Asia-Pacific. Maryann Keady, a freelance radio journalist and reporter for the ABC and SBS, writes that, in 2001, within the *Quadrennial Defence Review*, the United States had decided upon a new strategic priority—containing China. And Secretary of State Condaleeza Rice did not mince words when it came to what was expected of Australia. She stated, "All of us in the region, particularly long-standing allies, have a joint responsibility and obligation to try and produce conditions in which the rise of China will be a positive force in international politics, not a negative one."[11] This attitude that China represents a potentially negative force in East Asian affairs is prevalent amongst many academics and government officials in Australia and America. There are, as expected, new predictions of a new Cold War emerging in Asia, and an almost absolute certainty that conflict will occur between the U.S. and China during the twenty-first century. These judgments are stated without hesitation or reservation.[12] Of course, many concerned Australians ask, "What is our role within this troubling scenario?"

Keady, who is researching U.S. foreign policy and China at the Weatherhead Institute at Columbia University, writes that this perceived threat, represented by the China factor, is really more of a concern for the major regional powers—America, China, and Japan—than it is in reality for the majority of people in the region. Keady is resigned to the fact that a new Cold War is emerging in Asia-Pacific, and Australia will certainly play a role in this new power game. And, of course, sadly, she points out that it will be the "ordinary citizens" of the region who will be the ones who really pay the price for this new period of turbulence in Asia-Pacific.[13]

Though, Australia's overall role and purpose of being the "sheriff" in the South Pacific remains controversial and undefined. There is, however, one area of agreement between the major political parties in Australia. They (Australia) can and should play a more influential role in Asia-Pacific. How to achieve this goal is, once again, an ongoing argument within governmental and policy circles in Canberra, and in related institutions throughout Australia. Gareth Evans, called by former Labor Prime Minister Bob Hawke Australia's greatest foreign minister ever, believes that Australia has the capabilities to have a larger presence in the region, but it must stop evaluating and viewing every issue through the prism of the U.S. government. Though Evans does recognize America as being "the biggest dog on the global block," and this situation will remain the reality for the near future, it doesn't mean that Australia doesn't have an idea to contribute or a voice to be heard concerning vital global issues.[14] He is deeply disappointed by the current government's passive attitude toward accepting U.S. dominance:

> They (Howard government) can certainly do more than just lie on their back with their pink tummy exposed and their four paws waving and just soaking up whatever it is that the leader (Bush's America) of the universe wants to dispense, which has rather been, I'm afraid, the Australian reaction to so many of the U.S. initiatives.[15]

The former Australian foreign minister believes it is healthy, if not necessary, for *all* nations to express periodic disagreement amongst themselves over public policy. In the end, it makes for a better balanced, comprehensive, and functional policymaking process. Unfortunately, he does not see this occurring today, because almost everyone (large and small powers) immediately capitulates to the demands of the American government. Thus, Evans, currently the president and CEO of the Brussels-based independent NGO called International Crisis Group (ICG), who regularly visits the U.S. for approximately one week out of every month, has determined from numerous talks and visits with various U.S. officials in government, the U.S. Congress, and the American business community at large, that Australia's reputation is tarnished due to its sycophantic behavior toward U.S. policymakers. In the end, Evans states, "It accurately does reflect the reality that Australia is adopting very few independent policy positions of its own, and that I think over time it diminishes our effectiveness (in global affairs)."[16]

Alexander Downer, Australia's current foreign minister, also believes that Australia has a larger role to play in regional and international affairs. Though no one has called him the nation's greatest foreign minister ever, nevertheless, he has held the position longer than any individual in Australian history. And even his political critics have grudgingly admitted during several of my interviews in Australia that his performance has been consistent and steady, though they dislike elements of his interpretation of Australian foreign policy. Yet Downer's views are just as expansive as Evans' concerning the potential of Australia's contribution toward creating global stability and peace. He, however, does not interpret the recent U.S. geopolitical activities as negatively as Evans does, or, in fact, as some individuals do within the current leadership of the other two major political parties in Australia—Labor and the Greens. Thus, the argument continues, unyielding, over the proper and future direction of Australia within Asia-Pacific. Yet, during the course of my interview with Mr. Downer, in Canberra, there was no doubt in my mind that he certainly does have a view of Australia concerning its place in the world, America and its role in Asia, and how his perception of Australia is shaped by the current traumas affecting the present-day world itself.

Downer, Australia's foreign minister since 1996, believes that the dynamics of Asia-Pacific have indeed changed due to the rise of China. Downer mentioned during our interview, "First, China has substantially strengthened its position in Asia-Pacific. Secondly, its stature has grown tremendously, and they currently have more prestige than Japan. Third, the China factor is quite significant, and that is why China's power needs to be balanced in the region."[17] However, he does not believe China's power will be "balanced" by regional institutions. Downer observed, "I don't think you are going to get an Asian union in the near future. There is simply no consensus in the region for this to occur any time soon. However, over time, there might very well be a growing political momentum for an Asian free trade area (AFTA). I suspect that it would extend from northern China to New Zealand."[18]

In terms of Australian-U.S. relations, and America's role in Asia, the foreign minister spoke at the Asialink Chairman's Dinner in Melbourne, on 1 December 2005. He wanted to address a few of the major issues confronting Australia in the region. Asialink has strong ties in the Asia-Pacific business community and with a multitude of political organizations as well. Downer told his audience quite clearly, "The United States has an important role to play in the region, and we encourage an active U.S. presence . . . Our strong relationship with the United States is an asset that we bring to the region."[19] Nevertheless, Downer, though respectfully recognizing the historical importance of Australia's relations with America, also declared, "We engage with the region (Asia-Pacific) on our own terms. We pursue a foreign policy that is based on our own interests, just as other countries base their foreign policy on their own interests."[20]

And it appears that those "interests" are expanding, according to Professor Desmond Ball at the Australian National University. Professor Ball is considered to be one of the finest scholarly minds on issues concerning Australia's national defense—particularly on issues concerning tech-based weaponry. His background on this subject is quite extensive, including stints at the U.S. Pentagon, the Rand Corporation, and several other academic and governmental positions (there was a photo of him and former President Jimmy Carter in his office). In short, for over forty years, Professor Ball has studied and helped to create innumerable defense and military policies in America and Australia. Ball commented that "(Prime Minister) Howard's government has greatly expanded Australian operations. Island contingencies are becoming ever more important. Former Prime Minister Bob Hawke sent troops to the first Gulf War in 1991, but Howard currently has Australian troops in Iraq, Afghanistan, and upon three or four islands just off the northern shores of Australia. However, at this time, I believe that the Australian military is badly overstretched and that could lead to some problems down the road for the Howard government."[21]

Thus, unsurprisingly, there are vociferous *critics* and *supporters* of Australia's current foreign policy. However, at the present time, Downer and the Howard government are willing to provide America a bit more latitude in the implementation of their policies concerning Asia, and in defining Australia's role within those policies. The Howard government is simply *less* cynical than Evans, and many members of the Labor and Green parties, when evaluating the U.S. agenda for the region and the world. Finally, though, Downer does see China as a nation that will need constant scrutiny by the Howard government, because China will continue to try, on occasion, to dislodge Australia from the U.S. security orbit. He learned this geopolitical truth from his first encounters with the Chinese. Downer pointed out that the Chinese government "can be quite aggressive," and, in 1996, they attempted to "push us around" when we first came to power.[22] Thus, according to Downer, China's "divide and conquer" strategy has not, and will not, work because "everyone knows where we stand in the region. It's not a secret about our relations with the U.S. We (Australia) simply have a very different relationship with China."[23]

Australia's future role of being "America's Deputy Sheriff" in East Asia, particularly in Southeast Asia, will remain a politically sensitive subject, within Australia and in the region, due to the debated expectations of what America really wants Australia to achieve within the U.S. strategic framework for Asia-Pacific. Greg Sheridan, the senior foreign affairs editor for the *Australian*, Australia's only nationally published newspaper, wrote euphorically in his twice-weekly column, "Australia enjoys a fantastically good name across the U.S. and the Bush administration sees Australia, rightly in my view, as an important global ally."[24] In the same column, Sheridan completely agrees with American John Hillen, the assistant secretary of state for political-military affairs, who commented that Australia needs to upgrade their strategic planning to meet the current threats in Asia-Pacific.[25]

Sheridan's gushing support for American foreign policy makes for uncomfortable reading. One would think that a man of his journalistic stature might provide a more penetrating analysis of Australia's vital security interests, and about the lack of overall success of American policies—particularly in the Middle East. Instead, during our interview in June 2006, he presented himself as a shameless cheerleader of U.S. foreign policy—almost appearing to be groveling for the approval of the Bush administration. Tragically, Bush's policies are increasingly enshrouded with doubts, and their legitimacy and validity are now openly questioned by the majority of Americans, the Asia-Pacific community, and much of the world.

In Australia, two major foreign policy analysts have recently expressed their doubts about the wisdom (and implied potential danger) of Australia marching in "lockstep" with U.S. foreign policy. Owen Harries, one of Australia's leading commentators on international affairs, believes the "Iraq experience" has provided Australia with an extremely important lesson to learn and understand concerning future involvements with the U.S. and its global agenda.[26] Harries, who gave a widely read speech at the Lowy Institute for International Policy in Sydney during December 2006, did not mince words about what the *real* lesson was for Australia:

> What Australia must learn from the Iraq experience is that it should not commit itself to marching in lockstep with anyone—let alone a superpower which is simultaneously committed to an incredibly ambitious program of global

change, deeply divided domestically, and has the most inept president since Warren G. Harding in its White House. It (Australia) must learn to be as good an ally as it can be while maintaining its freedom of choice.[27]

Hugh White, a professor of strategic studies at the Australian National University, believes that Australia is faced with *two* fundamental foreign policy challenges today. First, Professor White believes there are new types of threats confronting Australia's future security—those being "non-state, sub-state and transnational"—which are now called the "new" security agenda. These were not present or prominent during the Cold War.[28] Second, White, a visiting fellow at the Lowy Institute for International Policy, believes that Australia is experiencing "profound change in the global distribution of power among states, especially in Asia, with uncertain strategic consequences."[29]

White is also deeply concerned that the U.S.-dominated international system will not welcome a powerful China or India with open arms. If this is indeed the case, then the potential for an increasingly unstable global environment will certainly have serious ramifications for Australia. In short, how does Australia defend its national and strategic interests—with the "old" security ties, or with the creation of new strategies to meet the "new" developments in Asia and the world?[30]

Hence, important issues and questions await answers. Future Australian governments will not be able to lean on Britain or America, as in the past, to provide them with relative security. It is the *speed* of change and its associated *transitional processes* that are forcing Australia to face the hard questions concerning its future strategic agenda: What can Australia *actually* contribute, from a diplomatic and military standpoint, to enhance the U.S. security agenda in East Asia? And what are Australia's own strategic needs and expectations? Are they realistic within a region that is experiencing incredible change so quickly in the twenty-first century? These vitally pertinent questions are unrelenting and will be further examined in this chapter.

BOOM TIMES IN THE LAND OF OZ

Perhaps, Australia's future geopolitical activities and policies concerning Asia-Pacific are debatable, but what is not in question is the country's economic growth for the last fifteen years. There are no doubts expressed by any of the major political parties in Australia about the current "boom times" throughout the country. The numbers are indeed impressive. And the national euphoria is continually splashed across the nation's newspapers, especially in the business sections.

In fact, there was a column in the *Sydney Morning Herald* that speculated that the Australian dollar might, in the near future, achieve parity with the American dollar for the first time since 1982. The reporter quotes Clifford Bennett, a chief financial strategist at FxMax, who predicted in the 1990s that the Aussie dollar would decline significantly in value against the U.S. dollar. Today, Bennett offers a different analysis: "As the Australian dollar climbs toward US80c, I think it is important for exporters to consider how far it may go . . . The answer is that the Australian dollar can reach $US1.00."[31] When two other Australian financial strategists were asked about this possibility, both said it was a long shot, but they did not dismiss it out of hand. One said it was a "huge call to make," and the other referred to Bennett's prediction as a "gutsy call."[32] Needless to say, good economic times engender a higher level of confidence and hope.

Looking at the raw data indicates that Australians' spirited economic outlook is certainly warranted—at least for the short term. And it is equally certain that the locomotive for Australia's financial windfall is Asia-Pacific, particularly China. First, let's look at the basic economic indicators that can quickly tell us the growth of the Australian economy. GDP (gross domestic product) per capita, in 2003, was $28,520. This represents a solid increase since 2000 ($25,477)—GDP has grown approximately 3 percent per year since 2000.[33] According to the *CIA World Factbook*, Australia's 2005 estimated GDP per capita will be $31,900.[34] In other words, if the CIA figures prove correct, since 2000, Australia's GDP will have risen approximately 25 percent—excellent growth in anyone's estimation. In 2005, according to the International Monetary Fund (IMF), the Australian economy ranked seventeenth (out of 162 countries listed in their report) in the world.[35]

The domestic budget, from 2000 to 2003, has shown a surplus in three of the four years.[36] And, in 2003, Australia represented 1 percent of world trade[37]—not bad for a country of only 20 million citizens—and its unemployment stands at a very low 4.9 percent.[38] Thus, GDP is up, budget surpluses are occurring, and more Australians are working. And the nation's short-term future (2005–2010) also appears bright and profitable. According to the Economist Intelligence Unit, which *forecasts* the future economic performances of countries in the world, Australia will experience solid and *real* GDP growth until 2010.[39]

This analysis is strengthened by the recent multibillion-dollar business deals, which occurred between 2004 and 2006, with China—involving the purchasing of iron ore, natural gas, and uranium.[40] In December 2006, the economic forecaster and industry analyst BIS Shrapnel publicly stated that the good times in the mining industry have not reached their peak. Within their own annual report entitled, "BIS Shrapnel's Mining in Australia,

2006–2021," their enthusiasm for the future health of Australia's mining industry remained undaunted.

> With an enormous amount of work in the pipeline and more projects still to commence, investment is forecast to rise another 11 percent over the next two years and peak in 2007–2008.[41]

Yet a note of caution was sounded by senior economist Richard Robinson, despite the boom times being experienced within the mining industry, primarily in the state of Western Australia. He mentions that there remain a few problems that continue to plague the industry—a lack of skilled labor and materials shortages. And, not unexpectedly, Robinson also reminds mining analysts that "a (possible) serious downturn in China would mean a bigger-than-expected correction in prices, investment, exploration and production."[42]

Despite the enormous profits from the last few years, the exporting of Australia's natural resources are not the only means of profiting from Asia. It is also believed that the future of the Australian tourist industry will be greatly enriched due to the millions of Asian tourists who are expected to visit "Down Under" in the next twenty years. The Australian Tourist Commission forecasted that perhaps over 20 million Asian tourists, in total, will arrive in Australia during this period. As a result, it is estimated that 2 million additional jobs will be created, and approximately $108 billion will be added to the national economy.[43] Finally, it appears that the presence of Asian students upon Australian university campuses will continue to grow in the next decade as well. Asian countries account for nine of the top ten intake countries—Hong Kong is number one, and the U.S. is the only non-Asian country in the top ten. In 1994, there were about 100,000 overseas students in Australia; that total grew to approximately 150,000 by the end of the twentieth century.[44]

When *all* these economic factors are *combined*, indeed, it is not hard to understand why many Australian pundits and voters believe there is nothing but "blue skies" ahead for the Australian economy. Asian dollars have breathed new life into the nation's economy in many different realms, and this *energy* has created a new sense of definition, purpose, and *ability* for Australia to play a larger role in the affairs of the region and internationally (i.e., Iraq and Afghanistan). To be specific, Australia's new accumulation of wealth has manifested itself, as world history has shown over and over again in various countries, into a new sense of national strength. And, again, as world history has continually shown, they are exercising this new-found strength without hesitation.

Australia's enhanced role in Asia-Pacific, especially in the South Pacific, has already been addressed in the prior section of this paper. And, of course, there are many individuals and groups reveling in this proactive period of Australian foreign affairs. However, I think it is appropriate and necessary to examine the current domestic situation in Australia. Henceforth, I think a few domestic problems (*debt, jobs, racism, and the environment*) need to be addressed in this section of my paper—all of which I believe could develop into major concerns if not properly addressed by the Australian government.

First, the country's external debt is now over $509 billion,[45] and its manufacturing sector is taking a beating from international competition—especially from their Asian competitors. Australian steel and automakers are screaming for help from the government to protect what is left of their industries. Their biggest gripe is with the historically low tariffs put upon foreign steel and auto parts, while their competitors have higher tariffs protecting similar industries at home.[46]

In the early 1980s, manufactured goods from foreign shores confronted a 25 percent Australian tariff upon entry into the domestic economy. Now, the tariffs have been lowered to less than 5 percent. According to automotive sources, the Australian components industry has suffered over 8,000 lost jobs.[47] Greens Senator Christine Milne stated in an interview in 2006 that Australia's manufacturing is slowly disappearing due to foreign competition. Senator Milne believes the Australian economy is depending too much upon its growing mineral export industry to pull the country through financially, while the nation is witnessing the hollowing out of Australian manufacturing—thousands of jobs are lost to their Asian competitors, especially China.[48] She is *not* a China-basher, but she is convinced that the Howard government's economic policies are insane and very destructive for the average Australian worker trying to earn a livable wage.[49]

Historically, the Australian people have always prided themselves on their sense of community, or *mate-ship* as they call it. However, recent times have shown a growing concern over the distribution of this newfound wealth within Australian society. In 2006, the Australian Federal Budget was announced by the nation's treasurer, Peter Costello, and great fan fair was expected about the large tax cuts that were to be given back to the Australian people. Yet, unexpectedly, the Australian taxpayers exhibited a detached coolness toward this new government giveback. The reason being is that many felt the money should be spent to improve the country. The polls taken after the tax cuts were announced provided credible evidence of the people's indifference to receiving more money from their government.[50] Green Senator Milne seemed to have captured the national angst concerning the new federal budget and its financial priorities. Senator Milne stated, "The (federal) budget reflects the soul of a nation."[51]

Thus, the biggest tax cut since the early 1990s was received with an unnerving silence amongst Australian voters. Dennis Shanahan, political editor at *The Australian*, wrote, "One of the biggest giveaway budgets on record has failed to deliver an electoral bounce to the Coalition (Howard's government), although it was one of the best-received in 15 years."[52] The reasons for concern by Senator Milne and Mr. Shanahan are considerable. Since 1996, the Howard government has created 1.81 million jobs, but the number of people on welfare ("outsiders") has increased to 1.75 million. These "outsiders" are not simply individuals presently unemployed, but individuals who will probably remain unemployed due to a lack of education or skills (or initiative) in the new technologically driven economy emerging in Australia since the 1980s.[53]

In 2005, the three biggest groups receiving the government's social benefits were families with children, retirees, and the "outsiders" (consisting of unemployed and disabled). The latter group received the least amount of government benefits. Whether this group is dealt with directly, or not, some feel, like the Brotherhood of St. Laurence's executive director Tony Nicholson, that this faceless group of unemployed men and women will come back to haunt Australian society. He points to the recent riots in Sydney's Macquarie Fields and Redfern, as examples of the anger and frustration that exist in these dark corners consisting of Australia's forgotten people.[54]

In December 2005, racial mayhem made an unseemly appearance in Australian society in one of the worst displays of public disorder in the nation's history at a Sydney beach just before Christmas. Several Lebanese youths got entangled in a scuffle with white Australian lifeguards. I mention the "race" element because white Australians went on the offensive against all Arabs, or perceived Arabs, in the Sydney area. In return, Arabs, of course, went on their own rampage because of the hostility directed at them. The unspoken factor, though widely recognized as the *roots* of this melee, was 9/11 and the Bali bombings, in 2002 and 2005, that killed over a hundred Australians. Prime Minister Howard immediately went on national television to condemn the racial violence, and emphatically stated that racism was not widespread in Australia.[55]

However, a poll taken by NEWS.com.au told a different story about Australia and Australians. Paul Cogan wrote, "Almost two-thirds of Australians believe there is underlying racism in the country, and four in 10 people believe it (their country) can be described as a racist nation."[56] The "war on terror," and over 300,000 Muslims living in Australia, represent a potentially toxic mix within the social framework of Australian society. It is safe to say, taking into consideration the current political climate throughout much of the world, especially toward Muslims in the West, that this will not be the last time such a conflagration will occur in Australia.

Finally, the environment has regained the attention of Australians. The topic of climate change, and the overwhelming evidence of its existence, have reawakened Australia out of its economic-centric absorption. Professor and scientist Tim Flannery, author of the critically acclaimed book, *The Weather Makers*, has honed in on the fact that Australia is on the verge of an aquatic catastrophe (i.e., massive water shortages), especially in its major cities. On the issue of climate change, Flannery (in a sense, Australia's Al Gore) said in an interview, "I agree with (the American) NASA's scientist James Hansen that the world is approaching a 'tipping point' within the decade, and that we will be scrambling to get the greenhouse gases out of the atmosphere."[57]

On the issues confronting Australia, Flannery was no less direct in his evaluation. He believes the issue of access to freshwater is currently threatening the future of Australia's major cities, particularly Perth and Sydney. Australia's environment is "delicately poised" and is very vulnerable to "extreme weather" events. If the Antarctic glaciers continue to melt at their current rapid pace, Flannery believes, "Australia's coastlines, port and shipping facilities would be negatively affected by rising water levels. In short . . . the nation's vulnerable environment representing a real threat to the future sustainability of the Australian economy because such a high percentage of our population lives close to (the) water."[58] On the subject of Australia's future energy needs, Flannery was stunned by the Howard government's commitment to use coal as its primary means to produce energy: "I think (Prime Minister) Howard's new statements stating coal represents the future energy for Australia is dangerous and stupid for Australia's economy and environment."[59]

In January 2006, three months prior to my interview with Dr. Flannery, the U.S. and Australia announced a pledge, a combined $127 million contribution, to an Asia-Pacific plan to reduce greenhouse gases by promoting the increased use of renewable energy sources and cleaner ways to use coal.[60] The emphasis upon using coal as a source of energy, and the refusal of both nations to sign the Kyoto Treaty, have produced great skepticism, duly noted by Professor Flannery, within the global community, concerning their *real* intentions and commitment toward producing a sustainable and safe environment for all people on the planet.

In an article, in May 2004, Flannery stated forthrightly at a forum held at Redfern's Australian Technology Park—just outside of Sydney, "There will be conditions not seen in 40 million years. The next fifty years offer Sydney the last chance to avoid catastrophic climate change that would devastate south-southeastern Australia."[61] As mention earlier, the Australian economic forecasts appear to support those who fervently believe that "blue skies" represent the nation's short-term prospects. However, there is credible evidence to indicate that the nation's long-term prospects are in doubt: Poverty, race, unemployment, and a dicey environment remain inescapable realities of Australia's future.

What will the next generation of Australians confront? Will the "blue skies" of tomorrow be sustainable, or does another future await this island continent? Its current ability to "serve two masters," and be an active player in global affairs, will be greatly diminished if domestic challenges are left unattended. Yale University historian Paul Kennedy strongly implied in *The Rise and Fall of the Great Powers*, that a nation's ability to project power is fundamentally based upon whether, or not, that country has the capability to maintain a vibrant and productive economy.[62] Hence, is Australia ready to confront its domestic economic and social challenges to maintain its influence in regional and international affairs?

DANCING WITH TWO PARTNERS—CAN IT LAST?

Australia's current levels of economic prosperity and its relative security have created an aura of the "perfect storm" phenomenon. Specifically, the nation's growing wealth and existing peace throughout the continent has provided a heightened sense of well-being for this country of 20 million citizens. In short, it's a country enjoying a "golden moment." I know those who read the sentence above will say, "Hold on, Doyle, aren't the Aussies directly involved in the war on terror in Afghanistan, Iraq, and other on-going military operations in the South Pacific?" The answer is yes, but with serious reservations.

Yes, Australia is indeed involved in the war on terror, but (at the time of this writing) their *military* has suffered only three deaths, and a handful of injuries, associated with the Afghanistan and Iraq wars. According to the website Unknown News, approximately 256,757 civilians and soldiers have been killed in both wars combined, and almost 544,000 have been wounded.[63] Ironically, Australian *civilian* casualties, especially due to the Bali bombings in 2002 and 2005, are far greater with a combined total of ninety-two deaths. Thus, Australian civilian casualties, by far, represent the greatest loss of life suffered by this proud nation.[64]

Henceforth, if we can agree that Australia's recent history shows it to be at a relatively elevated state of peace and prosperity, then we must take a closer look at why this reality exists, and what factors make this existence possible. In this section, I will examine three separate aspects of Australia's current foreign policy. First, I will look at the present-day security factors that enable Australia to participate, and project themselves, with more visible confidence in global affairs. Secondly, I will examine the current economic factors that provide Australia the financial wherewithal to involve itself externally, especially in military campaigns far from its shores. Finally, I will address what I believe to be an emerging dilemma confronting the foreign policy establishment in Australia. To be specific, the nation is currently dancing with two different and very powerful partners during this period of economic prosperity and relative national security. *The Nation*, an independent newspaper in Bangkok, Thailand, has stated the situation succinctly in an editorial: "How can Canberra remain a staunch and committed U.S. ally and at the same time maintain strong economic relations with Beijing?"[65] There are a lot of people in Australia and Asia asking the same question.

Presently, Australia's national security is being provided by the most powerful nation on earth, America, and its current and future economic vitality is situated in East Asia, particularly with China. Thus, if the predictions of some analysts are correct, concerning the strong possibility of the U.S. and China bumping into one another over an issue involving Asia-Pacific—which side will Australia support? It's not an easy question to answer, because the repercussions of such a decision can be potentially devastating for a country that has been historically, and remains to this day, vulnerable to outside forces. The "blue skies" thesis, concerning Australia's future, will become more cloudy and opaque as events unfold in Asia-Pacific.

Australia's current security status, due to an unquestioned American commitment in the form of the ANZUS Treaty (1951), has allowed it to use its rather small armed forces—approximately 52,000 overall—in conflicts further from home. Though, there are severe critics, primarily from the Left, of Prime Minister Howard's expansive foreign policies in the Middle East and the South Pacific, the actual troop deployments are less than 5,000 troops overall, according to Sheridan, a major voice in the Australian foreign policy debate. He mentioned that the uproar concerning Prime Minister Howard's current foreign policy is somewhat exaggerated because Australia has had a history of military interventions—usually at the behest of Great Britain or America.[66] Therefore, everyone knows that Australia's current involvement in the Middle East and the South Pacific is with the tacit support, and blessings, of the United States. However, Senator Milne points out that the Howard government has moved Australia away from its past support for multilateralism (U.N., the Non-Proliferation Treaty, etc.), which Australians have strongly supported since the end of WWII. Howard has decided since 9/11 to follow the Bush administration's penchant toward greater unilateralism—or at least the perception of this kind of action.[67]

However, this new policy emphasis has not gone unnoticed by Australian civilian and military analysts. Andrew Wilkie, who spent twenty years in the Australian Army as an infantry officer, and later worked for the Office of National Assessment—the CIA equivalent in Australia—for several years, states, "(Prime Minister) Howard is inclined toward creating a stronger Australia concerning national security matters—with a clear view of replicating the American agenda since 9/11."[68] However, Wilkie believes this policy methodology, and direction, are a mistake, because "Australia has lost its independence in terms of foreign policy and national security. We've become too obsequious toward Washington."[69]

It should be noted that Wilkie, a former military officer and intelligence analyst, courageously blew the whistle on the Howard government's willful distortion of government intelligence concerning Iraq and its alleged armaments—biological and nuclear. After writing a book, *Axis of Deceit*, telling why he exposed the Howard government's untruths about Australia's justifications for entering the Iraqi war, he left Sydney and moved to Tasmania. His book also provides specific examples on how Washington, London, and Canberra misled their respective citizenry about the nature of Iraq's potential as a military threat. Though his revelations shocked many throughout Australia, the mainstream media quickly dismissed his efforts as the ranting from a leftist dissenter and malcontent.[70]

Foreign Minister Downer acknowledges that the government's current foreign policies are not popular with many individuals or political parties in Australia, including his own, but he believes that eventually the positives will outweigh the negatives. The American connection has been very beneficial to Australia. Australia's voice is stronger and more influential due to its *special* relationship to the U.S., and this security factor represents the foundation of Australia's influence in East Asia. When asked about the Howard government's major foreign policy accomplishments since 1996, Downer proclaimed with pride that "Australia is now considered a major player in Asia-Pacific. We are more active than ever in the region. We have changed our status in the region from 'odd man out to odd man in.' It is not an exaggeration to say that Australia is a *real* global player and that we are a champion of freedom. We put our money where our mouths are."[71]

Yet there are words of caution concerning Australia's future balancing act in East Asia—between themselves, America, and their Asian neighbors. Professor Robert Ayson, director of studies at the Strategic and Defense Studies Centre at Australian National University, stated in a lecture given at the famous Australian War Memorial in Canberra, that Australia is currently caught between the U.S. and China's interests in the region, and that Australia's overall security priorities remain unclear. Professor Ayson also commented that Australia's economic future is based upon a volatile marketplace for its natural-resource-based economy. Thus, the financial situation for the country for the next twenty to thirty years is very unpredictable—and that will certainly affect defense spending.[72] Professor Derek McDougall also sees the two-masters thesis as a big question for Australia to answer. McDougall, an assistant professor of political science at the University of Melbourne, has written widely on the security factors concerning Asia-Pacific and observes that the two-master situation "would only arise over a major issue like Taiwan. Australia strongly supports the 'status quo' situation in Asia-Pacific."[73] He agrees that China does have leverage over Australia, economically, but Professor McDougall also points out that Australia balances China's influence with its relations with the U.S. How much longer can this situation continue—he believes no one really knows.[74]

From a military standpoint, Australia has no choice but to side with America in any military situation in Asia-Pacific. Former Australian Army General Peter Abigail, director of the Australian Strategic Policy Institute in Canberra, does not see the two-master question as the *main* question, or focus, for Australia. General Abigail, who spent thirty-seven years in the Australian Army, was appointed land commander of Australian forces from 2000 to 2002. To be succinct, he was responsible for *all* army forces and operations in Australia, as well as their overseas operations in East Timor, Bougainville and Afghanistan. General Abigail elaborated further, with greater detail, about the future of Asia-Pacific and Australia's current geopolitical situation within the region:

> The real issue in Northeast Asia is the China-Japan situation—who will dominate the region in the twenty-first century? China does not historically have hegemonic interests in the region, but it does like having influence in the region. China's real intention is to minimize future imperialism (i.e., U.S.) in the region. Australia is not just in a two-master dilemma, but is in a situation where all the countries in the region have an agenda. The great unknown is how the balance of power will evolve. However, Australia is finding out that the way power is used in Asia is changing, and the main reason for this change is the emergence of China. Therefore, your two-masters question is only part of a much bigger change in Asia-Pacific.[75]

Australia's recent economic prosperity is primarily based upon its extraction of the nation's natural resources, and selling them to foreign customers. In recent times, these minerals and gases have been sold primarily to Asian customers. Though, Japan remains their most important Asian relationship and trading partner in Asia, the emergence of China and its appetite for minerals, oil, natural gas, food, and technology has caused Australians to talk of boom times in the land of Oz.

According to the 2006 Index of Economic Freedom, created by the Heritage Foundation, all four of Australia's top export trading partners are situated in Asia-Pacific—Japan, China, the U.S., and South Korea. And three of Australia's top four import trading partners (U.S., China, Japan) are located in Asia-Pacific as well. Thus, the numbers don't lie—44 percent of Australian exports go to these four destinations, and 39 percent of their imports arrived from the three countries mentioned above.[76] Another information website, www.infoplease.com, lists Australia's top nine trading partners, six of which are in Asia-Pacific: Japan, China, U.S., South Korea, New Zealand, and Singapore.[77] To put an even finer point upon Australia's "enmeshment" within Asia, according to ABS Trade data on the Australian

Department of Foreign Affairs and Trade's database, statistics from 2001 to 2002 showed that Asia-Pacific represented eight of Australia's top traders, representing 51.2 percent of Australian trade.[78]

The final issue to be addressed in this section represents a question that I asked continually throughout my five-week trip through Australia in May–June 2006. Can Australia continue to dance with two different partners (i.e., China and America) in the twenty-first century? This specific question brought several of my interviewees to a moment of silence before they attempted to answer this complex and perplexing question concerning Australia's fate.

Robert Sutter, an analyst of Asian and Pacific affairs for over thirty years who now teaches at Georgetown University, had participated in a four-city discussion of Australia's future role in Asia in June 2004. After numerous academics, consultants, and government analysts examined the present situation in Asia-Pacific, the general consensus within the group was that "relations with the United States may be less close, and relations with China probably will continue to improve, the Australians seeing the two as either/or options was deemed unlikely. They advised Australia to stay close to the United States while it developed relations with China."[79] Sutter's findings, in 2004, were echoed two years later by many of those I interviewed, but several mentioned that this analytical consensus was conditional on whether or not America and China encountered a serious disagreement over a particular issue in Asia-Pacific, such as Taiwan, North Korea, or the growing tensions between China and Japan.

Former Australian Prime Minister Bob Hawke, who was a major supporter of reaching out and developing relations with China during his prime ministership (1983–1991), and who currently has significant business ties to China, analyzes this potential confrontational situation within Asia-Pacific in a coherent and realistic manner—based upon years of working with the U.S. and China, first, as the Australian prime minister and later on as a private citizen/businessman:

> Were it [a China-U.S. conflict] to come to a crunch, if the United States was stupid enough to support Taiwan, if Taiwan unilaterally moved toward independence and China reacted, and they [the U.S.] assume that we [Australia] would be coming in—it would be madness for us to do that, absolute madness. I think if that [a China-U.S. conflict] were to happen—that the stupid bloody U.S. administration were to move in the way—they would find themselves very much on their own. Particularly after the exhibition of ideology gone mad in Iraq, I don't think too many people would want to identify with another exercise of belligerent unilateralism.[80]

William Tow, professor of International Relations in the Research School of Pacific and Asian Studies at Australian National University, stated that "the post-WWII 'hub and spokes' Asia-Pacific defense structure is over, the U.S. now has symmetrical relations with their allies, and not asymmetrical as in the past."[81] In other words, bilateral relations representing the vital interests of *both* nations, separately, will be the new norm in regional security, and not a total commitment to one doctrine or strategy. Professor Tow also commented that "Australia approaches its regional security very cautiously, and the potential situation of having to make a 'U.S.-China choice' is to be avoided."[82] The danger of being in such a situation is understood without further elaboration. The ramifications, domestically and regionally, would obviously alter the future path and history of Australia and the region.

To make a final point on this sensitive subject concerning Australia's precarious situation in Asia-Pacific, I found an article in the Asian edition of *Time* magazine by Allan Gyngell titled, "Living with the Giants," that addressed this challenging subject directly, and with the knowledge that the next few years will determine whether Australia will be successful in its diplomatic efforts to navigate (or serve two masters) in increasingly dangerous waters within the Asia-Pacific region. Its present economic and security foundations are at risk, and yet there is no concise or understood strategy, or a blueprint that provides the exact details and methodology that will help them to avoid such a gut-wrenching dilemma. Gyngell writes:

> Australia will soon face foreign policy challenges different from any the country has experienced before. For the past 50 years, Asia's most important power, Japan, has been a staunch partner of the U.S. Australia has not had to make choices between its principal ally and its most promising market (China). But it may now face the uncomfortable challenge of having to maintain constructive relations with both Washington and Beijing. Its success in doing this will depend critically on two things: U.S. strategy towards its emerging Asian competitor, and China's own behavior.[83]

Common sense tells me that Australia will be confronted, in the relatively near future, with making a choice between America and China, due to an unexpected (aren't they all to some degree?) crisis emerging in Asia-Pacific. As in one's personal life, you can't have a wife and a mistress for very long before they discover each other—perhaps at the local grocery store. At *that* moment, you will have to *decide* which one you want to be with—and suffer the consequences of rejecting the other. For Australia, this choice, though acknowledged by its foreign policy establishment, is viewed as a worst-case scenario—but not dismissed. Who does Australia serve? At that moment, Australia's future relations with every country in Asia-Pacific will be affected. Does it have the courage and fortitude to remain neutral when America requests its participation in some crisis involving China in the region? Or does it dare to risk serious economic retaliation from China and its allies, due to supporting the Americans? This question grows in importance within Asia-Pacific, America, and China, but especially within Australia, every day.

CONCLUSION: DANGEROUS GAME IN ASIA-PACIFIC

Australia and Asia-Pacific find themselves in an ever-changing environment that fluctuates between economic euphoria and geopolitical tensions. Everyone in this region has something at stake—economically and militarily. No nation will be left unscathed if turbulent events overtake the region during the twenty-first century. Everyone must remain cognizant of the fact that things can quickly come unraveled for a number of reasons.

Henry Kissinger, former national security advisor (1969–1973) and U.S. secretary of state (1973–1977) during the Nixon and Ford administrations, is a longtime observer and veteran of Asia-Pacific. Several of the greatest challenges he confronted during his time in government were situated in this volatile region, particularly in Vietnam, Cambodia, and China. Kissinger, a government professor at Harvard University before entering the Nixon White House, analyzed the present situation in Asia-Pacific and acknowledges that this area of the world is experiencing rapid economic growth and dramatic prosperity, but he remains a "realist" in his observations about the future of this dynamic region. Kissinger writes,

> The stability of the Asia-Pacific region, the underpinning of its vaunted prosperity, is not a law of nature but the consequence of an equilibrium which will need increasingly careful and deliberate tending in the post-Cold War world . . . in Asia there is no pretense of collective security or that cooperation should be based on shared domestic values, even on the part of the few existing democracies. The emphasis is all on equilibrium and national interest. Military expenditures are already rising in all the major Asian countries. China is on the road to superpower status.[84]

My nine plus years of living, researching, teaching, and traveling throughout Asia-Pacific tell me Australia's attempt to serve two masters will, in the end, fail. The region is simply too volatile politically, and the historical and cultural relationships between the nations in the region are too complex. Australia's clever balancing act is essentially built upon sand and wishful thinking. Economic prosperity currently greases the wheels of diplomacy, and right now most of the countries in Asia-Pacific are cooperating with each other because they are visibly benefiting from regional cooperation and constructive negotiations. However, historical grievances continue to exist and, in several cases, remain unresolved.

It is vitally important to recognize, from a historical standpoint, that China and Japan have never been major powers at the same time. The nightmarish atrocities associated with Japanese militarism, since the late nineteenth century, are still fresh in the minds of most Chinese. Thus, I believe friction will continue to grow between these two rivals as they vie for the leadership of Northeast Asia. South and North Korea, the nations caught in between this power struggle, will have to be extraordinarily diplomatic not to be dragged into this dangerous struggle. Their own unification represents an extremely delicate situation, and yet my Korean friends told me, in 2005, that they believe no one in Northeast Asia really wants them to unify. And North Korea's firing of missiles into the Sea of Japan, in 2006, has only exacerbated the entire situation in Northeast Asia.

If North Korea's display of technological prowess wasn't enough to terrify everyone in Asia-Pacific, throw in these important factors: India is emerging as a power and will become a major competitor for China in Central and South Asia. The American empire is not quite ready to let the sun set on its position in the region. In short, it expects to maintain its hegemonic position in the region despite its failing wars in Iraq and Afghanistan. However, they are increasingly wary of China's military development in the region. Finally, Indonesia, the largest Muslim state in the world, is still recovering from a financial meltdown, political instability, and devastating tsunamis.

Indeed, Australia's future in balancing all these dangerous factors, and more, in an attempt to avoid taking sides in a crisis involving China (and its allies) and America (and its allies), is wishful thinking. This diplomatic and geopolitical challenge is truly daunting and unnerving for this lightly populated antipodal settlement.

Most analysts believe that it is China who holds the key to the future of Asia-Pacific. Though China has publicly stated, repeatedly, that they only seek a "peaceful rise" in Asia and throughout the world, their pronouncements have fallen, for a large group of Western and Asian analysts, upon deaf ears. These critics and observers point to the fact that China is aggressively seeking regional and global leadership. Specifically, the Chinese wish to regain their former vaunted status as the Zhongguo within East Asia. The analysis presented by these skeptics stands in stark contrast to China's public statements of peaceful development. Who is right?

Professor Desmond Ball, one of the leading analysts of the Asia-Pacific region at Australian National University, when asked directly whether war between the U.S. and China was inevitable during the twenty-first century, responded "*inevitable* was too strong a term, *probable* was the better and more accurate answer."[85] John Mearsheimer, the R. Wendell Harrison distinguished service professor of political science at the University of Chicago, writes that if China's economy continues to grow at the present rate (9–10 percent per year) then it will have the capacity to become stronger militarily. However, Mearsheimer cautions that this dual development in and of itself does not necessarily mean that China will become a threat to its neighbors, or to the American position in Asia, particularly in Northeast Asia. He reiterates that if China does become an aggressive economic and military hegemonic force within East Asia, then the U.S. would most likely (with Japanese and Korean approval) keep troops in the region to counter-balance China's growing influence.[86]

Therefore, according to Professor Mearsheimer, "it is clear that the most dangerous scenario the United States might face in the early twenty-first century is one in which China becomes a potential hegemon in Northeast Asia."[87] Mearsheimer, though, quickly points out that for this confrontational situation to occur the Chinese economy will have to continue growing at its current pace—a factor that no one can determine or accurately predict at this time.[88]

Yet there is no doubt in this writer's mind that China is seeking to regain lost prestige and influence in Asia-Pacific. In June 2001, China constructed the Shanghai Cooperation Organization (SCO), which currently includes six member nations: China, Russia, Kazakhstan, Kyrgyzstan, Tajikistan, and Uzbekistan. This organization accounts for 1.455 billion people, and its primary operating languages are Chinese and Russian.[89] There are reports that the SCO is trying to recruit Iran and other Middle Eastern nations. The United States views the SCO as China's attempt to secure an independent energy supply, and project its influence throughout the Caspian Sea region, and Eurasia, where major deposits of oil and gas exist. In short, China intends to project its growing power within the Eurasia region, without undue interference from the United States.

In December 2005, China also participated in the first East Asian Summit (EAS), the brainchild of former Malaysian Prime Minister Mahathir Mohamad. The EAS currently consists of sixteen nations, representing 50 percent of the world's population and 20 percent of global trade. It is an organization made up of primarily East Asian nations, but India, Australia, and New Zealand were invited to the inaugural meeting at Kuala Lumpur, Indonesia.[90] America was not invited. This was certainly noted in Washington, DC, and by experts of this region within the American foreign policy establishment.

I believe, from my years of living and traveling throughout the East Asian hemisphere, it will become increasingly difficult for Australian foreign policy to walk the geopolitical tightrope in Asia-Pacific. To put it simply, the region is evolving so quickly that the existing policy flexibility, and economic prosperity, that Australia has enjoyed the last fifteen years will begin to diminish. I believe China and America will clash, though all-out war is still a minute possibility. However, Australia will be confronted with the dilemma of making a *choice* between the two major powers. I believe they will continue to side with the U.S., but they *will* be punished economically by China and its supporters, perhaps severely depending on the nature of the crisis.

I also believe that Australians *will* become part of a new Pacific axis consisting of America, Australia, and Japan. In March 2006, a press release from Alexander Downer's foreign ministry announced a meeting between himself and the U.S. Secretary of State Condoleezza Rice and Japan's Foreign Minister Taro Aso, in Sydney, Australia, on 18 March 2006. The press release spoke of their "common cause," being "long-standing democracies," "working to maintain stability and security globally with a particular focus on the Asia-Pacific," "intensifying the strategic dialogue," and hoping to achieve "greater trilateral cooperation."[91]

The press release fell just short of announcing a new "tripartite" pact within Asia-Pacific. I am sure this cozy gathering of these three Pacific powers caught the attention of the Chinese leadership in Beijing, despite the group's "welcoming China's constructive engagement in the region."[92] The gesture toward multilateral cooperation with China came off a bit hollow and insincere. Dr. Zbigniew Brzezinski, a counselor and professor of foreign policy at the Center for Strategic and International Studies at Johns Hopkins University, believes the potentiality of a U.S.-Australia-Japan configuration to stymie China's rise to power in Asia is a nonstarter. Brzezinski stated unequivocally that "(a peaceful) equilibrium in East Asia will only be achieved by triangular diplomacy between the U.S., China, and Japan."[93] This triumvirate of powers represents "the new reality of East Asian power politics, but also its future hopes for maintaining prosperity and stability in the region."[94] Hence, Australia will be a *significant* player, but not a *key* player in Asia-Pacific during the twenty-first century.

Sheridan, the senior foreign affairs columnist for the *Australian*, though a bit over the top in his support for the Bush administration's policies at times, is quite succinct in his final analysis concerning the future of U.S.-Australian relations in the twenty-first century: "Australia and the U.S. disagree on many issues, but Australia understands that the U.S. provides security for them, and its U.S. relationship provides Australia leverage in its relations with Asian nations."[95]

Australia, since 9/11, has noticeably taken on an aggressive and more expansive role for itself in the affairs of the South Pacific. This perception was confirmed, in 2005, when U.S. President George W. Bush called Australia "America's Sheriff" in the region, and he described Australia as "a strategic and operational trailblazer."[96] Foreign Minister Downer commented, "China can be quite aggressive when they need to be, and they (China) will continue to attempt to dislodge Australia from the U.S. orbit, but they will fail. Everyone knows where we stand in the region."[97]

In closing, the "Australian paradox" in the twenty-first century will be a much more complex affair than many realize. Its potential for harm to the Australian economy, or its national security, is enormous. Many of those I interviewed in Australia told me that my topic of interest was extraordinarily important, and that most of the nation's citizens were not aware of the contradictory nature of Australia's economic and security policies. It is my hope that this chapter has addressed a few of the challenges that lie ahead for the Land Down Under within the Asia-Pacific region. The constantly evolving dynamics, economically and militarily, and the numerical diversity of cultures within the region, simply pose an insurmountable challenge for any government to attempt and create successfully an overarching foreign policy that will produce long-term stability and equilibrium for itself and the region.

In short, there are simply too many variables in play throughout Asia-Pacific. The major players are increasingly in competition with each other over regional leadership, and access to a diminishing supply of natural resources to fuel their national ambitions and economies. It is an area, physically, psychologically, and technologically, increasingly in need of dialogue and diplomacy because the region's wealth expansion has also increased its military capacity to do great harm to itself. Thus, it is imperative that the major players in the region take steps to rectify their differences, or the destructive power of modern weapon systems will do to them in the twenty-first century what they did to Europeans during the first half of the twentieth century.

Specifically, the ultimate *endgame* for Australia would be a regional crisis that forced them to chose, definitively, which direction their future lies— America or Asia. And this historic decision might very well end Australia's consecutive years of economic growth and prosperity that has been their experience since the early 1990s. This reality is not considered a strong probability by most regional observers. Nevertheless, a risk does exist that the future could be less sunny and warm for Australia, and the Australian people.

What awaits the land called "Oz" at the end of the yellow brick road? It is a crucial question, a soul-shattering question that the vast majority of Australians wish to avoid and never be forced to answer. Simply put, will the unfolding and unpredicted events of the twenty-first century allow, or deter, such a fate for Australia? Stay tuned.

NOTES

1. Stephen Blank, "Australia: A Sheriff with a Strategy," *Asia Times*, 2 October 2005.
2. Ibid.
3. Ibid.
4. Jeffrey Robertson, "Australia's Asian Ambitions," *Asia Times*, 2003.
5. Ibid.
6. Ibid.

7. John Pilger, "Bush's Sheriff," *The New Statesman*, 1 April 2004.

8. Ibid.

9. Ibid.

10. Ibid.

11. Maryann Keady, "Australia in the Region," zmag.org, 5 July 2006.

12. Ibid.

13. Ibid.

14. Australian Broadcasting Corporation, interview with Gareth Evans, by reporter Maxine McKew, broadcasted 20 September 2003.

15. Ibid.

16. Ibid.

17. Interview with Alexander Downer, 22 May 2006, Canberra, Australia.

18. Ibid.

19. Asialink Chairman's Dinner speech by Australian Foreign Minister Alexander Downer, 1 December 2005, in Melbourne, Australia.

20. Ibid.

21. Interview with Professor Desmond Ball, 24 May 2006.

22. Interview with Downer, 22 May 2006.

23. Ibid.

24. Greg Sheridan, "U.S. Sees Us as a Global Ally, a Vision Well Worth Sharing," *The Australian*, 29 June 2006.

25. Ibid.

26. Owen Harries, "After Iraq," Lowy Institute for International Policy, Sydney, Australia, December 2006, p. 9. This particular speech caught the attention of the major newspapers in Australia and America.

27. Ibid.

28. Hugh White, "Beyond the Defence of Australia: Finding a New Balance in Australian Strategic Policy," Lowy Institute for International Policy, Lowy Institute Paper, 16 October 2006, pp. 3–4.

29. Ibid.

30. Ibid., p. 4.

31. Jessica Irvine, "Aussie May Catch $US Next Year, Pundit Says," *The Sydney Morning Herald*, 13–14 May 2006, p. 41.

32. Ibid. (The two financial advisors referred to were Stephen Koukoulas, chief Asia-Pacific strategist at TD Securities, and Robert Rennie, chief currency strategist at Westpac. Both are situated in Australia.)

33. Economist.com, Country Briefings, Australia, Economic Data, 25 May 2004.

34. *CIA World Factbook*, Australia, 2006.

35. Wikipedia.org, the free encyclopedia, *International Monetary Fund* Statistics, 2005.

36. Economist.com, Country Briefings, Australia, Economic Data, 25 May 2004.

37. Australian Government, Department of Foreign Affairs and Trade, "Australian Trade Story in 2003," Fast Facts about Trade, found in July 2006.

38. Andrew Trounson, "Metals Giant Urges Tariffs," *The Australian*, 15 July 2006.

39. Economist Intelligence Unit (www.viewswire.com/index.asp?layout=VW-country).

40. Hamish McDonald, "BHP Reveals $11bn China Iron Ore Deal," *Sydney Morning Herald*, 2 March 2004. Nigel Wilson, "Australia-China LNG Deal Sealed," *Energy*

Bulletin (published by *The Australian*), 13 December 2004. Geoff Hiscock, "Australia, China Sign Uranium Deal," *CNN World News*, 2 April 2006.

41. Australian Associated Press, "Mining Boom to Continue," the *Mercury*, 11 December 2006. The *Mercury* has the largest circulation, and is the most important newspaper in the state of Tasmania.

42. Ibid.

43. *Asia Times*, "Asian Tourists Have Australia's Number," 1 May 1999. This article was retrieved from their "Oceania" section of their website.

44. Aree Chaisatien, "Asian Race for Diplomas Boosts Australia's Coffers," *Asia Times* (Oceania), 9 June 1999.

45. *CIA World Factbook*, Australia, 2006.

46. Trounson, "Metals Giant Urges Tariffs."

47. Ibid.

48. Interview with Christine Milne, 5 June 2006, Hobart, Tasmania.

49. Ibid.

50. Dennis Shanahan, "Voters Cool on Budget Tax Cuts," *The Australian*, 16 May 2006.

51. Federal Senator Christine Milne, *Australian Green Party Budget Reply*, 11 May 2006.

52. Shanahan, "Voters Cool on Budget Tax Cuts."

53. George Magalogenis, "The Old and the Poor Left Behind in Queue: Unemployment Is Down but More People Are on Welfare," *The Weekend Australian*, 10–11 June 2006.

54. Ibid.

55. Mike Corder, "Racial Unrest Strikes Australia," *Associated Press*, 12 December 2005.

56. Paul Colgan, "Australia Is Racist: Poll," *The Australian*, 6 March 2006.

57. Interview with Tim Flannery, 6 April 2006.

58. Ibid.

59. Ibid.

60. Michael Casey, "U.S., Australia Back Global Warming Plan," *Associated Press* Environmental Writer, 12 January 2006.

61. Anne Davies, Urban Affairs Editor, "Sydney's Future Eaten: The Flannery Prophecy," *Sydney Morning Herald*, 19 May 2004.

62. Paul Kennedy, *The Rise and Fall of the Great Powers: Economic Change and Military Conflict from 1500 to 2000* (New York: Random House, 1987).

63. Unknown News at myway.com provided the combined civilian and military deaths and injured statistics mentioned in my paper.

64. Wikipedia, *Bali Bombings 2002 and 2005*. I received the casualty statistics from this website for both bombings.

65. Editorial, Regional Perspective Section, "Australia Demonstrates the Art of Riding Two Horses," *The Nation*, 19 June 2006.

66. Interview with Greg Sheridan, Foreign Affairs Editor at *The Australian*, 13 June 2006, Sydney, Australia. *The Australian* is the only nationally published newspaper in Australia.

67. Interview with Senator Milne, 5 June 2006.

68. Interview with Andrew Wilkie, 5 June 2006, Hobart, Tasmania.

69. Ibid.

70. Ibid.

71. Interview with Alexander Downer, 22 May 2006.

72. The attributed material is taken from a conversation with Professor Robert Ayson at his campus office at Australian National University and later from notes I took at his lecture at the Australian War Memorial, 23 May 2006.

73. Interview with Professor Derek McDougall, 19 May 2006.

74. Ibid.

75. Interview with Australian Major General Peter Abigail, 22 May 2006.

76. "2006 Index of Economic Freedom," The Heritage Foundation, www.heritage.org/research/features/index/country.cfm?id=Australia.

77. http://www.infoplease.com/ipa/A107296.html.

78. Australia's Foreign and Trade Policy White Paper, March 2003; ABS trade data on DFAT STARS database, ABS regional services data 2001–2002.

79. Robert G. Sutter, *China's Rise in Asia: Promises and Perils* (Lanham, MD: Rowman & Littlefield Publishers, Inc., 2005), p. 287.

80. Interview with Bob Hawke, former Prime Minster of Australia (1983–1991), 4 June 2004.

81. Interview with Professor William Tow, 24 May 2006.

82. Ibid.

83. Allan Gyngell, "Living with the Giants," *Time-Asia* edition, 18 April 2005.

84. Henry Kissinger, *Diplomacy* (New York: Simon & Schuster, 1994), p. 826.

85. Ball interview, 24 May 2006.

86. John J. Mearsheimer, *The Tragedy of Great Power Politics* (New York: W. W. Norton & Company, 2001), pp. 400–401.

87. Ibid.

88. Ibid.

89. I acquired the information for this footnote from the Ministry of Foreign Affairs of the People's Republic of China website, 20 June 2006.

90. Wikipedia search, *East Asian Summit 2005*.

91. The Honorable Alexander Downer, Minister for Foreign Affairs, Australia, Press Release, 18 March 2006.

92. Ibid.

93. Interview with Professor Brzezinski, 8 January 2007.

94. Ibid.

95. Interview with Greg Sheridan, 12 April 2006.

96. Blank, "Australia: A Sheriff with a Strategy."

97. Downer interview, 22 May 2006.

Epilogue

Asia-Pacific in the Twenty-first Century: Pearl Harbor or Peace?

Though I briefly mentioned his interesting survey earlier in chapter 4, I think it's worth another look as I present my final overview of the Asia-Pacific Rim in the twenty-first century. David Rothkopf, author of *Running the World*, did an informal survey at the Carnegie Endowment for International Peace. Overall, almost 180 experts and scholars in various fields concerning America's international priorities responded to his questions. Rothkopf, a visiting scholar at the Carnegie Endowment for International Peace and CEO of the Rothkopf Group, was deputy undersecretary of commerce for international trade in the Clinton administration, decided to conduct an informal survey based upon the work of the Goldman Sachs analysis, in 2003, which identified the new emerging economic powers of the twenty-first century.[1] The eventual results were unexpected, but not too surprising to followers of global affairs.

As stated in chapter 4, Rothkopf's first question asks to identify America's *most important* ally, adversary, or critical player, during the next five years, with regard to the participant's areas of expertise. He then asks the same question concerning the next twenty years. Then he asks which country will be the *most likely* to be America's ally for the next five to twenty years. Finally, Rothkopf asks this group of global experts to identify the country *most likely* to be America's adversary, rival, or challenger.

This group of almost 180 accomplished individuals, who study and write on dozens of different topics that are important to U.S. global interests, chose the *same* country for every question mentioned above—China.[2] In short, at the prestigious Carnegie Endowment for International Peace, China will become, *potentially*, America's primary foe and/or friend during the first quarter of the twenty-first century. It is hard to think of the last time that such a consensus existed amongst American foreign policy analysts, perhaps, since the darkest days of the Cold War and the existence of the Soviet Union.

At British Prime Minister Tony Blair's last press conference of the year in December 2005, I watched and listened to a reporter asking Blair what he thought of China's becoming, according to some estimates, the fourth largest economy in the world. The prime minister showed no emotion whatsoever. He shrugged his shoulders and stated that if China continues to grow at its present rate, it will be the largest economy in the world in the near future. His voice had the tone of one accepting the reality of his times.[3]

There is no doubt about it, the twenty-first century and the Asia-Pacific region, especially China and America, will dominate the headlines as history unfolds at the beginning of a new millennium. The alliances and friendships created after WWII, in this volatile area, appeared to be dated, no longer pragmatic, and simply insupportable for many nations. In the end, power and glory, without a doubt, will drive events between China and America, but to what end? Pearl Harbor or peace? Can *new* history be made? Is humanity *capable* of creating it? Or are we *doomed* by the kind of war and destruction that litters the history of mankind?

The twenty-first century is in its opening stages. What will occur, or evolve, during the first century of the new millennium rests within the realm of guesstimate. However, having spent close to a decade in Asia-Pacific, I have witnessed the rise of nationalism and the movement toward greater economic and political autonomy in all the countries that I had lived in or visited. These dramatic indigenous developments are having a critical effect upon the future direction of the region. Thus, these dynamic forces were the topical focus of my research and writing of this book. I wanted to discover and examine the post-WWII history, and the challenges and issues concerning future cooperation and unity amongst the major partners of the post-WWII security structure—put in place by the U.S.—and how China's phoenix-like rise in Asia-Pacific, in the twenty-first century, is causing a serious reevaluation to occur amongst all the alliance members.

It is not false hyperbole or hollow rhetoric to state that there are serious storm clouds emerging on the horizon for this nation's foreign policy and military establishments with concern to Asia-Pacific. As expected, there is a growing list of vociferous critics, realists and internationalists both, who are seriously questioning America's future role in this vital region. They do not see U.S. influence and power becoming irrelevant, but they are increasingly certain that America will have to make a number of fundamental and serious adjustments with concern to its future hegemonic role in Asia-Pacific.

The following areas, I believe, must be addressed and dealt with honestly and decisively for the U.S. to maintain a credible and substantive role in Asia-Pacific during the twenty-first century. The list below identifies a number of categories and issues (economic, environmental, political, and military) confronting America in this crucial region:

1. **Geography**: The U.S. has a significant presence in Asia, but it is not an Asian power.
2. **Environment**: Throughout Asia-Pacific the environment represents a time bomb that could undermine economic development and regional stability very quickly.
3. **Finance**: China, Japan, South Korea, and the rest of Asia-Pacific understand how fragile their economic situation really is. How much longer can Asian banks keep financing America's gigantic national debt and trade deficits?
4. **East Asia Summit**: Will this first-ever summit, in December 2005, represent the beginning of an independent and unified region—economically and militarily?
5. **Nationalism**: Toxic patriotism and the danger of rectifying the past—Taiwan represents the greatest danger of these two factors converging in China.

Professor Robert Sutter, an instructor in Georgetown University's School of Foreign Service, acknowledges that the issues mentioned above are indeed daunting for the U.S. and its future status in East Asia during the twenty-first century. However, Sutter, who has over thirty years of experience analyzing Asian and Pacific affairs for a multitude of U.S. agencies and governmental entities such as the CIA and the State Department, and as a staff member on the U.S. Senate Foreign Relations Committee, made some insightful and interesting observations concerning the present-day realities facing the U.S., China, and East Asia in the twenty-first century. Professor Sutter states that the possibility of an independent trade bloc developing in East Asia is "thin" or "small," because there is a significant degree of mistrust and wariness amongst Asians towards each other. He emphasized that "in East Asia, no one wants to be dominated."[4]

Sutter's analysis of U.S.-China relations is one of hope and caution. He mentioned that the *key* word to describe this delicate relationship is "hedging." Both countries are "hedging" toward each other, which means that both countries are taking steps to ensure that they are well positioned if something goes awry between them. He points to U.S. Secretary of State Condolezza Rice's visit to East Asia, in March 2005, as the origins of this new regional policy toward China. Sutter, at this time, does not see China as an aggressive power, because the Chinese government's

primary objective is to manage its economic growth properly. China's main dilemma is to reform domestically as soon as possible. The internal social implications, if they fail, will be very important for the future status of the Chinese Communist Party. Thus, the Chinese government is preoccupied by domestic problems, and not by foreign affairs or trying to dominate or intimidate its neighbors. The whole issue of countries in East Asia choosing China or America in a situation involving Taiwan is pure fantasy. It is long-standing history that countries throughout East Asia have determined not to be trapped into a war with China over Taiwan.[5]

GEOGRAPHY: WHERE YOU LIVE DETERMINES HOW YOU LIVE

Within the real estate industry, the old axiom is "location, location, and location." Thus, geography matters. This truism is often overlooked in American foreign policy. We constantly hear of new technologies that allow America to project its power globally—with greater speed and without hindrance. Hysterical cheerleaders within the corporate media, such as Thomas Friedman of the *New York Times*, preach about a "flat world" existing during this current stage of globalization. Yet, even in flat worlds, geography remains important. The fact of the matter is that America's ability to support long-distanced military operations will be difficult in the best of conditions. The current Iraqi war has shown how difficult it is to properly arm and supply tens of thousands of soldiers situated thousands of miles from the homeland.

Therefore, I believe, Asia-Pacific's breathtaking physical dimensions and potential scope of operations represent an even more daunting logistical task for U.S. military planners. If a future military crisis occurs in the region, especially involving China, the Pentagon will be faced with a monumental challenge that may be just beyond their current capabilities—if we exclude a nuclear strike. If it metastasizes as a regionwide conflict, then literally millions of U.S. troops would be needed to even have a chance to neutralize China's massive population advantage in a war of attrition.

Looking at the expansive Pacific region (64 million square miles[6]) boggles the mind when you consider the current and immense challenges confronting U.S. military strategists within the Pentagon. Real threats such as terrorism, nations developing nuclear weapons programs, an emerging China, increasing nationalism, and natural catastrophes are just a few of the major dilemmas facing an "overstretched" Pentagon at this point of the American empire. The U.S. government has made it quite clear that it does not want any future hegemonic military challengers to its well-established global preeminence.[7] The U.S. military expenditures are now hovering around $500 billion per year—and that is not including the hundreds of billions already spent on the Iraqi and Afghan wars.

The only territory in East Asia that America can guarantee a future military presence on is Guam because it remains a U.S. territory. As a consequence, after the Philippines' government asked us to leave in 1991, Guam was the recipient of millions of dollars for the purpose of substantially upgrading its military facilities. Its geographic location is also advantageous, particularly for military operations in Southeast Asia. Andersen Air Force Base was the home base for the B-52 bombers that tormented North Vietnam, Cambodia, and Laos during the Vietnam War.

Though, relatively secure for now, the multitude of U.S. bases in Japan and South Korea are, nevertheless, granted to exist by these respective governments. In the unpredictable world of power politics, it would not be the first time that an assumed ally asked the "occupying" power to leave their country due to changing political circumstances. Hence, politics is always volatile, and policies often change on a dime, due to extenuating circumstances beyond the control of the major power. Currently, U.S. troops are situated in key areas in Northeast Asia—Okinawa, mainland Japan, and South Korea. Okinawa (Japan) is situated perfectly for U.S. forces to deal with potential trouble involving Taiwan or North Korea.

However, not everything is peaches and cream for the American military in either location. Okinawans are growing more belligerent about the presence of U.S. bases and the valuable real estate they occupy on the main island. American efforts to build new facilities on Okinawa have faced fierce resistance from the local citizens. In South Korea, the U.S. military has decided to move its troops about forty miles south of Seoul, the nation's capital, and build new military facilities for a reduced number of U.S. personnel.

I taught in Okinawa, mainland Japan, and South Korea for the University of Maryland's Asian Division during the late 1990s. There was no doubt in my mind that the political climate had changed dramatically in these locales. The Berlin Wall came down in 1989, and the Soviet Union dissolved in 1991. Hence, the question was often asked by many citizens in these Asian nations—why are the Americans still here? The question, though, was a bit disingenuous because many of these individuals also knew the Cold War was over only in Europe. However, in East Asia, tensions still existed due to combative political ideologies and unhappy memories from WWII, especially in Northeast Asia. A U.S. presence was still necessary and supported, for the most part, by these regional governments.

However, there are a few emerging and important stories that, I believe, are developing "under the radar" with concern to the U.S. public. This news vacuum is not a surprise to those of us who follow foreign news, especially from Asia. The American corporate-owned news services have cut back dramatically on overseas news coverage since the fall of the Berlin Wall and the demise of the Soviet Union. Though, it has improved due to the fallout from 9/11, but mostly in its coverage of the Middle East.

Nevertheless, I will provide a brief and distinct overview of three consequential situations emerging in East Asia. In my opinion, they have the potential of bringing *Asia* back into the living rooms of America in the very near future. If these regional stories materialize into greater importance, it will become impossible for the U.S. government and its citizens to ignore them.

The Spirit of Governor Masahide Ota and the U.S. Military on Okinawa

Okinawa's Governor Masahide Ota, who was elected twice in the 1990s, believed it was time for the American bases to be given back to the people of Okinawa. Governor Ota was continually painted by the U.S. military as anti-American, and possibly a Communist supporter. This transparent American propaganda had very little effect upon the native population who strongly supported Ota's agenda to rid the island of American bases. Yet, in a rather odd and convoluted methodology, it also succeeded in convincing most Americans on Okinawa that their being there was absolutely legitimate.

However, the U.S. bases, during my time on Okinawa, encountered a constant and ever-growing grassroots movement that attempted to rid the island of its occupying force. This growing swell of discontent amongst the vast majority of citizens on Okinawa often confused and frustrated Americans who insist upon seeing themselves as saviors of the perceived ignorant and underdeveloped wretches on this island.

A good example of the nonstop misinformation campaign on Okinawa was the unchallenged acceptance, by American soldiers and dependents, of the fact that Okinawa's economy would soon collapse without the financial windfall associated with the American bases. In reality, Governor Ota told me that this was simply a falsehood. He showed me the government statistics that clearly indicated that the U.S. bases and soldiers only accounted for approximately 5 percent of the island's total revenue. Yet, when I told colleagues of mine about this irrefutable financial fact, supported by (Okinawa) government documentation, I was met with either total indifference, or I was told that Governor Ota was just a scheming anti-American radical.

In 1999, I taped a television interview with Governor Ota, at his office in downtown Naha—the island's capital, just after he had lost his bid for a third term as Okinawa's governor. We addressed several issues such as his real views concerning the U.S. bases on Okinawa, why he lost his bid for re-election, what the future for the island would be, and what he would do in retirement. It was a solid interview. It was eventually aired on an independent cable television station operating at Camp Butler, a major facility for the U.S. Marine Corps near Kadena Air Base—the largest U.S. air base in East Asia. I was stunned to find out that my interview of Governor Ota was the first ever shown, on Okinawa, to U.S. troops and military dependents on Armed Forces Radio and Television Stations (AFRTS).

It dawned upon me immediately, that the visceral anger shown toward Ota was conducted without the American military personnel ever knowing who the hell this man really was, or what he truly represented in reality. In other words, the U.S. military's high command, on Okinawa, did their thinking for them. The military's successful propaganda campaign against this native son of Okinawa remains impressive. In hindsight, the U.S. military, in Japan, especially upon Okinawa, had convinced a majority of its soldiers and dependents that Governor Ota hated Americans, and that his views did not represent the sentiments of the majority of citizens on Okinawa. It was pure lies on both counts.

Yet all of this intense indoctrination was accomplished without the soldiers, or their dependents, ever laying eyes upon Ota, or listening to him on their radios or televisions. I have no doubt that British writer George Orwell, author of *1984*, would be quite impressed. Nevertheless, the mood on Okinawa has remained unchanged. The U.S. military's efforts to build new facilities on the island have failed. A resolute island-based nationalism has emerged and will remain a potent force until fundamental restructuring has occurred with concern to the presence of the U.S. bases. American security concerns are colliding with anticolonial nationalism on Okinawa. The eventual result will be compromise favoring the native population, or there will be acts of open rebellion—similar to those exhibited since the early 1970s.

Kim Dae-jung and the "Sunshine" Policies on the Korean Peninsula

In South Korea, President Kim Dae-jung's Sunshine policies and his subsequent meeting with the North Korean leader, Kim Jong-il, in June 2000, meant that the Korean peninsula was going in a new direction. And, for the most part, the Korean people, especially the young, supported future unification of the two Koreas. In my recent trip to South Korea, in 2005, I noticed that Koreans seemed calmer and more deliberate in their political activities. A new self-confidence was very apparent to this observer.

I asked Professor Bruce Cumings, who teaches Asian and Korean history, at the University of Chicago, whether my initial evaluation of Korean political behavior was accurate, or was I just immersed in wishful thinking. Professor Cumings immediately smiled and nodded in agreement concerning my description of a new and confident Korea. He said that democracy is taking hold in Korea, and that the Koreans are getting more confident in running their own affairs. We both agreed that the country simply felt different, but we perceived it as being a good development—though not so good for American influence.[8] In short, as Bob Dylan sang, "the times they are a'changin'"; this was very true for South Korea, and even North Korea, in 2005.

My conversation with Professor Cumings occurred due to my being invited to the fifth commemoration of the 15 June summit that took place between Kim Dae-jung and Kim Jong-il, at North Korea's capital, Pyongyang, in 2000. After talking with Choi Kyung Hwan, the executive secretary to Kim Dae-jung at the Kim Dae-jung Presidential Library at Yonsei University, about former President Kim's activities since he left office in 2002, he enquired whether I would like to attend the international conference recognizing the fifth anniversary of this momentous event in Korean history. The conference was held at the fashionable Shilla Hotel in downtown Seoul. And I should note that the lunch served after the morning sessions was simply outstanding.

In my mind, Kim Dae-jung was putting on a first-class conference to impress upon Korean and foreign dignitaries that his courageous diplomatic initiative, in June 2000, represented a turning point in the country's post-WWII existence. In short, it was a first-rate meeting, with a high public profile, indicating that Korea was indeed on a new path. In 2007, there is cautious hope for Korea, both in the North and the South. Perhaps, both Koreas can finally escape the suffocating shadow of the Cold War, which keeps the peninsula trapped in a time warp, ideologically and militarily, in the twenty-first century.

The Bush administration, however, has remained distant and indifferent toward the North-South dialogue since the very beginning of its reign in Washington, DC. Yet, despite no support from their American occupiers, the current South Korean president, Roh Moo-hyun, made a surprise appearance and gave a ringing endorsement for the continuation of the process. And, as a sign of hope and progress for the future, Korea's friends and supporters in Asia, America, and Europe made their presences felt at this international conference:

1. *Qian Qichen*, the former vice premier in China
2. *Donald Gregg*, former U.S. ambassador and currently the chairman of Korea Society in the U.S.
3. *Irmgard Schwaetzer*, the former vice minister for foreign affairs in Germany (during the process of German unification)
4. *Mikhail Gorbachev*, former president of the Soviet Union—Russia
5. *Bruce Cumings*, professor of Asian history at the University of Chicago
6. *Don Oberdorfer*, Johns Hopkins University's Nitze School of Advanced International Studies
7. *Yu Xintian*, president of the Shanghai Institute for International Studies, China[9]

After the conference ended, one definitely got the impression that the Bush administration was significantly behind the geopolitical curve in understanding the political trend evolving upon the Korean peninsula in the twenty-first century.

(Postscript: It appears that an important first step toward creating a peaceful Korean peninsula has finally occurred in February 2007. North Korean leader Kim Jong-il has tentatively approved a major agreement to shut-down his nation's primary nuclear reactor at Yongbyon within sixty days. Assistant Secretary of State Christopher Hill had worked for three years to reach this agreement with North Korea. As a result, international inspectors will be allowed back into North Korea to investigate any location in the country for nuclear activity. In return, the U.S., China, Russia, and South Korea will provide an emergency shipment of fuel oil and humanitarian aid. If the agreement is *fully* carried out, the U.S. has committed itself to discussing the ending of its standoff with North Korea. In short, this tentative agreement possibly represents the first *real* attempt to defuse and dilute the geopolitical tensions that have existed between the U.S. and this hard-core and isolated Communist entity since the end of the Korean War in 1953.[10]

It is also important to note the considerable influence that China and its leader, President Hu Jintao, has exercised during these intense negotiations. China, without a doubt, played *the* key role in finally getting North Korea back to the negotiating table, and getting this agreement hammered out and acceptable to all parties. John Bolton, the former U.S. representative at the U.N., and a political hard-liner during his time in the Bush administration, bitterly denounced the agreement because it sent the wrong message to other countries who act badly in world affairs. Perhaps, the earlier immaturity and simplistic bravado exhibited by several members of the Bush administration in exercising American foreign policy, in Asia and the Middle East, has been replaced by a more measured and mature perspective on the realities confronting the world's only superpower.[11])

The Rising Sun—Stuck in a Geopolitical Box

The Japanese are finding themselves increasingly troubled by regional events that represent uncomfortable scenarios, with limited options or solutions, due to a foreign policy that originates and is often implemented outside their direct control. As expected, there is a growing mood within Japan's elite to create an independent foreign policy that more clearly reflects the country's national interests in its external affairs. Though grateful to the U.S. for providing a protective umbrella during the Cold War, and for American efforts in rebuilding Japan after WWII, most Japanese, today, know this era has passed. And, in 2007, the new threats—North Korea's nuclear weapons program, possible Korean unification, potential Taiwanese independence, and the rise of China—are complicated and extremely important issues for the future security of Japan. Yet many observers in Japan believe that there is a real danger that exists due to U.S. policies within the region; many Japanese feel they might be inadvertently dragged into a military conflagration without their consent or consultation.

Let's consider the following (potential) crises: a) the rise of China, economically and militarily, challenging the regional leadership of an unnerved Japan; b) the prospect of North Korea's creating or using a nuclear weapon, which causes sleepless nights; c) Taiwan deciding to seek true independence from China, and depending on U.S. direct (and Japan's indirect) assistance to stave off a Chinese military response; and d) finally, the real possibility of a unified and powerful Korea situated a 120 miles off their shores, producing mixed and unsettling thoughts due to Japan's brutal occupation of this nation from 1905 until 1945. Japan's occupation of Korea remains controversial, and extraordinarily sensitive; a combination of anger and fear are lying just beneath the public faces of these two powerful nations in Northeast Asia.

Therefore, if one looks upon these real, and potentially destructive, developments within the region, it is not hard to understand the internal stress and the growing chorus of voices demanding a greater degree of autonomy for the nation's foreign policy. These voices for internal reforms—with concern to Japan's relations to the U.S.—are now evident by the stronger public displays of nationalism within the nation. This mixture of fear and anger, directed primarily toward China, represents echoes of the past, the 1920s and 1930s, which can be—if acted upon—a real danger to regional stability during the first decade of the twenty-first century.

One of the most public voices concerning Japan's taking a harder line with the U.S. and exercising a greater degree of autonomy is the outspoken governor of Tokyo, Shintaro Ishihara, who wrote a controversial best seller in 1989 called, *The Japan That Can Say 'NO'*.[12] His voice was once feared within the ranks of Japanese politics, because many felt he wanted to be prime minister and take Japan down the road of militarism again. Though elected to the Japanese Diet (he resigned in 1995) and as governor of Tokyo in 1999—a position he still holds—Ishihara never became prime minister. However, his beliefs and sentiments concerning Japan's role in Asia, and its relations with the U.S., were clearly evident in the sudden shake-up of Prime Minister Junichiro Koizumi's cabinet in 2005.[13]

Prime Minister Koizumi's appointment of Taro Aso, as Japan's new foreign minister, had an immediate effect within Northeast Asia. Aso caused a significant stir, particularly within South Korea, when he insisted that Koreans had adopted Japanese names willingly during Japan's occupation from 1910 to 1945. Koizumi also chose Shinzo Abe as his new cabinet chief—as expected, Abe succeeded Koizumi as Japan's prime minister in

2006. Abe also created quite a stir because he refused to say that Japan's defeat in WWII was regrettable.[14] It appears that Ishihara's aggressive and nationalistic utterances, in the 1990s, are now reemerging within the mainstream of Japanese politics. Thus, one must ask, what does this mean for the future of Japan? And how do their Asian neighbors judge such controversial opinions or views by such high-profiled individuals within the Japanese government?

Eugene Matthews, a senior fellow at the Council on Foreign Relations, in 2003, wrote that "a little healthy nationalism may be just what Japan, with its faltering economy, needs most."[15] Matthews, however, does acknowledge that the recent diplomatic language of the Japanese government has become more aggressive and nationalistic, particularly with concern to North Korea and its nuclear weapons program. Shigeru Ishiba, Japan's defense minister, has issued a direct warning to North Korea concerning a possible preemptive strike—if Japan felt its immediate security was threatened. Matthews writes, "Not long ago, such comments would have been unthinkable outside the extreme right-wing of Japan's political discourse. Today, however, this kind of language is becoming more and more common."[16]

History has shown over and over again that unbridled nationalism can easily lead to expansionism and militarism overseas, and instability and upheaval at home. The American, French, Japanese, Chinese, and Russian nationalistic surges, during their respective histories, are specific examples of what can happen when fervent nationalism runs amuck—in terms of death, destruction, and violence. In short, a nation's leaders must exercise caution when stirring up the nationalistic pot. What you may have intended to conceive or develop, if history is our barometer, is often quite different from what you actually achieve.

ENVIRONMENT: MOTHER NATURE'S REVENGE?

All one hears about these days are trade, profits, growth, and rising standards of living. Yes, it's true that millions are rising up from poverty and heading toward that undefined but, nevertheless, sought-after middle-class status in their respective countries throughout Asia. The supporters of globalization, particularly those in the West, and their basic mission of turning the world into one giant big-box store (i.e., Wal-Mart) are ecstatic. Yet the more mature, sober, and less-emotional observers are asking disturbing questions about the future of such a venture. It appears the one unavoidable link in this chain of success throughout Asia is the natural environment—including oil, gas, and freshwater. Many global experts and students of such matters agree that there are simply not enough natural resources to go around. Thus, the fundamental and unavoidable question becomes, simultaneously, simple and terrifying: Who gets the natural resources of this world?

Some observers point toward the eventuality of a great-power conflict in Asia. Others indicate that a compromise of sorts will be created to avoid a major military confrontation over such materials. America and China are, of course, often linked together in these potentially dangerous scenarios. Yet what about the smaller Asian powers who are pushed to the periphery of the grand chessboard called global politics? How will they respond? It is hard to believe that they will accept their permanent second-class (maybe, even Third World) status willingly and without resistance. Globalization, even with its recognized flaws, has undeniably lifted hundreds of millions of people out of abject poverty.

What happens when these individuals discover that their newly acquired lifestyles represent just a mere moment of economic bliss? How long do you think it will take for instability, perhaps rioting, to occur due to the fact that their respective national governments simply could not obtain the necessary natural resources to maintain their current living standards? Would it be too radical to say that anarchy would soon occur in these countries? These potential political and social dilemmas represent frightening and troubling questions for those who seek global peace and stability in the twenty-first century. Thus, I believe, it is absolutely imperative that the world's most powerful nations must construct a resource-sharing plan. I simply do not believe tens of millions of people will passively and willingly accept abject poverty again, today, after experiencing just a taste of First World economic prosperity (i.e., improved housing, food, clothing, technology, and leisure time). A failure to meet these expectations will have massive ramifications for any leader or nation.

According to Michael T. Klare, presently the Five College Professor of Peace and World Security Studies at Hampshire College, who has written extensively on the potential conflict associated with the diminishing amount of crucial resources (oil, gas, and water, specifically) in our world today, we have arrived at a crucial point in human history.[17] Klare is unequivocal on the growing dangers associated with growing global demand and the ability of regions, or nations, having direct access to these irreplaceable natural resources (i.e., oil, gas, and water). He describes in his work the real threat, in the near term, to the present economic stability in Asia—both in the developed and developing countries alike.[18] It's becoming increasingly clear that access to these limited natural resources is emerging as the primary concern for countries within the East Asian hemisphere.

For instance, on the matter of water, I would like to examine briefly the disturbing situation developing in Australia. Though a case can certainly be made for China's water problems, I will focus upon them later on in this section when I examine the fast-approaching oil and gas challenges in Asia.

The developing water crisis within Australia, particularly for two of its major cities—Sydney and Perth—is one of great concern for a nation who has experienced fifteen years of steady economic growth and prosperity. Some could say that Australians are witnessing a form of environmental or weather shifting that is perfectly natural but unstoppable, though man's influence can not be discounted. Therefore, the declining levels of annual rainfall, the lowering of water levels in their respective dams and groundwater systems, and a continued and growing need for water have created a high level of anxiety and concern for the short-term economic futures of both cities.[19] Thus, both of these state capitals, one in the west and the other in the east, are facing a similar threat to their future viability. Simply put, the ebbs and flows of Mother Nature can indeed have a devastating effect upon a nation's economic fortunes.

Specifically, Australia's future economic prosperity might well evaporate along with the current freshwater supplies for Sydney and Perth. In 2005, Dr. Tim Flannery, author of the highly acclaimed book, *The Weather Makers*, and a widely published public intellectual on environmental and scientific matters, wrote that the current water shortage for both major cities may be just a prelude of future calamities for Australia, and other parts of the world, if some serious thought is not conducted on how to reallocate, create, and better preserve this diminishing resource.[20] Without fear, nor favor, the goddess of the natural world is bringing an unprecedented crisis to the Land Down Under. Australia might, if serious ideas and solutions are not discussed and developed, represent an example of how a nation's economic viability is jeopardized due to a lack of imagination and commitment toward confronting an immense challenge that is irrepressible and unrelenting. Hence, the acute shortage of freshwater is forcing Australians to face its aquatic shortcomings. In fact, Australia might well be *the* test case on how a developed nation deals with one of the fundamental natural resource questions confronting all global citizens and nations in the twenty-first century—maintaining access to freshwater.

Finally, I believe it's necessary to talk about oil, and the potential chaos and turmoil that this finite natural resource could cause amongst the major economic and military powers in the relative near future. Of course, for the purpose of this book, and due to the current geopolitical situation in East Asia, I think its proper to exam the oil situations in the U.S. and China. Professor Klare's book, *Blood and Oil*, and Lutz Kleveman's book, *The New Great Game: Blood and Oil in Central Asia*, both focus on the potential for military conflict amongst the major powers over their accessibility to oil, which maintains their (perceived entitlement?) economic and lifestyle expectations. Klare's book provides statistical graphs indicating the dramatic future rise in American and Chinese oil consumption by the year 2020.[21] However, Klare's research also indicates that both countries will become increasingly dependent upon foreign sources of oil, while their domestic production will remain either stagnant, or will steadily decline during the period—2000 to 2020.[22]

Kleveman's book focuses upon the importance of Central Asia, particularly the Caspian Sea, for all the industrialized countries in the world, and how the competition for the gas and oil that lies in this region represents a potentially dangerous situation. He titled his chapter on China, "The Waking Giant," and this seems quite appropriate. Kleveman, an American-based journalist—born in Germany—who studied at the London School of Economics and has written for *Newsweek*, CNN, *Der Spiegel*, and the *Independent*, provides a quality overview of the potential conflicts that could originate in a region ("Eurasia") that has often been described as one of the most important landmasses in the world. The famous British geographer, Halford Mackinder, author of the famous essay, "The Geographical Pivot of History," in 1904, stated with absolute certainty the future and long-term geopolitical importance of this massive landmass that stretched from Europe to Asia—"the conception of Euro-Asia."[23]

In essence, Mackinder believed that whatever nation or nations were able to control this key and strategic region would become *the* dominant power in world affairs.[24] Ironically, just over a hundred years later, due to the world's desperate search for oil and gas, Eurasia has once again gained center stage, but perhaps for all the wrong reasons. Kleveman's last section of his book, "Angry Young Men: An Epilogue," deals with the potential for conflict in the region between the U.S., Russia, and China. He believes the competition for oil and gas does not have to end in conflict between any of the major parties. However, according to the author, who has traveled extensively throughout the region, the new "Great Game" for Eurasia is one fraught with danger due to first, America's bloody and destructive war in Iraq and second, America's insatiable appetite for oil—especially for their SUVs.[25] In a real sense, both of these factors represent scorpions caught in a nationalistic bottle—one representing American foreign policy directed toward energy acquisition (associated with terrorism), and the other representing a combination of American cultural vanity and the reckless wasting of fossil fuels. Tragically, both of these dangerous practices may inadvertently end up destroying America's influence and stature as the world's lone superpower.

EAST ASIA SUMMIT: A NEW DIRECTION FOR ASIA?

On 14 December 2005, America and the West might have witnessed a historical epoch in East Asian history. The location of this potential historical transformation was Kuala Lumpur, Malaysia. The first East Asia Summit

(EAS) took place—sixteen nations participated, and the United States and most of the West were not invited. Thus, the ten members of ASEAN and six other nations within the scope of the East Asian hemisphere attended the inaugural meeting.[26] This meeting, though undefined in its real meaning or significance to Asia and the West, in and of itself, represents a new confidence and desire amongst Asian nations to exercise and solidify their economic and regional power in a world that is increasingly balkanized into regional blocs. Siddharth Varadarajan wrote in the Indian newspaper, the *Hindu,*

> Despite the onset of the World Trade Organization with its emphasis on "most favored nation" status, there has been an explosion in preferential trading areas (PTAs) around the world. Asia has its share of bilateral PTAs, but there is nothing at the multilateral level to match what Europe, North America, and South America have done. At the same time, intra-Asian trade has risen dramatically.[27]

Initial comments concerning the significance of the first EAS meeting were guarded, but revelatory. John Howard, Australia's prime minister since 1996, stated, "The symbolism of the first meeting is very important. We'll clearly talk about issues that affect the region, we'll talk about the threat of pandemics, we'll talk about terrorism, we'll talk about economic issues."[28] Howard also said, "I see the East Asia Summit as an important development. (However,) I certainly don't see it replacing the premier role of APEC."[29] Observers of the region acknowledge the first EAS as the brainchild of former Malaysian leader Mahathir Mohamed, who originally did not want any non-Asian countries to participate, especially Australia. He sees Australia as America's "Deputy Sheriff" in the region, and that Australia's views are in reality, de facto, America's views. Mahathir was overruled by ASEAN members.

However, Australia's presence was not the only problem emerging before the EAS meeting in late December 2005. Of course, China and Japan took swipes at each other over the participation of Australia, New Zealand, and India at the first summit. China's official government newspaper, *People's Daily,* stated, "ASEAN diplomats believe Japan is trying to drag countries outside this region such as Australia and India into the community to serve as a counter-balance to China."[30] The state-controlled paper also speculated upon an unspoken alliance emerging at the EAS meeting: "Analysts say, Japan would most probably dish out the 'human rights' issue and draw in the United States, New Zealand, and Australia to build up U.S., Japan-centered Western dominance."[31] Obviously, the Chinese leadership, like former Malaysian Prime Minister Mahathir, looked upon non-Asian participants as being part of a greater effort to dilute (or contain) the potential power of this new organization. And China, without a doubt, saw its own influence diminished by the presence of non-Asian countries and India.

Japan, without the usual diplomatic ambiguity or subtlety of language, took an aggressive position concerning its own role at the EAS conference. Taro Aso, Japan's current foreign minister, described Japan as Asia's "thought leader."[32] In essence, Aso asserted (arrogantly?) that this was Japan's destiny within the parameters of this organization: "A thought leader is one who through fate is forced to face up against some sort of very difficult issue earlier than others."[33] And, finally, if destiny wasn't a strong enough argument for the Japanese delegation at the first EAS meeting, then the foreign minister reminded his Asian counterparts that it was Japan who provided $21 billion to assist them during the darkest days of the 1997–1998 financial meltdown—even though Japan was suffering from its own financial woes.[34]

The U.S. government did not react to this upcoming inaugural EAS meeting with institutional disregard, or regional indifference. In fact, there was a concerted push to ensure access, or full participation, at the EAS being available to all nations who sought it. In February 2005, UPI editor and journalist Martin Walker wrote that U.S. Secretary of State Condolezza Rice commented to Singapore Foreign Minister George Yeo, "The East Asia summit should be open to any country that wants to join."[35] In March, Secretary Rice stated, during her visits to Japan and South Korea, that the Bush administration expected its longtime allies to fully support their (U.S.) desire in creating an open East Asian system. On a subsequent trip to India, Rice also expressed the Bush administration's determination "to help India become a world power."[36]

What does this mean for America and its future in the region? It means that the U.S. government is taking quite seriously that the EAS could quite possibly manifest itself into a real challenge to U.S. hegemony throughout the Pacific Rim in the twenty-first century. Neil Francis, a fellow at the Weatherhead Center for International Affairs at Harvard University, believes the potential creation of an East Asian union represents a significant development on many levels. First, the sixteen EAS participants would possess approximately 60 percent of the global population, and have a combined GDP greater than the European Union. Secondly, such a union could constructively ameliorate the present-day Sino-Japanese tensions. In turn, such a result could enable the Asia-Pacific Rim to fundamentally redesign and transform the existing post-WWII American hegemonic framework into a new *regional collective* that would represent increased economic, political, and military autonomy and independence.[37]

Therefore, not unexpectedly, America is asserting its present-day influence and power to undercut any attempt to isolate it from the conference rooms and economic summits throughout East Asia that may create a new *Asia*-oriented agenda for the region without proper regard, or respect, for U.S. considerations or input. Martin Walker writes, "However far this burgeoning friendship between the United States and India is to go, it is clear that Washington, Tokyo and New Delhi all seem to agree on one thing; that the future of Asia is far too important to be left to the East Asians alone."[38] Yet America's influence is in relative decline due to the steady economic ascendance of China, South Korea, India, a (slowly) resurgent Japan, and the Asia-Pacific region overall.

It was however noted in an article published by the Yale Center for the Study of Globalization and written by journalist Daniel Sneider, foreign affairs columnist for the *Mercury News* and a Pantech fellow at Stanford's Shorenstein Asia Pacific Research Center, that President Bush's foray throughout Northeast Asia, in November 2005, encountered a new and profound regional trend that the U.S. will have to contend with in the very near future:

> Beneath the polite appearance, however, there is no less a challenge to American leadership in Asia. While Washington fiddled, a powerful momentum has been building up in Asia toward the formation of an East Asian Free Trade Area or, more ambitiously, an East Asian Community, modeled on the European Community. Led by China, the East Asian grouping pointedly excludes the United States.[39]

This emerging trend, though a surprise for many Americans, actually represents a natural progression of development for many longtime observers of Asia. In 1995, for instance, Chalmers Johnson, founding president of the Japan Policy Research Institute and professor emeritus of political science at the University of California, Berkeley and San Diego campuses, wrote that after the end of the Cold War in 1991, three global trends emerged without question—one of them being regional economic integration. In 1960, the Asian economies represented perhaps only 4 percent of global production. However, by 1990, Asia's economic prowess is now in the neighborhood of 25 percent. And, if current trends of economic development continue until 2000, Asian economies may possess up to 33 percent of world productivity.[40]

In 1995, Professor Johnson had surmised that the "most important fact about the post-Cold War Asia-Pacific region is Japan's growing economic dominance, and the degree to which this is causing integration among the nations of the region."[41] Though Johnson had stressed the crucial economic role of Japan, in 1995, he did not dismiss the future role of China. The author states,

> The second major issue affecting the future of Asia is the deeply destabilizing effects on all the Southeast Asian nations of even the idea of "Greater China"— of China as a civilization rather than just a country—not to speak of any moves that might be made toward achieving its reality . . . In most parts of Southeast Asia, with the possible exception of Thailand, where the Chinese have been

assimilated more than elsewhere, the presence, and success, of the Chinese creates significant political problems. This is why it is in the interest of the Pacific countries, including Japan, to curb China's overseas claims.[42]

Sean Randolph, president and CEO of the Bay Area Economic Forum and former staff member in the U.S. Congress, wrote, in 2003, "In a global economy characterized by slow growth at best, Asia will once again outperform all other regions in 2003."[43] Randolph, who has held various economic and Asian policy positions at the U.S. State Department and at the White House, believes that one of the reasons for the region's continued success is due to one important commonality amongst Asian economies—there is a new emphasis on the development of domestic markets. Thus, this internalized focus by Asia, domestically and regionally, reduces the region's necessity of relying upon exports to Western markets for maintaining its economic prosperity.[44] The author, like Professor Johnson, sees China's emergence having a profound effect upon the region—economically, militarily, and politically. He writes, speculatively, "If current trends continue, and China can avoid economic and political instability, it is likely in the next decade to emerge as a key player in both the global and regional economies, with political influence to match."[45]

I believe one more factor should be addressed concerning the Pacific Rim when determining what might happen as the twenty-first century unfolds—nationalism. It is on the rise throughout Asia—and many analysts are worried that it could lead to the type of destruction (human and material) experienced and witnessed in the region during the 1930s and 1940s. It is no small matter, indeed. Journalist Victor Mallet, in July 2005, wrote in the globally respected *Financial Times*, "Even in peacetime, nationalism in East Asia is not an abstract concept but a matter of flesh and blood."[46] What are the roots of this noticeable rise in nationalistic fervor, particularly in northeastern Asia? Mallet points to the difficult relations between China and Japan. There is South Korea desiring a larger role in this particular region. And, finally, the continued pursuit by Japan in gaining a permanent seat upon the U.N. Security Council has the Chinese and Koreans worked into an emotional frenzy.

Akihiko Tanaka, a politics professor and director of the Institute of Oriental Culture at Tokyo University, writes about the "vicious cycle of nationalism and counter-nationalism" that represents a real threat to regional peace and stability. Professor Tanaka points to two primary reasons for the rise in nationalism in Northeast Asia.[47] First, China does not see itself as being historically "whole" due to Taiwan's periodic pronouncements of achieving independence in the near future, and the Korean peninsula remains a relic of the Cold War, being divided along the thirty-eighth parallel. Finally, the end of the Cold War has provided an opportunity for countries, such as China and Japan, to release some pent-up nationalistic energy that has been bottled up for nearly fifty years.[48] Tanaka indicates that the recent historical transition from the tense-filled years of the Cold War to an era that remains undefined has created—in a sense—a sort of cultural and political vacuum in Asia. Professor Tanaka explains, "During the Cold War there was a clear split . . . there was a balance of power. Now it's over, there is an imbalance of power. The factors comprising nations—people, ethnic groups, religion and so on—all those became apparent."[49]

In short, after the Cold War, the people and nations of East Asia rediscovered their *history*, and a passionate desire emerged to create a new future for the region. Perhaps, in the relatively near future the West will look upon the East Asia Summit, which occurred in December 2005, as an irrefutable historical "tipping point." In short, Asia-Pacific is in the process of shedding the last vestiges of humiliating Western colonialism, such as economically exploitative treaty ports, the forced signings of "unequal treaties," the ravages of imperial wars, the nuclear shadow cast over the region during the Cold War, and finally the dominance of globalization imposed upon them by institutions created in the West.

Perhaps, in its final form, a new road map—economically and politically—will be collectively constructed, designed, and implemented by all Asian governments. Perhaps, such a "road map" will ultimately establish a new era in East Asia—and in the process reestablish the region's rightful place in global affairs.

HALFORD J. MACKINDER AND THE ASIA-PACIFIC RIM IN THE TWENTY-FIRST CENTURY

By an ironic twist of fate, geography, history, and Halford J. Mackinder's "heartland" thesis are in play again—specifically, in East Asia and the Pacific Rim. However, I am tweaking Mackinder's primary argument of the importance of Eurasia (the "pivot area") and its role in achieving global dominance—that was expounded before a small audience on a cold winter night, in London, England, at the Royal Geographical Society in 1904.[50] In 2007, and for the next twenty-five years in the twenty-first century, it is my belief that there will be a new heartland emerging in the world. Accordingly, in 2007, Mackinder's heartland, in my opinion, will no longer be located in East-Central Europe, Central Asia, and Russia, but instead will be situated further east and south, primarily Central Asia, East Asia, and South Asia, and will include several of the Pacific Rim nations as well.

This new "pivot area" will be situated between Siberia Russia in the north and the Northern Territory of Australia in the south, and from the recently created "-stan" countries in Central Asia to Taiwan on the eastern side of the

Taiwan Straits. Within this new geographical paradigm, the following factors are present: 1) It has most of the world's largest and fastest-growing economies; 2) the "Asia-Pacific Rim" workforce represents some of the hardest-working and most educated people in the world; and 3) finally, the Asia-Pacific Rim's energy future, particularly within Central Asia, is globally acknowledged and quantified by oil and gas experts—which makes this new pivot area a potential economic dynamo for decades to come during the twenty-first century.

Henceforth, whichever nation or nations emerge on top—within this new pivotal heartland—will dominate the world economically, perhaps even militarily, during the twenty-first century. And the U.S. is part of this geodrama, because it has an extensive and extended military presence throughout the region. Though America is not considered an *Asian* nation, it is a *Pacific Rim* power without a doubt.

Mackinder's original thesis is still respected and defined in modern-day geopolitical literature by foreign policy mavens like Zbigniew Brzezinski, President Jimmy Carter's national security advisor from 1977 to 1981, whose book, *Grand Chessboard*, published in 1998, focused upon Eurasia's heartland as still representing the key "chessboard" in the world's geopolitical affairs.[51] You could say, to some degree, our current and increasingly disastrous wars in Iraq and Afghanistan represent irrefutable evidence that American foreign policy continues to reflect Mackinder's thesis. His geopolitical stratagem, "Who rules the heartland commands the World Island; Who rules the World Island commands the World,"[52] could legitimately be used to explain the American military presence in the Middle East (a part of Mackinder's "pivot area")—the heartland of the world's future energy supply. However, there is increasing evidence that points to the East Asian hemisphere and the Pacific Rim as, perhaps, the new paradigm in global affairs as the twenty-first century unfolds.

Chalmers Johnson, a former professor of Asian history at the University of California–San Diego and CIA analyst, has written about the present-day global presence and power of the American empire, and the number of U.S. military installations (725) situated throughout the world. In his book, *The Sorrows of Empire*, he focuses upon the one region that has recently received intense attention from the American government—the former Soviet states: Azerbaijan, Kazakhstan, and Turkmenistan. The dissolution of the Soviet Union, in 1991, has initiated new American efforts to develop (dominate?) the region's energy sources. According Professor Johnson, "The modern race to control the oil and gas resources of the region has begun. It was led by American-based multinational oil companies, soon to be followed by the U.S. military in one of its more traditional and well-established roles: protector of private capitalist interests."[53]

Johnson's work describes the oil and gas deposits within these three republics as being significant for future global energy needs. Interestingly, the scientific sources he uses to support his thesis concerning this region are the U.S. Department of Energy and the infamous *Cheney Report* (put together from secret talks with energy companies in 2001). For instance, Azerbaijan and Kazakhstan are considered to have proven oil reserves equal to the oil findings in the North Sea.[54] And Turkmenistan is considered to have the eighth largest gas reserves in the world.[55] Finally, but not surprisingly, the U.S. has already built their largest (named Chief Peter J. Ganci, Jr.) military garrison at Manas, Kyrgyzstan—which is located in the eastern part of the former Soviet "–stan" territory, to go along with their other two air bases at Bagram and Mazar-i-Sharif, located in northeastern Afghanistan. These air bases are also situated relatively close to China's western frontier.[56] I believe these bases are not just there for controlling the region's energy sources, but to "softly" contain any expansionist impulses the Chinese may entertain for Central Asia in the future.

In terms of economic prowess, East Asia and the Pacific Rim are certainly becoming more prominent, if not dominant in several manufacturing sectors. And, of course, China appears to be the primary economic locomotive for Asia-Pacific economic growth for at least the next decade, with Japan and South Korea remaining major forces in finance, trade, and manufacturing. In Southeast Asia, Singapore, Indonesia, and Australia will also play crucial economic roles in Asia-Pacific, and their efforts toward maintaining security—patrolling sea lanes, maintaining port security, focusing on terrorist preemption activities, and enhancing overall regional stability—will be absolutely imperative if Asia-Pacific is to continue to grow economically, and construct a higher profile in global affairs.

It is estimated that the *Pacific Rim* is home to an estimated 30 percent of the world's population and 20 percent of global (GNP) gross national product. These figures represent almost all the Asian nations that border the Pacific Ocean, or are lumped into this region by their geographical proximity, except Russia (Siberia). Thus, this territory extends from China in the north to Australia in the south, from Myanmar in the west to New Zealand in the east. It is a region with a stunning degree of cultural and ethnic diversity and interconnectedness. Dean Collinwood's book, *Japan and the Pacific Rim*, indicates there are twenty-one countries or administrative entities along or near the Asian side of the Pacific Ocean, plus an almost uncountable number of islands throughout the largest body of water on earth.[57]

Thus, I believe the core of this new global *heartland*—the Asia-Pacific Rim region—will represent the vortex of global affairs during the twenty-first century. Its extraordinary economic growth, since the end of WWII, is greatly due to its dedicated, educated, and energetic workforce, and to its strategic and centrally (government) directed economic policies. Finally, the region's relatively untapped energy, which includes the Caspian Sea region and western China, makes this area potentially an even more intimidating juggernaut, economically and politically. If development continues at its current pace, the Asia-Pacific Rim region will certainly be positioned to challenge and compete with NAFTA (North American Free Trade Area) and the EU (European Union) for global economic primacy. Presently, the major economic locomotives pulling the region toward development and prosperity are China, Japan, and the "Asian Tigers" (South Korea, Taiwan, and Singapore).

However, according to Kent Calder, director of the Reischauer Center for East Asian Studies at SAIS–Johns Hopkins University, the future relations between China and Japan represent the key factor in Asia-Pacific's continued ascendance. These two Asian powerhouses represent approximately 75 percent of the region's economic activity. They also represent half of the region's total expenditures for military hardware. Hence, Professor Calder positions himself in the "realist" camp when it comes to defining the future implications between these two behemoths. His China-Japan analysis sees danger for America and the world, due to a significant degree of *bad* history existing between the two nations since the late nineteenth century. And, presently, there are serious regional hegemonic, military, and energy challenges confronting them both during the opening decades of the twenty-first century.[58] Calder also points out how the potential flashpoints—the Taiwan Strait and the Korean peninsula—represent very different kinds of geopolitical challenges and threats to China and Japan, respectively.[59]

China's stature, within the Pacific Rim, would benefit greatly *if* Taiwan reunited with the Chinese mainland, and if North and South Korean unification became a reality as well. Thus, China's hegemonic status in the region, already being the number one trade partner for Taiwan, Japan, and both Koreas, would certainly rise to a new level of recognition. Japan, on the other hand, would suddenly find itself confronted with two powerful neighbors (China and Korea), economically and militarily, in Northeast Asia. Japan would also have to acknowledge (at least, privately) that China's influence has expanded, and, perhaps, will someday eclipse its own in shaping Asia-Pacific affairs. This real potentiality has not gone down well in Tokyo.[60] Professor Zbigniew Brzezinski, author of *The Choice: Global Domination or Global Leadership*, sees China's rise to political supremacy in Asia as inevitable. He stated, in 2007, during an interview, "China will become the political leader in East Asia in the near future—in a decade or so."[61]

This new reality is emerging already in conjunction with the search for oil and gas in the East China Sea (Chunxiao gas fields) between China and Okinawa (Japan), which has already sparked an intense debate about the issue of sovereignty—and who owns what part of the East China continental shelf. Military activity, particularly by the Chinese, though presently minis-cule, only heightens the nationalistic emotions in both nations.[62] Due to these potential and real developments, Calder believes the U.S. can still be the "essential power" in Asia, by stabilizing the relations between China and Japan. Maintaining constructive and functional relations between these two Asian powers will help not only America, but the world at large.[63]

Yet there are other "realists" who have also examined China closely, and have come away less than enthralled by the future prospect of its becom-ing a major Asian power. Internally, these critics have pointed out that China has profound weaknesses, institutionally and structurally, which could seriously undermine their stunning growth levels and plunge the country into chaos and create a significant degree of instability throughout the Pacific Rim. Minxin Pei, a senior associate and director of the China Program at the Carnegie Endowment for International Peace, is not one of those overwhelmed or overly impressed by China's "economic miracle." Professor Pei exposes severe flaws within China's economic and govern-mental structures, and states, "China may be rising, but no one really knows whether it can fly."[64]

The reasons for skepticism, stated by Professor Pei, are persuasive and substantial concerning China's future development. First, the nation's banking system is simply overwhelmed by the influx of foreign invest-ment into the country, and its domestic financial situation is a profit killer as well. Approximately 30 percent of China's current GDP is being ab-sorbed by a banking system drowning in nonperforming loans ("bad pa-per"). Some China observers, such as Dr. Pei, believe the financial system itself may suddenly implode due to the structural fragility of China's fis-cal house.[65] Despite this fundamental weakness within China's financial structure, there continue to be literally hundreds of journal, magazine, and newspaper articles, and dozens of television stories and documen-taries, every month, praising China's stunning financial ascendance. Yet there is substantive evidence that clearly indicates that international in-vestors are actually getting a much greater return on their investments in India, rather than in China.[66] This bit of interesting and valuable knowl-edge is not widely known by the general public, or perhaps even by in-vestors themselves.

Also, the nature of China's command economy makes it less transparent, and its methodology of doing business is often not accessible to outside scrutiny, as some economic investors and observers would prefer. In fact, Lester Thurow, the widely read and globally respected economist at MIT, has written that he thinks China's annual growth figures are fudged a bit. Thurow believes that those 9 percent, or 10 percent, annual growth figures that catch the attention of financial analysts throughout the world simply don't hold up upon closer scrutiny. What is the basis of his argument?

First, Professor Thurow strongly implies that there is a certain degree of deception to the national process of data collection, because "China has a bottom-up reporting system and a top-down promotion system."[67] In short, Beijing hands out promotions based upon good economic numbers—and Thurow states the local leaders know this before they send their economic reports to the national government. Secondly, he questions the "statistical consistency" and quantification of data by the Chinese government itself. Thurow refutes the Chinese government's sparkling statistical declarations by applying statistical logic, and, thus, using it to examine the reality of China's urban and rural income development rates:

> China admits that there has been little or no growth in the countryside in the last 15 years. A total of 70 percent of Chinese citizens live in the countryside. Do a little simple algebra. If a country grows at 10 percent and 70 percent of its citizens do not enjoy any growth, how fast do the incomes of the other 30 percent have to grow? The answer is 32 percent. Shanghai and other Chinese cities are growing rapidly, but they are not growing 32 percent a year.[68]

Thurow's analysis appears to quantitatively refute the media hype and hysteria concerning China's overall economic development. Professor Pei also points out in his own article that the "wealth gap" is enormous in China. The top 1 percent of Chinese families control more than 60 percent of the nation's wealth (compared to 5 percent in the U.S.). And the Beijing government controls approximately 38 percent of Chinese GDP.[69] Obviously, one can clearly see that China's economic wealth is not equitably distributed, nor has it promoted political pluralism within the Middle Kingdom.

Nevertheless, China's stunning growth over the past quarter century has had a profound effect upon its regional and global standing. Allan Behm, a strategic analyst and former senior Australian defense department official, stated, "(China) has the world's largest and most dynamic population coming into its own as an economic, political and strategic force."[70] Behm is not wrong, but neither is Thurow or Pei. Hence, the question asks itself—Can China continue to grow, at its present rate, if significant *individual* and *provincial* economic imbalances remain unaddressed by the central government? Not likely, because the common worker and the local governments in the poorer regions of China, will want substantive evidence that the national government is committed to their betterment. In short, workers will expect better pay, and local governments will demand substantial investment into their local communities by the national government.

Those *imbalances*, mentioned above, will only be exacerbated because there is emerging qualitative evidence that indicates China's current rate of economic growth will not be sustained during the next couple of years, according to the World Bank. China experienced 10.4 percent growth in 2006, but this could quite possibly drop to 8.7 percent by 2008. The primary reasons for the approximately 20 percent decline in annual growth, according to the Associated Press story, is due to "high investment rates and excess capacity in several sectors dominated by state-owned enterprises [that] leave open the possibility of a sharp decline in investment."[71] If this momentary economic decline evolves into a lengthy trend, China's well-being and Asia-Pacific's future stability may be tested sooner than anticipated.

In the final analysis, America, Australia, China, Japan, South Korea, and the other national entities throughout the Asia-Pacific Rim are now standing at the proverbial crossroads in the twenty-first century. Their future economic prosperity and security will be achieved only if there is a serious collective effort by the major powers within the region. However, the key question remains unanswered at this time—can this vast region consisting of multiple cultures, ethnicities, languages, and political ideologies find enough common ground to continue its global ascendance in the twenty-first century? What will it be—Pearl Harbor or peace?

The next twenty-five years will determine whether the Asia-Pacific Rim finally emerges, as predicted by many analysts and scholars, as the new economic-military axis in global affairs. Or will this period of history, as some suspect, be remembered for the lost opportunities toward creating a greater peace and prosperity throughout the region? America, Australia, China, Japan, and South Korea will certainly play key roles in the region's destiny. But, I believe, America and China have a golden opportunity to redirect history and, perhaps, establish a new historical path that will permit both nations to coexist and provide visionary leadership, economically and militarily, within the Asia-Pacific Rim region. Therefore, despite credible historical evidence to the contrary, I simply do not believe, at this time, that the bloody and destructive hegemonic wars of yesteryear represent the inevitable fate of America and China in the twenty-first century.

NOTES

1. David Rothkopk, *Running the World: The Inside Story of the National Security Council and the Architects of American Power* (New York: Public Affairs, 2005), Chapter 13.

2. Ibid.

3. British Prime Minister Tony Blair's final press conference in 2005. I saw this event on C-SPAN on 26 December.

4. Interview with Robert Sutter, 28 December 2006.

5. Ibid.

6. Dean W. Collinwood, *Japan and the Pacific Rim* (Dubuque, IA: McGraw-Hill/Dushkin, 2006), p. 13.

7. U.S. Government, "U.S. National Security and Strategic Report 2002." This document was retrieved from a U.S. government website, White House.

8. Conversation with Bruce Cumings that took place at the International Conference to Commemorate the fifth anniversary of the 15 June South-North Joint Declaration. The conference was held at the Shilla Hotel in Seoul on 13 June 2005.

9. Conference Program: International Conference to Commemorate the fifth anniversary of the 15 June South-North Joint Declaration. All the individuals mentioned above spoke at the conference, except Mikhail Gorbachev, who sent a taped message.

10. Bill Powell, "North Korea Has Agreed to Shut Down Its Nuclear Program," *Time*, 26 February 2007, pp. 32–33.

11. Ibid.

12. Shintaro Ishihara, *The Japan That Can Say 'No': Why Japan Will Be First among Equals* (New York: Simon & Schuster, 1990).

13. Anthony Faiola, "Tokyo Maverick Just One of the Crowd Now," *Washington Post Foreign Service*, 13 November 2005, p. A20.

14. Ibid.

15. Eugene A. Matthews, "Japan's New Nationalism," *Foreign Affairs*, November/December 2003.

16. Ibid.

17. Michael T. Klare, *Resource Wars: The New Landscape of Global Conflict* (New York: Henry Holt and Company, 2001) and Lutz Kleveman, *Blood and Oil: The Dangers and Consequences of America's Growing Dependency on Imported Petroleum* (New York: Henry Holt and Company, 2004). Both books warn readers of the real dangers for America due to its pursuit of oil throughout the world.

18. Ibid.

19. Tim Flannery, *The Weather Makers: The History & Future Impact of Climate Change* (Melbourne: The Text Publishing Company, 2005), Chapter 13, "Liquid Gold: Changes in Rainfall."

20. Ibid.

21. Klare, *Resource Wars*, pp. 63, 166.

22. Ibid.

23. Halford J. Mackinder, "The Geographical Pivot of History," *The Geographical Journal*, April 1904, Vol. 23. Mackinder was a reader in geography at the University of Oxford.

24. Ibid.

25. Kleveman, *The New Great Game*, pp. 255–64.

26. Parliament of Australia website. Primary sources: Dr. Frank Frost, Analyst and Policy Foreign Affairs, Defense and Trade Section; Ann Rann, Information and E-links Foreign Affairs, Defense and Trade Section.

27. Siddharth Varadarajan, "Asian Interests and the Myth of Balance," *The Hindu*, 27 December 2005, www.zmag.org.

28. ABC Online, "East Asia Summit Won't Replace APEC Role: Howard," 14 December 2005, www.abc.net/au.

29. Ibid.

30. Rich Bowden, "Battle Looms over Inaugural East Asia Summit," *World Press*, Contributing Editor, Sydney, Australia, 11 December 2005.

31. Ibid.

32. Ibid.

33. Ibid.

34. Ibid.

35. Martin Walker, "Walker's World: Battles around New Asia Summit," *The Washington Times*, 2 April 2005.

36. Ibid.

37. Neil Francis, "For an East Asian Union—Rethinking Asia's Cold War Alliances," *Harvard International Review*, Fall 2006, Vol. 28, No. 3, pp. 75–76.

38. Walker, "Walker's World."

39. Daniel Sneider, "Asia's Polite Reception to Bush Masks Declining U.S. Influence: Growing Regional Cooperation Threatens U.S. Preeminence in East Asia," *YaleGlobal* online, 17 November 2005.

40. Chalmers Johnson, "The Empowerment of Asia," *Pacific Rim Report*, October 1995, *Pacific Rim Report* #1.

41. Ibid.

42. Ibid.

43. R. Sean Randolph, "Asia in the World Economy: Globalization, Growth, and the Changing Structure of Trade," *Pacific Rim Report*, May 2003, *Pacific Rim Report* #28;

44. Ibid.

45. Ibid.

46. Victor Mallet, "A Stir in Asia: Nationalism Is on the Rise, Even as the Region's Economies Intertwine," *Financial Times*, 19 July 2005, p. 15.

47. Ibid.

48. Ibid.

49. Ibid.

50. Mackinder, "The Geographical Pivot of History." This famous essay was reprinted in the December 2004 issue of *The Geographical Journal*, Vol. 170, Part 4.

51. Zbigniew Brzezinski, *Grand Chessboard: American Primacy and Its Geostrategic Imperatives* (New York: Basic Books, 1998).

52. *Halford John Mackinder*, Wikipedia, the free encyclopedia.

53. Chalmers Johnson, *The Sorrows of Empire: Militarism, Secrecy, and the End of the Republic* (New York: Henry Holt and Company, 2004), p. 169.

54. Ibid.

55. Ibid.

56. Ibid., pp. 169–71.

57. Collinwood, *Japan and the Pacific Rim*, pp. xiv–1.

58. Kent E. Calder, "China and Japan's Simmering Rivalry," *Foreign Affairs*, March/April 2006, Vol. 85, No. 2, p. 129.

59. Ibid., p. 131.

60. Ibid., pp. 131–32.

61. Interview with Professor Brzezinski, 8 January 2007.

62. Calder, "China and Japan's Simmering Rivalry," pp. 130–31.

63. Ibid., p. 139.

64. Minxin Pei, "The Dark Side of China's Rise," *Foreign Policy*, March/April 2006, p. 40.

65. Ibid., p. 34.

66. Ibid. Professor Pei writes that, between 1999 to 2003, judging from six major industrial sectors (ranging from autos to telecom), Indian companies delivered

rates of return on investment that were 80 percent to 200 percent higher than their Chinese counterparts.

67. Lester Thurow, "China's Statistics Don't Add Up," *The Banker*, 2 August 2004.

68. Ibid.

69. Pei, "The Dark Side of China's Rise," pp. 35, 39.

70. David Lague, "Coming to Terms with China's Ascent," *International Herald Tribune–Asia-Pacific*, 7 November 2005. I retrieved this article from the *International Herald Tribune*'s website. It is one of the better newspapers covering Asia-Pacific.

71. Associated Press (Asia/Pacific), "Economic Growth in China Set to Slow, World Bank Predicts," *The Wall Street Journal*, 14 December 2006, p. A6.

Postscript

My Journey through China, Japan, and South Korea, Spring 2007

I decided to write a postscript to my book because of the lag-time between my finishing the original manuscript and the actual date of publication. To be specific, I finished the writing of this book in March 2007, but the book itself was not to be published until late-August 2007. Thus, this time-gap represented approximately five months. Most individuals would view this timeframe as short and, perhaps, inconsequential. However, in relation to Asia-Pacific and its rapid development and transformation, a five-month gap is enormous. My initial instincts were proven correct, as there has been a torrent of events within the region since the completion of the original manuscript. However, I must warn the reader that this section of the book may be a bit scattered in its presentation of the information I have acquired or witnessed during this time period.

Therefore, what I have decided to do within this postscript is to keep the book as current and relevant as possible for the reader. Hence, I have approached this section of the book with a two-fold objective: First, I wanted to write about the major events that have occurred since March 2007 and second, I wanted to write about my experiences from my journey to China, Japan, and Korea in May–June 2007. I believe both objectives will enhance the book's overall effectiveness in its presentation of the modern complexities and diversity that exist throughout Asia-Pacific.

In March 2007, Australia and Japan signed a new and far-reaching security agreement. It caught the nations of Asia-Pacific by surprise, especially China. Paul Kelly, a senior foreign policy analyst for *The Australian*, the nation's only nationally published newspaper, wrote, "For decades Australia's status in Asia has been defined by its alliance with the U.S. The new test is whether Australia's status in Asia will be defined by security ties with Japan.

For Australia, this is a new and challenging event."[1] Kelly also indicates that Japan is steadily moving toward normalization as a power in the region. As a result, China and South Korea are watching this Japanese progression very carefully and with a sense of wariness.[2]

Dennis Shanahan and Patrick Walters also wrote an article in *The Australian* stating that the Chinese were less than pleased by this security agreement: "The security aspect has aroused the attention of Chinese representatives in Canberra, who have informally expressed concern about the deal's 'lack of transparency.'"[3] As I mentioned in chapter 6, Australia continues to walk the proverbial tightrope in Asia-Pacific between its post-WWII relationships with the U.S. and Japan on one side, and its evolving but cautious relations with the People's Republic of China on the other.

In June 2007, Australian foreign minister Alexander Downer, during a trip to Japan for a four-way meeting of defense ministers and foreign ministers from the two nations, suggested that a new security forum be created concerning northeast Asia. Downer stated, "Australia is interested in the question of the possible evolution of a Northeast Asian security mechanism" that might eventually emerge out of the current six-party discussions that are focused upon North Korea's nuclear program.[4] Thus, as mentioned earlier in the book, Australia continues to assert itself on regional matters by aggressively pursuing a new regional security agenda that will create more peace and stability during the twenty-first century.

In April 2007, Eric Talmadge, a reporter for the *Associated Press*, wrote that the space race in Asia has become more heated, intense, and potentially dangerous than at any time since the end of the Cold War. He points to China's destruction of a satellite in space by a land-based missile, North Korea's testing of a missile near Japan, the Japanese initiating a multimillion dollar spy satellite program, India's preparation for a lunar mission, and Pakistan's promotion of a new and more powerful warhead.[5] China's foreign ministry vigorously denied that the anti-satellite missile test was a threat to the U.S. and that the test itself does not represent a process to militarize space. Christopher Hill, the assistant secretary of state for Asian affairs, believes the Chinese should be more forthcoming about these types of military activities and that increasing transparency with concern to its military budget would be greatly beneficial for increasing the level of trust between the U.S. and China.[6]

Nevertheless, America's subsequent criticism of China's anti-satellite missile test appears somewhat disingenuous, according to an article also published in April 2007, by *The New York Times*. Reporters Michael Gordon and David Cloud uncovered the fact that the U.S. government was clearly aware of China's anti-satellite test, but decided to wait until after its occurrence to respond publicly because it didn't want "to let Beijing know how much the United States knew about its space launching activities."[7] Gordon and Cloud also indicate that three months after China's launching, a debate continues within the Bush administration on whether they were too indecisive in their actions concerning the Chinese and their new space-technology capabilities. The reporters surmised "the events show that the [Bush] administration felt constrained in its dealings with China because of its view that it had little leverage to stop an important Chinese military program."[8]

In the June 4th issue of *Asia Weekly*, the editorial staff answered some pressing questions in their "Focus" section of the magazine concerning China's growing military budget. They point to the U.S. 2006 Quadrennial Defense Review that declared China "the greatest potential military rival to the U.S."[9] A rational-minded individual must ask, How does the U.S. expect China to react to such a declaration within their most important military analytical report? Yet, the editors do acknowledge that China's growing military expenditures "bother Washington," and that the U.S. government "is more concerned that Beijing has yet to explain its motivations for the policy change, and the overwhelming suspicion that China is spending more on defense than it admits."[10]

Professor Noam Chomsky wrote in his bestselling book, *Hegemony or Survival*, that America's current promotion of missile defense "is only a small component of much more ambitious programs for militarization of space, with the intent to achieve a monopoly on the use of space for offensive military purposes."[11] Chomsky also points out that the Chinese are clearly aware of the potential consequences for them if the U.S. acquires an effective missile defense system. Professor Chomsky states directly, "China is well aware that it is a target of the radical nationalists designing policy in Washington, and presumably the prime intended recipient of the message in the National Security Strategy that no potential challenge to U.S. hegemony will be tolerated."[12] In short, America is closely watching the technological developments related to missiles and space in Asia and it is rapidly pursuing a missile defense system that will neutralize any potential advancements (or threats) created within the region.

In late-May 2007, the Pentagon's own annual report to the U.S. Congress also focused on the "China threat". The report indicates that, "while Beijing had maintained its traditional focus on the Taiwan Straits, it also seemed to be looking at projecting its growing military strength beyond the island of Taiwan."[13] The report further states that "analysis of China's military acquisitions and strategic thinking suggests Beijing is also generating capabilities for other regional contingencies, such as conflict over resources or territory."[14] Is a new cold war emerging in East Asia? Probably not, for the time being. However, there is no doubt within the U.S. military establishment that China's evolution as an Asian power is indeed causing serious anxiety and consternation within the hallways of the Pentagon.

Finally, one article published in the *Financial Times*, "Dragon Fleet: China Aims to End the U.S. Navy's Long Pacific Dominance," written by Mure Dickie and Stephen Fidler, gave an in-depth analysis of what is transpiring within China's naval establishment. The Chinese are in the process of building a navy capable of neutralizing the power of the U.S. Navy within the Taiwan Straits.[15] Another article I read on this subject used the Orwellian term "area denial". In short, China hopes to minimize the U.S. Navy's effectiveness and presence if they decide to invade Taiwan. China remains determined to bring all *recognized* Chinese territories under its flag at some point in the future. It's China's potential methodology in achieving this dream that continues to concern its Asia-Pacific neighbors.

Economically, the Chinese juggernaut continues unabated. Its economy grew at a mind-boggling 11.1 percent during the first quarter of 2007. China's real economic growth has averaged more than 10 percent per quarter over the last four years. This astounding growth, according to critics, is due to the Chinese hierarchy being very cautious in their economic decision-making and planning. Hence, China has been able to avoid any unexpected or unwanted economic jolts that could derail its rising prosperity.[16] However, according to Thomas P. M. Barnett, a highly respected geostrategist, the Chinese government must produce over 20 million new jobs every year "to keep this juggernaut moving forward."[17] So far, the Beijing government has basically met the employment needs of its people. But, the question remains—for how long? No one really knows, but perhaps longer than many people believe.

According to the World Trade Organization (WTO), China had surpassed the U.S. as the world's second-largest exporter in the middle of last year! And, if its expected linear economic rise continues, China will overtake Germany in 2008. A twenty-one-page WTO report states that, "China's merchandise trade expansion remained outstandingly strong."[18] It is safe to say that the U.S. is starting to feel the "China pinch" throughout its domestic economy. Its major industries, especially the U.S. auto industry, are under full attack by the economic tsunami emerging from Asia-Pacific. Michigan's auto industry, which has been badly damaged by low sales, inconsistent quality, and intense foreign competition, is fighting for its very existence. Tens of thousands of blue-collar workers and thousands within the management ranks have been laid-off permanently. Yet, the hemorrhaging has not stopped.

Sadly, the Big Three in Detroit continue to experience diminishing sales and continued financial losses, despite their draconian downsizing efforts to turn things around. Unfortunately, the Big Three's collective futures don't appear to be any brighter. China is currently developing its own cars that will compete with U.S. models in the American and Chinese marketplaces within the next couple of years.

The Wall Street Journal published an article in April 2007, which shows that China is in the process of producing quality luxury cars. The Shanghai Automotive Industry Corporation has produced a luxury car called the Roewe 750 that will cost between $30,000 and $36,000. This is $7,000 less than a comparable U.S. model from GM such as the Buick LaCrosse. Overall, car sales have increased 35 percent in China, and Chinese automakers are planning to introduce new models every year.[19] What does this mean for U.S. automakers that have relocated in China?

Recent evidence indicates that their lucrative profits may soon diminish. Already, GM profits are beginning to fall in China—they fell 19 percent in the final quarter of 2006.[20] And in the U.S. market, Japan's Toyota commanded a 17.2 percent market share (up from a 15.8 percent last year) according to their 2007 first quarter figures. Though GM showed a modest increase to 23.5 percent, the Big Three's first quarter (2007) U.S. market share continues to fall, slipping to 51.8 percent from 52.9 percent.[21]

Critics believe that GM has provided China with too much technology concerning car production, and in the near future, Chinese autos, especially eco-cars designed to meet the new environmental standards, will become fully competitive with their U.S. rivals.[22] In the final analysis, due to diminishing profits, increasing competition, and growing Chinese consumer nationalism, it appears that the long-term prospects for U.S. automakers in China may not be as bright, or as promising, as originally believed by auto executives in Detroit a few years ago. Thus, again, the Big Three may discover in the near future that Chinese consumers, like their American counterparts, are simply no longer interested in buying what they are selling.

In May 2007, Craig James, the chief economist for Commsec, stated that China had overtaken Japan as Australia's biggest trade partner. The combined export-import numbers concerning Australian trade for the first quarter of 2007 indicated that at $52.7 billion, China had finally surpassed Japan ($50.6 billion).[23] James commented that "Japan became the manufacturer to the world, particularly of electrical and electronic items, but has now passed that baton to China . . . Japan still draws our iron ore and coal but China has also taken over that principal role from Japan."[24]

Perhaps it is this new economic reality within Asia-Pacific, and increasing competition for markets amongst countries such as Australia, that is causing relations between these two Asian powerhouses to become a bit strained. Chinese scholar Zhang Tuosheng, a researcher with the China Foundation for International and Strategic Studies, writes "it is vital to both countries to seize this opportunity to propel bilateral relations into a new mutually beneficial era."[25]

I believe the future stability of northeast Asia depends upon both nations finding enough common interests to coexist during a period of great change and volatility. Unfortunately, finding common interests may be difficult to achieve. In May 2007, the Japanese Diet took the controversial first step toward revising Japan's pacifist constitution. Article 9, which prohibits war, is one part of Japan's constitution that Japanese Prime Minister Shinzo Abe is particularly interested in rewriting.[26] You can be certain that China and Korea are not amused by this new development.

Some strongly believe, however, that Abe is stoking nationalistic emotions with his efforts to revise the Japanese constitution to boost his sagging popularity in Japan. The latest polls show that the beleaguered prime minister's popularity is at its lowest level since he took office in September 2006.[27] The recent suicide of his farm minister, Toshikatsu Matsuoka, in late May 2007 due to persistent rumors of massive corruption within his ministry, has further eroded the prime minister's credibility with the Japanese populace.[28]

On the issue of trade between Australia and China, it is important to note that the greatest percentage of Aussie exports to the Middle Kingdom involve its natural resources. Thus, it should not come as a surprise that many within the Australian business community remain concerned that only 4 percent of the nation's exports to China are manufactured goods. Conversely, just the opposite trade ratio exists for Chinese exports to the Land Down Under. In short, nearly *all* of China's exports to Australia are manufactured goods. Mark Joiner, an ANZ international economist, believes these economic figures once again show "how closely Australia's trade fortunes were linked to the commodity sector."[29] Yet, it appears that the selling of commodities will remain quite healthy for years to come according to Australian Treasurer Peter Costello: "Booming economies in China and India will keep demand for Australian resources growing at a healthy pace despite increased competition from other mining nations."[30]

It appears then, that Australian Prime Minister Bob Hawke was correct in his judgment in May 1986 when he gave a speech at Nanjing University defining Australia's future relations with China: "For Australia, the development of China is not simply a matter of academic interest. . . . The implications are vital for us because we are, with you, part of the Asia-Pacific region and we have the capability to be a partner in your development."[31] Over twenty years later, Hawke's words appear eerily prophetic.

Interestingly, two recent events have occurred within the Australian government. Both are related to the selling of resource commodities to China. First, the Australian government announced that its 2007–2008 annual defense budget is being increased by 10.6 percent. This spending surge represents the largest annual increase in defense spending by Australia in thirty years. Simply put, Australia is expanding its military capabilities in the Pacific region. Ironically, it is being paid for by Chinese government contracts.[32]

However, there was a troubling development that caught the eye of many Australians. In June 2007, the Dalai Lama will be visiting eight cities in Australia within a ten-day period. Yet, his visit has already created controversy due to the flip-flopping behavior of Australian Labor Party leader Kevin Rudd, who initially refused to meet the religious leader, but quickly changed his stance due to public pressure. Rudd, who may be the next Australian prime minister, appeared weak and vacillating in the eyes of critics and voters. Many believe that Rudd was acknowledging the fact that China does not like foreign representatives meeting the Dalai Lama.

In short, China was strongly influencing the behavior of one of Australia's leading politicians, and perhaps future prime minister. Bob Brown, a prominent federal senator representing the Australian Greens, said, "It was a big mistake. It was a great opportunity for the Opposition Leader to show he was more in tune with Australians but he missed that opportunity—what a pity."[33] It should be noted that in June 2007, Australian Prime Minister John Howard did visit with the Dalai Lama despite loud protestations from the Chinese government. China stated that future relations with Australia could be affected because the Chinese government interpreted the visit by the religious figure as a form of meddling in the domestic affairs of their country. The Howard government denied such accusations.[34]

In the spring of 2007, a grassroots environmental movement emerged with great force within China because the people were "calling for action to address years of industrial pollution."[35] It is believed that China's environmental condition is already approaching apocalyptic proportions, especially due to its burning of coal which provides 70 percent of the nation's power.[36] As a result, there is a major push to develop and promote wind power in China. It is hoped that by 2020, China will be one of the world's largest wind power markets.[37] If China fails, the implications for the rest of the world could become quite serious. Significant amounts of sulfur dioxide and carbon dioxide from China are already traveling across the Pacific, causing acid rain in North America and Europe.[38] Harvard professor John Holdren states, "[China's] dependence on fossil fuels is already causing big problems, such as international tension over access towards oil and gas supply, air pollution, and climate disruption."[39]

CHINA: INTERVIEWS AND OBSERVATIONS

I visited Beijing (11 May–23 May) and Shanghai (23 May–29 May) primarily during my time in China. In my opinion, Beijing has more cultural and historical importance, but Shanghai represents the future—good and bad—for many Chinese. It has become the most important Chinese city, and its history is truly fascinating and intriguing. At the end of my tenure in China, I realized that I had acquired a greater knowledge and respect for this ancient nation. Finally, I left with several impressions and perspectives concerning the Chinese people, my students, and the beautiful cities that I visited for almost three weeks:

1. Population density—Beijing and Shanghai both possess well over 16 million people and growing.
2. Urban planning will become increasingly more important in China's future.
3. It is estimated that Beijing and Shanghai already have 3 million cars apiece, and it is believed that a thousand new cars are added to their daily respective totals. China expects to have 140 million vehicles by 2020.
4. The Chinese still ride approximately 450 million bicycles. However, the major cities are being rebuilt primarily for the use of cars in the twenty-first century. The older generation still tends to ride bikes and the younger generation wants cars. Obviously, one's financial standing in modern China is the key factor in determining personal transportation.
5. There are thousands of apartment complexes; private home ownership is not an important issue in urban China. Home ownership is more likely in rural China.
6. There is incredible energy in urban China; cities are vibrant and somehow function quite well despite the crushing numbers.
7. There is non-stop building occurring everywhere in Beijing and Shanghai. Over six hundred sites were being worked on for the 2008 Olympics in Beijing.
8. Pollution levels are significant and a major threat to urban vitality.
9. Chinese people are generally very optimistic about the future, though economic inequality is becoming a real problem, especially in the rural areas.
10. My students at North China University of Technology were energetic and inspiring—they were eager to learn more about American culture and history. I provided five three-hour lectures on U.S. diplomatic history and my wife, Mimi, also gave a three-hour lecture on the fundamentals of learning the English language.

I was also fortunate to interview four interesting individuals concerning present-day China, domestically and internationally. One of the self-discoveries that surprised me during my encounters and travels was the degree of openness expressed by the people I met. The individuals that I interviewed, and my two hundred-plus students at North China University of Technology were often very direct about their feelings about China, its future, and its political system.

I also sensed a profound patriotism and pride amongst the Chinese concerning their society and their recent economic successes. All those I met supported the government's economic reforms and were quick to tell me that political reforms are also occurring, if slowly. Finally, they represented a new generation of Chinese who are experiencing broader freedoms and economic opportunities. Each of them told me that the days of immediate repression, or possible imprisonment, for ill-tempered remarks about the government and its policies was a thing of the past. Though, it was still considered dangerous to publicly challenge the government, and the media remains tightly controlled by the government.

An excellent example of censorship of China's media occurred during my first night in Shanghai at the Pacific Hotel, located across the street from the People's Square in the city's downtown area. I was watching a BBC news program concerning the publication of Amnesty International's 2007 report on global human rights and political repression. When the representative for the organization was about to talk about specific Asian countries, the television screen went black. I first thought the cable had shut down, but I checked the other channels and they were fine. It dawned on me that I had just witnessed government censorship of television programming. I was correct. The BBC broadcast came back on at the very end of the Amnesty International segment. I later thought—what is worse?—the government censoring the news in China, or U.S. corporations manipulating the news in America? China is worse, because at least you receive part of the story in the corporate-owned U.S. media.

I am now going to present a few of the Chinese perspectives that I encountered during my journey in China. I interviewed the following individuals during my stay in Beijing and Shanghai. These individuals' names are in **boldface** in this section of the postscript:

Zhang Boshu, an assistant research fellow at the Chinese Academy of Social Sciences (CASS) in Beijing, was the most outspoken of the three scholars concerning China's political system and society. Boshu acknowledged that his comments and writings criticizing the government's policies had prevented him from being promoted to lecturer within the CASS. He also stated that his boss had often warned him that his critical academic work would harm his advancement as a scholar. Yet, he did not retreat from his political commentary.

Boshu believes China's biggest challenge is to figure out a way to change its one-party system without revolution. He thinks that reformers, intellectuals, and ordinary people need to work together to change the system. Though he admits that change has occurred in some areas, civil law and society in China are just starting to develop. Boshu is not an idealist; he points to the legal and legislative systems as being inadequate. Thus, he contends that political and human rights, and civil society, will not function well in China until the legal and legislative systems work properly. Nevertheless, he remains optimistic about China's future, but he also realizes that the necessary political reforms will be hard earned.

Zhang Zhi Rong, an associate professor in the School of International Politics at Peking University in Beijing, is a leading scholar on China's foreign policy, particularly in East Asia. Professor Zhang believes that history continues to play an enormous role in the relations between East Asian nations in the twenty-first century. Generally, Professor Zhang believes China has improved its relations with all the countries in East Asia, though relations with Japan are still difficult at times. He believes the major issues between China and Japan are (recent) history, Taiwan, and trade. The significant issues between China and the U.S. are the four "T"s: Taiwan, Tibet, Tiananmen Square, and trade. Between China and Australia, the major issues are Tibet and trade. However, Zhang believes there are no major issues or disputes between China and South Korea.

Professor Zhang asserts that there are two key factors to creating a stable Asia-Pacific in the twenty-first century—the continued presence of the U.S. in the region, and China and Japan working together. He emphasized that China and America view their relationship from three perspectives: globally, regionally, and bilaterally. And he believes that Japan will also continue to be a very important factor in the region because it views itself as a coleader in Asia-Pacific alongside the United States. Professor Zhang thinks that Japan views Asia-Pacific from four different perspectives:

1. The U.S.-Japan Security Alliance
2. The four regional "dragons": South Korea, Hong Kong, Taiwan, and Singapore
3. The four new small regional "dragons": the Philippines, Malaysia, Indonesia, and Thailand
4. China

Finally, Professor Zhang is concerned about the Korean peninsula because it has been the focus of several wars and regional tensions since 1895. Presently, North Korea represents a real threat to regional stability—and to Japanese security. However, he is convinced that North Korean leader Kim Jong-il wants to reform his country slowly, using China as his model for fundamental changes. Zhang notes that South Korean aid is very important for North Korea's future development, but he remains somewhat baffled as to why former South Korean President Kim Dae-jung's "sunshine policies" were not more successful for the Korean peninsula.

Guo Tao, dean of the Office of International Cooperation and Exchanges at North China University of Technology in Beijing, was a former interpreter with the World Health Organization (WHO) and the United Nations (UN) during the 1980s. He has taught for over twenty-five years and he has seen China, especially his hometown Beijing, change dramatically. Yet, he perceives China's reform process as a fragile development. For this reason, Guo has little patience for reformers like Zhang Boshu because he believes a significant uprising by the people could spell the end of China's economic progress. Thus, the legal and legislative reforms that Boshu desires would end as well. The country would be enveloped in chaos. Having grown up poor in Beijing, Professor Guo is convinced that the significant social changes and economic improvements over the past thirty years must be maintained and continued, or China could experience internal upheaval and violence. He also believes that China could irrefutably become a *real* danger for the future stability of Asia-Pacific and the world, if there was a sudden collapse from within.

Professor Guo emphasized that the U.S. must understand that China is not intimidated by America's military power. Though China greatly respects the U.S., it does not like to be told what to do, or be lectured, by the American government. China interprets these activities as external acts designed to interfere in their domestic affairs. Also, according to Guo, the Chinese see themselves as heroic individuals in terms of helping the weak in society. Thus, China is not a threat to its neighbors, though Professor Guo admits that China can indeed be aggressive when it needs to be, but the Chinese are not interested in creating a global empire (e.g., British Empire). Therefore, he insists that there is no credible reason to see China as a threat because, in reality, it is moving towards the mainstream of world affairs—economically, politically, and socially. Perhaps change is occurring in China, but not as fast as the U.S. would like.

CHINA: ECONOMIC JUGGERNAUT

While visiting Shanghai, I had the opportunity to visit two Chinese joint business ventures—Dow Chemical (U.S.-China) and Volkswagen Automotive (Germany-China). Both visits provided great insights concerning the dramatic rise of China's industrial prowess, and why the West had better prepare itself for more intense competition from the Middle Kingdom.

On 24 May, my wife and I rode in a minivan from the Pacific Hotel for over two hours, outside of Shanghai, to visit the Dow facility in Jiangsu province. The facility itself is located in a massive and still expanding industrial park called Zhangjiagang. Our host was an extremely bright and gregarious individual named **Henry Ling**. He was the site leader in charge of overseeing all manufacturing and engineering at this particular Dow plant. Henry was educated in Australia after his family was allowed to leave

China in 1978. He graduated in 1986 from St. George Technical College located in Sydney with a degree in electrical engineering. Henry returned to China because there were better job opportunities for someone with his educational background. His family remained in Australia.

Henry Ling is an excellent example of the ambition and energy displayed by the new generation of Chinese workers who, since 1978, have enthusiastically embraced Deng Xiaoping's radical economic reforms. Deng's bold and dramatic departure from Mao's rigid communist orthodoxy, which had existed as the basis of Chinese life since the successful 1949 revolution, was in essence a new and visionary belief that China had to change course and develop economically. Though, Henry realizes that Deng's decision to send the military into Tiananmen Square in 1989 to put down the student protests will taint his legacy. He also strongly believes that future historians will see Deng Xiaoping as a visionary leader who changed China forever. According to Henry, Deng is much more popular than Mao amongst the younger generations because they see him as a regular guy. In fact, it was an image that Deng wanted to cultivate. Mao continues to be seen as a demigod in many respects. But it is Deng who is seen as being responsible for the recent economic resurgence of China and for giving the Chinese people a new sense of pride in themselves and their country.

Henry was quick to point out that Chinese society is indeed opening up, and that a new sense of freedom and tolerance is being felt throughout China—even religion can be practiced as long as it is not a threat to the government. Though, of course, these societal developments within China are not comparable to the established civil liberties and constitutional freedoms in the American community. Nevertheless, according to Henry, most Chinese young people and adults are now more interested in business, pop culture, and consumerism rather than quoting chairman Mao. Communist orthodoxy is no longer a concern amongst the populace; they instead wish for "good government" and more transparency with concern to government activities. Corruption and the environment are becoming major issues for China and its future stability as a society.

Finally, Henry provided me with an interesting "rule of thumb" relating to the economic development of cities in China. He said that there are three classification tiers:

a) Tier One—cities that had Starbucks, McDonald's, and Kentucky Fried Chicken
b) Tier Two—cities that had McDonald's and Kentucky Fried Chicken
c) Tier Three—cities that only had Kentucky Fried Chicken

Dow has twelve plants in China, including Hong Kong and Taiwan. The plant that I visited in Zhangjiagang has approximately 250 employees (all

Chinese from what I saw) and it had approximately $250 million in sales last year. The plant itself is in the process of expansion and its sales are expected to double in three years. I saw and spoke to several employees during my visit. It seemed most of them were in their twenties. They were very bright and energetic. The engineers (again, young) were graduates from the best schools in China. Henry said it was very difficult to keep them because they were being offered better salaries from other companies in China. Hmmm, sounds very much like the American corporate world!

My visit to the Shanghai-Volkswagen Automotive Company (SVW) was arranged by Li Guang Wen, general manager of Shanghai Kyokuto Shokai and Kyokuto Shokai in Tianjin, China, and the husband of Guilan Wang, the director of the International Program at Central Michigan University. I met Mr. Li shortly before my trip to China. His main office is in Tianjin, but he contacted his associates in the Shanghai office, Zhang Hongyi and Yuee Wu, to assist us with our trip to SVW. Both were simply wonderful. Their generosity was unending. In fact, Ms. Wu contacted her husband, a medical doctor, to treat my wife, Mimi, who had contracted a cold during our travels. Visitors to Shanghai could not have asked for better ambassadors than Mr. Li, Mr. Zhang, and Ms. Wu. My gratitude is boundless.

Our visit to Shanghai-Volkswagen was very interesting for several reasons. First, the plant itself was the first car-making joint venture after China began its reforms and opened its doors to the outside world. In fact, today Chinese and German shareholders each own 50 percent of the operation. Secondly, I wanted to see Chinese autoworkers in action. Having visited car plants in America and South Korea, I was interested in evaluating the skill level of Chinese autoworkers. Though our tour of the plant was brisk, you were still able to get a good idea about the overall process. SVW produces approximately 450,000 units annually. The SVW facilities are located in Anting International Auto City, just a short car trip from downtown Shanghai. There were numerous auto companies located in this "city".

Finally, I noticed that there was not as much reliance upon the use of robotics to produce an SVW product. For instance, compared to the Korean car makers Hyundai and Kia, the Chinese SVW operation appeared to be using many more workers in its overall process. However, this is *not* a liability in terms of profitability because the average manufacturing worker in China earns approximately $0.67 per hour. In North America, the average hourly wage for both an American and a Canadian manufacturing worker is over $23.00 per hour. Go ahead and do the math. China has an unimaginable advantage in terms of its overall labor costs, plus SVW has no medical costs because the government provides a national health program for its citizens. No wonder Detroit is going bankrupt. When China starts to export quality, low-cost autos to the U.S. marketplace, perhaps as early as 2008, it may be game-set-match for the American auto industry.

REVISITING THE LAND OF THE RISING SUN

On 31 May, I returned to Japan for the first time since 1999 to attend a six-day international conference at International Christian University (ICU) titled, "A Grand Theory of Peace: The Fate of the Peace Movement and Pacifism after September 11th". Prominent academics such as Richard Falk, who spent forty years teaching at Princeton University, and Yoshikazu Sakamoto, who is professor emeritus at the University of Tokyo, provided the keynote addresses. I was responsible for providing commentary on their presentations. Later, on Monday afternoon during the following week, I gave my own seminar lecture concerning the future of Asia-Pacific in the twenty-first century at the Kawaguchiko/Win Lakehill Hotel, located near Mt. Fuji. The poster for the ICU conference had my name listed—in bold print—at the bottom of a list of important guests. No problem, it only took me fifteen years to finally see my name on an international conference poster!

More importantly, I unexpectedly discovered an extremely interesting fact about ICU during the two-day conference at this location. The former chairman of the ICU Church, Mr. Takeshi Suto, informed me that this aesthetically beautiful and tranquil campus was the former location of the Nakajima Aircraft Company that built the Japanese Zero Fighter Plane before WWII. In the early postwar years, the Nakajima plant was dismantled and, in 1952, ICU opened its doors at this very same location and had their first graduating class in 1956. The institution has dedicated itself to teaching numerous courses on global peace and tolerance. Cynics say a leopard never changes its spots, but clearly ICU does not represent that analogy. Conversely, ICU irrefutably shows that a people, and a nation, can indeed reform and redeem themselves and set out on a new course of human existence in this world.

Just a few thoughts on Japan during my initial six-day visit: In 1999, when I left Japan to teach in the U.S., this proud nation found itself in the thralls of economic stagnation. However, things are beginning to turn around. National unemployment is at its lowest level in nine years—3.8 percent. Japanese companies are hiring again, and wages and consumer spending are expected to increase as a result.[40] Trade with China has been one of the primary reasons for Japan's steady economic growth. I visited a local sporting goods store near my hotel in Tokyo and found that almost every pair of athletic shoes and a large percentage of the sports clothing were made in China. But trade in China is not the only arena of success for Japanese products. As mentioned earlier in this chapter, in May 2007, Toyota claimed 17.2 percent of the U.S. auto market. Japan's most prominent automaker trailed only GM (23.5 percent), but they surpassed Ford Motor Company again for the fifth time.

Walking for several hours around the local community, I was reminded how compact and precise the Tokyo communities remain. The main roads are often narrow, two-lane venues and many roads within neighborhoods are barely big enough for a mid-size automobile to travel. I walked back to my hotel from ICU after the 10:30 am Sunday church service conducted by Reverend Paul Johnson, an American from South Dakota. He has made Japan his home. Reverend Johnson is married to a Japanese woman and they have three children. He felt very grateful to be the university minister in such a beautiful setting. During my walk back to the Hotel Mets, I passed literally dozens of small shops that fit comfortably within their respective neighborhoods. Unlike urban settings in China, Hong Kong, or South Korea, Japanese urban apartment complexes are often smaller in size and height, rather than the fifteen-, twenty-, or thirty-storied structures that are a common sight in the aforementioned areas.

SOUTH KOREA: PROSPEROUS ASIAN DRAGON

I was in South Korea only for six days. I spent much of it visiting my wife's family. However, I did visit the Kia Motors Company and I toured the Gyeonggi provincial government house thanks to the generosity of my brother-in-law, Heun-Jae Lee.

I also noticed that the prices for commodities and services in South Korea had risen sharply. I am not sure why this has occurred, because the exchange rate for the U.S. dollar remains very advantageous to American tourists. And salaries have not increased that much in South Korea within many realms of work. Yet South Koreans rank at the top for "working excessively" according to the International Labor Organization's 160-page report, "Working Time Around the World," published in June 2007. Among developing countries, South Korea ranks second (49.5 percent) in the world with concern to its citizens laboring more than forty-eight hours per week. Only Peru had a higher percentage (50.9 percent) of its labor force working forty-eight-plus hours per week than South Korea. By comparison, the U.S. had only 18.1 percent of its labor force working beyond forty-eight hours in a week.[41]

JAPAN ONCE MORE

I returned to Japan on 12 June, a week after my departure at the close of the ICU/CEO conference. In the interim, as mentioned above, I traveled to Seoul, South Korea. Then I returned with my wife to Japan and traveled on the famous bullet train to Hiroshima, Kyoto, and Tokyo until 17 June.

In Hiroshima, my visit to the Atomic Dome, a surviving structure that has come to symbolize one of the great tragedies in human history, was quite moving and troubling. I just could not wrap my mind around the level of devastation that was visited upon this beautiful city at 8:15 am on the morning of August 6, 1945. Even though I visited the Hiroshima Peace Memorial Museum and saw the photographs and charred clothing associated with the atomic bombing of this city, my imagination simply did not (could not) operate at the appropriate level to understand the horrific circumstances of that day.

However, two things did attract my attention at the museum. First, the portrayal of Japan's actions in WWII was not denied or sugarcoated. Secondly, the spirit of the people of Hiroshima was awe-inspiring. Literally, within forty-eight hours after the bombing, they began the process of rebuilding their city. Photos of their activities stayed with me. I visited the Atomic Dome three times, and I came away each time deeply troubled and worried about whether the world truly understands how destructive these weapons really are. On a positive note, we visited the world-famous Miyajima Shrine just outside of Hiroshima. My only disappointment in Hiroshima was that the local baseball team was out of town. I have never seen a professional baseball game in Japan. Nevertheless, the visit to Hiroshima was a powerful and wonderful experience for me.

Finally, I want to personally thank Keiichi Morioka for his kindness and generosity of spirit in helping Mimi and I with our hotel and travel plans during our time in Japan. Keiichi was a former student of Mimi's at Central Michigan University's English Language Institute. He took a day off from work to show us the beauty of Hiroshima and Miyajima, and he introduced us to wonderful restaurants to enjoy the local cuisine.

Our visit to Kyoto was special because we visited the awe-inspiring Kyoto Imperial Palace, the UNESCO World Heritage listed Nijo Castle, and several temples. The city was older looking than Hiroshima because it was not bombed or completely devastated by U.S. air corps during WWII. However, Mimi and I were nearing physical exhaustion by this stage of our trip. We boarded the bullet train to Tokyo with tired enthusiasm because we knew we were heading home. We spent an uneventful afternoon and night in a Tokyo suburb and took the bus the next morning to Narita Airport and flew home on United Airlines, via Chicago, to Lansing, Michigan. Whereupon, officially ending our thirty-seven-day Asian sojourn through China, Japan, and South Korea.

Note to the Reader: The individuals, interviews and other sources mentioned in this postscript will not be listed in the acknowledgment or bibliography sections of my book because this section of the text was written so closely to the publication deadline.

NOTES

1. Paul Kelly, "Security Accord Flags New Japan," *The Australian*, 13 March 2007.

2. Ibid.

3. Dennis Shanahan and Patrick Walters, "Our Military Ties with Japan Worry China," *The Australian*, 10 March 2007.

4. The Associated Press, "Australia Calls for Security Forum," *International Herald Tribune*, 7 June 2007, p. 3.

5. Eric Talmadge, "Heated Space Race Under Way in Asia," *Associated Press*, 14 April 2007.

6. *Associated Press*, "China Denies Intent to Militarize Space," 22 January 2007.

7. Michael R. Gordon and David S. Cloud, "U.S. Knew of China's Missile Test, but Kept Silent," *The New York Times*, 23 April 2007.

8. Ibid.

9. Editorial Staff, "China's Military Budget: Are The Defense Spending Figures Accurate?," *Asia Weekly*, 4 June 2007, p. 12.

10. Ibid.

11. Noam Chomsky, *Hegemony or Survival: America's Quest For Global Dominance* (New York: Henry Holt and Company, 2004), p. 225.

12. Ibid., p. 227.

13. Hu Xuan, "Pentagon Report Clouds Facts, Says Analyst," *China Daily*, 28 May 2007, p. 2.

14. Ibid.

15. Mure Dickie and Stephen Fidler, "Dragon Fleet: China Aims to End the U.S. Navy's Long Pacific Dominance," *Financial Times*, 12 June 2007, p. 9.

16. Bill Powell, "Is China's Economy Overheating?," *Time*, 19 April 2007.

17. Thomas P. M. Barnett, "China: The Slated Near-Peer," *Esquire*, May 2007, p. 114.

18. Bradley S. Klapper, "WTO: China Overtakes U.S. in Exports," *Associated Press*, 12 April 2007.

19. Gordon Fairclough, "GM's Chinese Partner Looms as a New Rival," *The Wall Street Journal*, 20 April 2007.

20. Ibid.

21. *The Japan Times*, "Toyota Models Grab 17.2 Percent Share of Huge U.S. Market," 3 June 2007, p.9.

22. Joe McDonald, "Chinese Automakers Showcase Eco-Cars," Associated Press Business Writer, 22 April 2007. I used Fairclough and McDonald's articles as sources for this note.

23. David Uren, "China Emerges as Our Biggest Trade Partner," *The Australian*, 5 May 2007.

24. Ibid.

25. Zhang Tuosheng, "Despite Sticking Points, Relations Enter New Era," *China Daily*, 11 April 2007, p. 10.

26. *China Daily*, "Japan Takes First Step in Revising Pacifist Charter," 15 May 2007, p.1.

27. *The Japan Times*, "Abe Rating Hits New Low," 16 June 2007, p.1.

28. Ibid.

29. Uren, "China Emerges as Our Biggest Trade Partner."

30. Sid Morris, "China to Continue Feeding the Boom," *The Australian*, 8 May 2007.

31. Speech by Australian Prime Minister Bob Hawke, "Australia-China Relations," Nanjing University, 23 May 1986.

32. Patrick Walters, "Defense Spending Jumps 10.6 pc to $22 Billion," *The Australian*, 8 May 2007.

33. Maria Hawthrone and Nick Ralston, "Leaders' Backflip: Pressure Forces Quick Rudd Rethink on Meeting Dalai Lama," *The Mercury*, 17 May 2007, p. 4.

34. *The Japan Times*, "Australia's Howard Meets Dalai Lama: China Furious," 17 June 2007, p. 3.

35. Maria Hvistendahl, "The China Experiment: Inside The Revolution to Green the Biggest Nation on Earth," *Seed Magazine*, May/June 2007.

36. Ibid.

37. Simon Ward, "Is The Answer Blowing in the Wind?," *Beijing Talk*, May 2007, pp. 6–7.

38. Hvistendahl, "The China Experiment," May/June 2007.

39. Yan Zhen, "Global Balancing Act 'Challenge for China'," *Shanghai Daily*, 26–27 May 2007, p.1.

40. *The Korean Times*, "Japan's Jobless Rate Hits Nine-Year Low," 30 May 2007, p. 12.

41. *The Korean Herald*, "Korean Workers Toil 'Excessively' ILO Says," 8 June 2007, p. 3.

Bibliography

BOOKS

Acheson, Dean. *Present at the Creation: My Years in the State Department* (New York: W.W. Norton & Company, 1969).

Baker, Peter, and Susan Glasser. *Kremlin Rising: Vladimir Putin's Russia and the End of Revolution* (New York: Scribner's, A Lisa Drew Book, 2005).

Berger, Suzanne. *How We Compete: What Companies Around the World Are Doing to Make It in Today's Global Economy* (New York: Currency, a division of Random House, 2005).

Bix, Herbert P. *Hirohito and the Making of Modern Japan* (New York: HarperCollins Publishers, 2000).

Blainey, Geoffrey. *In Our Time: The Issues and the People of Our Century* (Melbourne: Information Australia, 1999).

Bolton, Geoffrey. *The Oxford History of Australia—Vol. 5* (Melbourne: Oxford University Press, 1996).

Bracken, Paul. *Fire in the East: The Rise of Asian Military Power and the Second Nuclear Age* (New York: HarperCollins Publishers, 1999).

Breen, Michael. *The Koreans: Who They Are, What They Want, Where Their Future Lies* (New York: St. Martin's Griffin, 2004).

Brown, Lester R. *Plan B 2.0: Rescuing a Planet under Stress and a Civilization in Trouble* (New York: W.W. Norton & Company, 2006).

Brzezinski, Zbigniew. *Grand Chessboard: American Primacy and Its Geo-strategic Imperatives* (New York: Basic Books, 1998).

Brzezinski, Zbigniew. *The Choice: Global Domination or Global Leadership* (New York: Basic Books, 2004).

Chace, James. *Acheson: The Secretary of State Who Created the American World* (New York: Simon & Schuster, 1998).

Chambers, John H. *A Traveler's History of Australia* (New York: Interlink Books, 2002).

191

Cohen, Warren I. *The Cambridge History of American Foreign Relations—Volume IV: America in the Age of SOVIET Power, 1945–1991* (New York: Cambridge University Press, 1993).

Collinwood, Dean W. *Japan and the Pacific Rim* (Dubuque, IA: McGraw-Hill/Dushkin, 2006).

Cumings, Bruce. *Korea's Place in the Sun: A Modern History* (New York: W.W. Norton, 1997 & 2005).

Day, David. *Claiming a Continent: A New History of Australia* (Sydney: HarperCollins Publishers, 2001).

Dower, John W. *Embracing Defeat: Japan in the Wake of World War II* (New York: W.W. Norton & Company/The New Press, 1999).

Evatt, H. V. *Australia in World Affairs* (Sydney: Angus & Robertson, 1946).

Ferguson, Niall. *Colossus: The Price of America's Empire* (New York: Penguin Group USA, 2004).

Ferguson, Niall. *The Cash Nexus: Money and Power in the Modern World, 1700–2000* (New York: Basic Books, 2001).

Ferguson, Niall. *The War of the World: Twentieth-Century Conflict and the Descent of the West* (New York: The Penguin Press, 2006).

Flannery, Tim. *The Weather Makers: The History & Future Impact of Climate Change* (Melbourne: The Text Publishing Company, 2005).

Gaddis, John Lewis. *The Cold War: A New History* (New York: The Penguin Press, 2005).

Gittings, John. *The Changing Face of China: From Mao to Market* (New York: Oxford University Press, 2005).

Harrison, Selig S. *Korean Endgame: A Strategy for Reunification and U.S. Disengagement* (Princeton: Princeton University Press, 2002).

Hutton, Will. *The Writing on the Wall: Why We Must Embrace China as a Partner or Face It as an Enemy* (New York: Free Press, 2006).

Ishihara, Shintaro. *The Japan That Can Say 'No': Why Japan Will Be First among Equals* (New York: Simon & Schuster, 1990).

Jentleson, Bruce W. *American Foreign Policy: The Dynamics of Choice in the 21st Century* (New York: W.W. Norton & Company, 2004).

Johnson, Chalmers. *Blowback: The Costs and Consequences of American Empire* (New York: Henry Holt and Company, 2000).

Johnson, Chalmers. *The Sorrows of Empire: Militarism, Secrecy, and the End of the Republic* (New York: Henry Holt and Company, 2004).

Jones, Howard. *Crucible of Power: A History of U.S. Foreign Relations since 1897* (Lanham, MD: S.R. Books, 2001).

Kennedy, Paul. *The Rise and Fall of the Great Powers: Economic Change and Military Conflict from 1500 to 2000* (New York: Random House, 1987).

Kim, Byong-Kuk. *Kim Dae-jung: Hero of the Masses, Conscience in Action* (Seoul: Ilweolseogak Publishing Company, 1992).

Kim, Dae-jung. *Prison Writings* (Berkeley: University of California Press, 1987).

Kim, Il-sung. *On the Building of the People's Government* (Pyongyang, Korea: Foreign Languages Publishing House, 1978).

Kim, Tae-Hyo, and Brad Glosserman, editors. *The Future of U.S.-Korea-Japan Relations: Balancing Values and Interests* (Washington, DC: Center of Strategic and International Studies, 2004).

Kissinger, Henry. *Diplomacy* (New York: Simon & Schuster, 1994).

Kissinger, Henry. *Does America Need a Foreign Policy? Toward a Diplomacy for the Twenty-first Century* (New York: Simon & Schuster, 2001).

Klare, Michael T. *Blood and Oil: The Dangers and Consequences of America's Growing Dependency on Imported Petroleum* (New York: Henry Holt and Company, 2004).

Klare, Michael T. *Resource Wars: The New Landscape of Global Conflict* (New York: Henry Holt and Company, 2001).

Kleveman, Lutz. *The New Great Game* (Atlantic Monthly Press, 2003).

LaFeber, Walter. *The Clash: U.S.-Japanese Relations throughout History* (New York: W.W. Norton & Company, 1997).

Lee, David, and Christopher Waters, Editors. *Evatt to Evans: The Labor Tradition in Australian Foreign Policy* (Australian National University: Allen & Unwin, 1997).

Mahan, Alfred Thayer. *The Influence of Sea Power upon History* (originally published in 1890).

Mearsheimer, John. *The Tragedy of Great Power Politics* (New York: W.W. Norton & Company, 2001).

Menzies, Sir Robert Gordon. *The Measure of the Years* (Victoria: Cassell Australia LTD, 1970).

Molony, John. *History of Australia: The Story of 200 Years* (Victoria: Penguin Books of Australia, 1987).

Moon, Chung-in, and David I. Steinberg, editors. *Kim Dae-jung Government and Sunshine Policy: Promises and Challenges* (Seoul: Yonsei University Press, 1999).

Murphey, Rhoads. *East Asia: A New History* (New York: Pearson/Longman, 2004).

Nye, Joseph. *Bound to Lead: The Changing Nature of American Power* (New York: Perseus Publishing, 1991).

Nye, Joseph S., Jr. *Soft Power: The Means to Succeed in World Politics* (New York: Public Affairs, 2004).

Oberdorfer, Don. *The Two Koreas: A Contemporary History* (New York: Basic Books, 2001).

Perkins, John. *Confessions of an Economic Hit Man* (New York: Plume Book, 2006).

Pilger, John. *A Secret Country* (Victoria: Vintage Books, 1992).

Rothkopk, David. *Running the World: The Inside Story of the National Security Council and the Architects of American Power* (New York: Public Affairs, 2005).

Shenkar, Oded. *The Chinese Century: The Rising Chinese Economy and Its Impact on the Global Economy, the Balance of Power and Your Job* (Upper Saddle River, NJ: Wharton School Publishing, 2006).

Smith, Patrick. *Japan: A Reinterpretation* (New York: Pantheon Books, 1997).

Sutter, Robert G. *China's Rise in Asia: Promises and Perils* (Lanham, MD: Rowman & Littlefield Publishers, Inc., 2005).

Takaki, Ronald. *Strangers from a Different Shore: A History of Asian Americans* (New York: Little, Brown and Company, 1998).

Terrill, Ross. *The New Chinese Empire: And What it Means for the United States* (Cambridge, MA: Perseus Books Group, 2003).

Zinn, Howard. *A People's History of the United States, 1492–Present* (New York: HarperCollins Publishers, 1999).

BOOK REVIEWS

Asahina, Robert, "All the Enemy's Mercy, in Asia . . . ," *The Washington Post*, 24 July 2005, concerning the book, *Surviving the Sword: Prisoners of the Japanese in the Far East, 1942–1945* (New York: Random House, 2005).

ARTICLES

Achcar, Gilbert, "Assessing China," www.zmag.org, 25 June 2005.

Alagappa, Muthia, Editor, *Asian Security Order: Instrumental and Normative Features* (Stanford: Stanford University Press, 2003), including David Kang, "Acute Conflicts in Asia after the Cold War: Kashmir, Taiwan and Korea."

Ali, Mahir, "Fight Them on the Beaches? Australia's Identity Crisis and the Sydney Riots," *ZNet/Australia*, 20 December 2005, pp. 1–3.

Armstrong, Charles K., "South Korea and the United States: Is the Love Affair Over?," 6 June 2005, http://hnn.us/articles/12241.html.

Asia Times, "Asian Tourists Have Australia's Number," 1 May 1999.

Associated Press, "Economic Growth in China Set to Slow, World Bank Predicts," *The Wall Street Journal*, 14 December 2006.

Associated Press, "Ford to Invest in Plants and Get Tax Breaks," *The New York Times*, 23 December 2006.

Australian Associated Press, "Mining Boom to Continue," *The Mercury*, 11 December 2006.

Ban, Ki-Moon, "For Permanent Peace: Beyond the Nuclear Challenge and the Cold War," *Harvard International Review*, Summer 2006.

Beehner, Lionel, "The Rise of the Shanghai Cooperation Organization," *Council on Foreign Relations*, 12 June 2006.

Bix, Herbert P., "Hirohito and History: Japanese and American Perspectives on the Emperor and World War II in Asia," *ZNet/Activism*, 30 July 2005.

Blair, British Prime Minister Tony, final press conference in 2005, C-Span, December 26.

Blank, Stephen, "Australia: A Sheriff with a Strategy," *Asia Times*, 2 October 2005.

Bowden, Rich, "Battle Looms over Inaugural East Asia Summit," *World Press*, Contributing Editor, Sydney, Australia, 11 December 2005.

Bradsher, Keith, "China Seeking Auto Industry, Piece by Piece," *The New York Times*, 17 February 2006.

Branford, Becky, "Lingering Legacy of Korean Massacre," *BBC News Online*, 18 May 2005.

Brown, Lester R., "China Is Replacing U.S. as World's Leading Consumer," *New Perspectives Quarterly*, Spring 2005.

Bruemmer, Emily, "Join the Club: Japan's Security Council Bid," *Harvard International Review*, Summer 2006.

Burkman, Thomas W. "Japan and the League of Nations: An Asian Power Encounters the European Club," *Wilson and the League of Nations, Part 2* (www.24hourscholar .com).

Calder, Kent E., "China and Japan's Simmering Rivalry," *Foreign Affairs*, March/April 2006, Vol. 85, No. 2.

Casey, Michael, "U.S., Australia Back Global Warming Plan," *Associated Press* Environmental Writer, 12 January 2006.

Chaisatien, Aree, "Asian Race for Diplomas Boosts Australia's Coffers," *Asia Times* (Oceania), 9 June 1999.

Clark, Gregory, "No Rest for 'China Threat' Lobby," *Japan Times*, 7 January 2006.

Cohen, Jerome A., "Law in Political Transitions: Lessons from East Asia and the Road Ahead for China," *Council on Foreign Relations*, 25 July 2005.

Colgan, Paul, "Australia Is Racist: Poll," *The Australian*, 6 March 2006.

Collier, Joe Guy, "Growth in China Gives GM a Boost," *Detroit Free Press*, 6 January 2006.

Commonwealth of Australia, "Advancing the National Interest," *Australia's Foreign Affairs and Trade Policy White Paper*, 2003, Chapter 1.

Commonwealth of Australia, *Australia's Foreign Affairs and Trade Policy White Paper*, 2003, Appendix 2.

Cooper, William H., Specialist in International Trade and Finance, Foreign Affairs, Defense and Trade Division, "U.S.-Japan Economic Relations: Significance, Prospects, and Policy Options," *Congressional Research Service*, updated 28 February 2005.

Corder, Mike, "Racial Unrest Strikes Australia," *Associated Press*, 12 December 2005.

Cumings, Bruce, "The World Shakes China," *The National Interest*, Spring 1996.

Davies, Anne, Urban Affairs Editor, "Sydney's Future Eaten: The Flannery Prophecy," *Sydney Morning Herald*, 19 May 2004.

Dickie, Mure, Kathrin Hille and Demetri Sevastopulo, "Report Strikes Beijing Nerve at Politically Sensitive Time," *Financial Times*, 21 July 2005.

Downer, The Honorable Alexander, Minister for Foreign Affairs, Australia, Press Release, 18 March 2006.

Doyle, Randall, "The Reluctant Heretic: George F. Kennan and the Vietnam War, 1950–1968," *Grand Valley Review*, Vol. 27, Spring 2004.

Drezner, Daniel W. website (www.danieldrezner.com), including Sachdev, Ameet, "Trade, China and Steel," published in *Chicago Tribune*, August 2005.

Dumbaugh, Kerry, "China-U.S. Relations: Current Issues and Implications for U.S. Policy," *CRS Report for Congress*. Congressional Research Service, The Library of Congress, 20 January 2006.

Editorial, "China, the Word's 4th Largest Economy?" *Asia Times*, 14 December 2005.

Editorial, Regional Perspective Section, "Australia Demonstrates the Art of Riding Two Horses," *The Nation*, 19 June 2006.

Fackler, Martin, "New Optimism about the Japanese Economy after a Black Decade," *The New York Times*, 7 December 2005.

Faiola, Anthony, "Tokyo Maverick Just One of the Crowd Now," *Washington Post Foreign Service*, 13 November 2005.

Fallows, James, "Postcards from Tomorrow Square," *The Atlantic Monthly*, December 2006.

Fong, Mei, "So Much Work, So Little Time," *The Wall Street Journal* (Weekend Edition), 23–24 December 2006.

Francis, Neil, "For an East Asian Union—Rethinking Asia's Cold War Alliances," *Harvard International Review*, Fall 2006.

Frederick, Jim, "Why Japan Keeps Provoking China," *Time* (Web Exclusive), 10 December 2005.

French, Howard W., "Anger in China Rises over Threat to Environment," *The New York Times*, 19 July 2005.

Fullilove, Michael, "Ban's Debut Is Chance for Asia to Step into Spotlight," *Financial Times*, 19 December 2006.

Golley, Jane, "Contemplating China," *ANU Reporter*, Autumn 2006.

Gregg, Donald, and Don Oberdorfer, "A Moment to Seize with North Korea," *The Washington Post*, 22 June 2005.

Gyngell, Allan, "Living with the Giants," *Time-Asia* edition, 18 April 2005.

Haass, Richard N., "What to Do about China," *U.S. News and World Report*, 20 June 2005.

Halliman, Conn, "China: A Troubled Dragon," *Foreign Policy in Focus*, 11 May 2006.

Harries, Owen, "After Iraq," Lowy Institute for International Policy, December 2006.

Heginbotham, Eric, and Christopher P. Twomey, "America's Bismarckian Asia Policy," *Current History*, September 2005.

Hiscock, Geoff, "Australia, China Sign Uranium Deal," *CNN World News*, 2 April 2006.

Irvine, Jessica, "Aussie May Catch $US Next Year, Pundit Says," *The Sydney Morning Herald*, 13–14 May 2006.

Johnson, Chalmers, "No Longer the 'Lone' Superpower: Coming to Terms with China," Japan Policy Research Institute, March 2005, JPRI Working Paper No. 105.

Johnson, Chalmers, "The Empowerment of Asia," *Pacific Rim Report*, October 1995, *Pacific Rim Report #1*.

Kaplan, Robert D., "How We Would Fight China," *The Atlantic Monthly*, June 2005.

Keady, Maryann, "Australia in the Region," www.zmag.org, 5 July 2006.

Kelly, Paul, "Hanson, a Symptom of a Deeper Problem," *Paradise Divided: The Changes, the Challenges, the Choices for Australia* (Australia: Allen & Unwin, 2000), pp. 142–53.

Kim, Dae-jung and Yonsei University (Organizers), "From Stalemate to New Progress for Peace in Korea," International Conference to Commemorate the Fifth Anniversary of the 15 June South-North Joint Declaration, June 2005.

Kissinger, Henry, "China Shifts Centre of Gravity," *The Australian*, 13 June 2005.

Klare, Michael T., "Containing China," www.zmag.org, 18 April 2006.

Klare, Michael T., "Revving Up the China Threat," *The Nation*, 24 October 2005.

Mackinder, Halford J., "The Geographical Pivot of History," *The Geographical Journal*, April 1904, Vol. 23. Reprinted in a Special Edition in December 2004, Vol. 170, Part 4.

Magalogenis, George, "The Old and the Poor Left Behind in Queue: Unemployment Is Down but More People Are on Welfare," *The Weekend Australian*, 10–11 June 2006.

Mallet, Victor, "A Stir in Asia: Nationalism Is on the Rise, Even as the Region's Economies Intertwine," *Financial Times*, 19 July 2005.

Matthews, Eugene A., "Japan's New Nationalism," *Foreign Affairs*, November/December 2003.

Maynard, Micheline, and Martin Fackler, "Toyota Is Poised to Supplant GM as World's Largest Carmaker," *The New York Times*, 23 December 2006.

McDonald, Hamish, "BHP Reveals $11bn China Iron Ore Deal," *Sydney Morning Herald*, 2 March 2004.

McGeown, Kate, "Raking Over South Korea's Colonial Past," *BBC News Online*, 19 August 2004.

Mearsheimer, John, "The Rise of China Will Not Be Peaceful at All," *The Australian*, 18 November 2005.

Mekay, Emad, "U.S. Warned on War Spending and Deficits," www.zmag.org, 1 October 2006.

Office of the Secretary of Defense, "The Military Power of the People's Republic of China," *Annual Report to Congress*, 2005.

Pan, Esther, "China's Angry Peasants," *Council on Foreign Relations*, 15 December 2005.

Pei, Minxin, "The Dark Side of China's Rise," *Foreign Policy*, March/April 2006.

Pilger, John, "Bush's Sheriff," *The New Statesman*, 1 April 2004.

Randolph, R. Sean, "Asia in the World Economy: Globalization, Growth, and the Changing Structure of Trade," *Pacific Rim Report*, May 2003, *Pacific Rim Report #28*.

Recknagel, Charles, "World: Global Spending on Military Tops $1 Trillion, Nears Cold War Peak," *Radio Free Europe/Radio Liberty*, 8 June 2005.

Rigol, Natalia, "A Game of Giants: The Future of Sino-U.S. Relations," *Harvard International Review*, Spring 2005.

Robertson, Jeffrey, "Australia's Asian Ambitions," *Asia Times*, 2003.

Shambaugh, David, "Rising Dragon and the American Eagle—Part 1," *YaleGlobal* online, 20 April 2005.

Shambaugh, David, "The Changing Nature of the Regional Systems in Asia-Pacific," lecture, Chicago Council of Foreign Affairs, 26 January 2006.

Shanahan, Dennis, "Voters Cool on Budget Tax Cuts," *The Australian*, 16 May 2006.

Sheridan, Greg, "U.S. Sees Us as a Global Ally, a Vision Well Worth Sharing," *The Australian*, 29 June 2006.

Shorrock, Tim, "China's Elite Clearly Split over Foreign Policy," *Asia Times*, 15 February 2002.

Sneider, Daniel, "Asia's Polite Reception to Bush Masks Declining U.S. Influence: Growing Regional Cooperation Threatens U.S. Preeminence in East Asia," *YaleGlobal* online, 17 November 2005.

Spence, Jonathan D., "The Once and Future China," *Foreign Policy*, January/February 2005.

Sustar, Lee, "Containing China: The United States on the Asian Chessboard," *International Socialist Review*, July–August 2006.

Talmadge, Eric, "U.S. Troops in Asia Undergo Transformation," *Associated Press*, 16 November 2005.

The Detroit News, "GM, Ford See Sales in China Jump," 9 January 2007.

The Economist, "The Sun Also Rises: A Special Issue on Japan's Economic Revival," 8–14 October 2005.

Thottam, Jyoti, "Where the Good Jobs Are Going," *Time*, 28 July 2003, www.time.com.

Thurow, Lester, "China's Statistics Don't Add Up," *The Banker*, 2 August 2004.

Trounson, Andrew, "Metals Giant Urges Tariffs," *The Australian*, 15 July 2006.

Turner, David, "Tokyo Home Prices Start to Rise for First Time in 13 Years," *Financial Times*, 2 August 2005.

Varadarajan, Siddharth, "Asian Interests and the Myth of Balance," *The Hindu*, 27 December 2005, www.zmag.org.

Vaughn, Bruce, "Australia: Background and U.S. Relations," *CRS Report for Congress* (updated 14 July 2004).

Wakamiya, Yoshibumi, and Tsuneo Watanabe, "Yomiuri and Asahi Editors Call for a National Memorial to Replace Yasukuni," www.zmag.org, 19 February 2006.

Walker, Martin, "Walker's World: Battles around New Asia Summit," *The Washington Times*, 2 April 2005.

White, Hugh, "Beyond the Defence of Australia: Finding a New Balance in Australian Strategic Policy," Lowy Institute for International Policy, Lowy Institute Paper, 16 October 2006.

Wilson, Nigel, "Australia-China LNG Deal Sealed," *Energy Bulletin* (published by *The Australian*), 13 December 2004.

Wilson, Robert, "China Exports Take Aim at Australia," *The Australian*, 29 March 2006.

Yardley, Jim, "China Chemical Spills Spur Plan to Guard Water Supply," *The New York Times*, 12 January 2006.

Yardley, Jim, "China's Next Big Boom Could Be the Foul Air," *The New York Times*, 30 October 2005.

INTERVIEWS

Abigail, Peter, 22 May 2006.

Ayson, Robert, 23 May 2006.

Ball, Desmond, 24 May 2006.

Brzezinski, Zbigniew, 8 January 2007.

Chomsky, Noam, 2 January 2006 (email correspondences).

Downer, Alexander, 22 May 2006.

Flannery, Tim, 6 April 2006.

Hawke, Bob, 4 June 2004.

McDougall, Derek, 19 May 2006.

Milne, Christine, 5 June 2006.

Oberdorfer, Don, 28 December 2006.

Shan, Patrick Fuliang, 20 October 2006.

Sheridan, Greg, 12 April 2006 & 13 June 2006.

Sutter, Robert, 28 December 2006.

Tow, William, 24 May 2006.

Wilkie, Andrew, 5 June 2006.

Zhang, Yuping, 25 April 2006.

Zinn, Howard, conversations, correspondences, public lectures, 1994–2007.

OTHER SOURCES

ABC Online, "East Asia Summit Won't Replace APEC Role: Howard," 14 December 2005, www.abc.net/au.

Asialink Chairman's Dinner speech by the Australian Foreign Minister Alexander Downer, 1 December 2005, in Melbourne, Australia.

Australian Broadcasting Corporation, interview with Gareth Evans, by reporter Maxine McKew, broadcasted 20 September 2003.

Australian Government: Department of Foreign Affairs and Trade, "Australian Trade Story in 2003," Fast Facts about Trade, retrieved in July 2006.

Parliament of Australia website; Primary Sources: Dr. Frank Frost, Analyst and Policy Foreign Affairs, Defense and Trade Section; Ann Rann, Information and E-links Foreign Affairs, Defense and Trade Section.

CIA World Factbook, Australia, 2006.

Conference Program: International Conference to Commemorate the Fifth Anniversary of the 15 June 2000 South-North Joint Declaration.

Conversation with Professor Bruce Cumings (University of Chicago) took place at the International Conference to Commemorate the 5th Anniversary of the 15 June South-North Joint Declaration; The conference was held at the Shilla Hotel in Seoul, South Korea on 13 June 2005.

Conversation with Professor Robert Ayson (Australian National University) in his office and from my notes taken during his lecture at the Australian War Memorial, 23 May 2006.

Economist Intelligence Unit (www.viewswire.com/index.asp?layout-VWcountry).

Economist.com. Country Briefings, Australia, Economic Data, 25 May 2004.

Lecture given by Professor Merle Goldman (Emeritus Professor, Boston University) at Alma College (Michigan), 16 October 2006. Professor Goldman's lecture was about present-day China and its future.

Milne, Australian Federal Senator Christine. *Australian Green Party Budget Reply*, 11 May 2006.

Ministry of Foreign Affairs of the People's Republic of China website, 20 June 2006.

Ross, David, interview of Chalmers Johnson, "Fickle, Bitter, and Dangerous," 1 April 2004, *ZNet/Activism*.

The Heritage Foundation, "2006 Index of Economic Freedom." www.heritage.org/research/features/index/country.cfm?id=Australia.

Thomas Jefferson Papers (an electronic archive), The Massachusetts Historical Society, Unknownnewsatmyway.com.

U.S. National Security and Strategic Report 2002 (Obtained from a U.S. government website).

Wikipedia.org search: *East Asian Summit 2005, Bali Bombings 2002 and 2005, Halfrod John Mackinder, International Monetary Fund Statistics, 2005.*

About the Author

Dr. Randall Doyle teaches East Asian history, history of the Pacific Rim, and American diplomatic history at Central Michigan University. He has taught, studied, and lived in Asia, Australia, Europe, and North America during his academic career. In 2007, Dr. Doyle was invited to lecture on the history of American foreign policy at North China University of Technology (Beijing) and at International Christian University (Tokyo). Professor Doyle's primary geographical areas of interest are Asia-Pacific, Australia, and the United States. His primary subject areas of historical research and writing are the environment, politics, and foreign policy.

Professor Doyle's current research and next book will focus upon the possible roots of war in Asia-Pacific; specifically, how the major powers in the region are continually seeking a greater share of the world's natural resources and a larger degree of influence and power, and how history represents a road map in understanding these economic and political trends. Finally, the book will define how all these specific factors will *affect* America's leadership in this vital region as the Pacific Century transforms the world in the twenty-first century.

In 2004, he was awarded a research fellowship from the Bob Hawke Prime Ministerial Research Centre (University of South Australia) to study the origins of the Asia-Pacific Economic Cooperation (APEC). He was also a visiting research scholar at the University of Tasmania in 2003–2004, and in the offices of Green Party Federal Senator Bob Brown and Green Party Tasmanian House Leader Peg Putt in Hobart, Tasmania. Professor Doyle has been a cohost and commentator on various television and radio programs concerning U.S. political affairs and American foreign policy during stints in Okinawa, Nevada, and Michigan. Professor Doyle's first encounter with Asia and U.S. foreign policy occurred during his military service in the United States Navy (1976–1980). He was stationed overseas at U.S. naval communication bases located in Western Australia and Guam.